HERTFORDSHIRE & BEDFORDSHIRE AIRFIELDS IN THE SECOND WORLD WAR

D1347434

Other counties in the series include:

BERKSHIRE, BUCKINGHAMSHIRE & MIDDLESEX
CAMBRIDGESHIRE
DEVON & CORNWALL
DORSET
ESSEX
HAMPSHIRE
KENT
LEICESTERSHIRE & RUTLAND
LINCOLNSHIRE
NORFOLK
NORTHAMPTONSHIRE
NOTTINGHAMSHIRE & DERBYSHIRE
OXFORDSHIRE
SUFFOLK
SURREY
SUSSEX
WILTSHIRE
YORKSHIRE

HERTFORDSHIRE & BEDFORDSHIRE AIRFIELDS IN THE SECOND WORLD WAR

Graham Smith

COUNTRYSIDE BOOKS
NEWBURY, BERKSHIRE

COUNTRYSIDE BOOKS
3 Catherine Road
Newbury, Berkshire

To view our complete range of books,
please visit us at
www.countrysidebooks.co.uk

ISBN 1 85306 585 4

The cover painting is by Colin Doggett and shows Mosquito FBVIs of
No 487 (RNZAF) at Hunsdon.

Designed by Mon Mohan

Produced through MRM Associates Ltd., Reading
Printed by Woolnough Bookbinding Ltd, Irthlingborough

CONTENTS

Map of the Hertfordshire Airfields   7

Map of the Bedfordshire Airfields   8

1 Setting the Scene • Royal Air Force •   9
   Flying Training Command • USAAF • Airfields

2 Bovingdon (Hertfordshire)   58

3 Cardington (Bedfordshire)   71

4 Cranfield (Bedfordshire)   79

5 Gransden Lodge (Bedfordshire)   91

6 Hatfield (Hertfordshire)   106

7 Henlow (Bedfordshire)   120

8 Hunsdon (Hertfordshire)   129

9 Little Staughton (Bedfordshire)   143

10 Luton (Bedfordshire)   157

11 Nuthampstead (Hertfordshire)   165

12 Podington (Bedfordshire)   179

13 Sawbridgeworth (Hertfordshire)   192

14 Tempsford (Bedfordshire)   204

15 Thurleigh (Bedfordshire)   219

16 Twinwood Farm (Bedfordshire)   234

17 Other Airfields   241

18 Civilians at War   253

Bibliography   274

Index   277

ACKNOWLEDGEMENTS

I am, again, deeply indebted to a number of people for assisting me during the preparation of this book, especially with the provision of photographs; Norman G. Richards of the Archives Division of NASM, Nigel Lutt of the Bedfordshire & Luton Archives & Records Service, Peter S. Robinson of Cranfield University, Nicola Smith of London Luton Airport, and the Archives & Local Studies of Hertfordshire County Council.

I thank Helen Millgate for her kind permission to use an extract from *Mr Brown's War*. As usual I am grateful for the very willing help of the staff of Galleywood Library.

Graham Smith

HERTFORDSHIRE'S WORLD WAR II AIRFIELDS

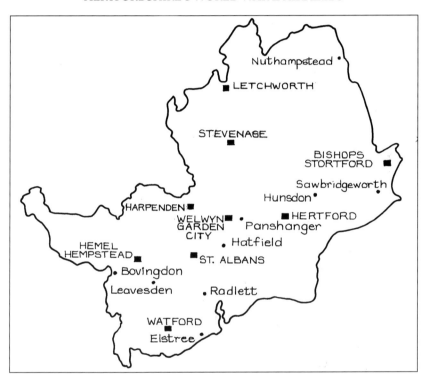

BEDFORDSHIRE'S WORLD WAR II AIRFIELDS

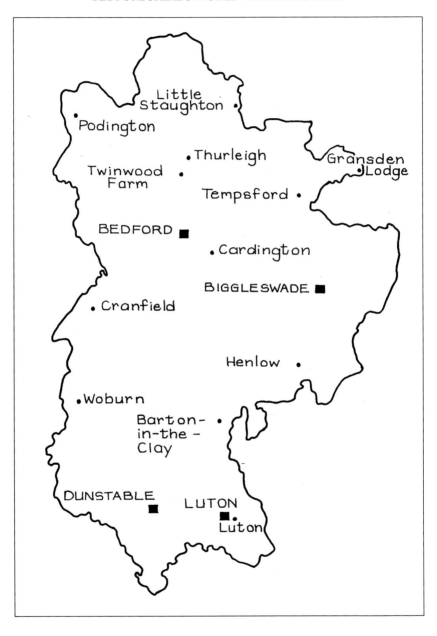

Little
Staughton

Podington

Thurleigh

Gransden
Lodge

Twinwood
Farm

Tempsford

BEDFORD ■

Cardington

BIGGLESWADE ■

Cranfield

Henlow

Woburn

Barton-
in-the-
Clay

DUNSTABLE ■

LUTON
■
Luton

I

SETTING
THE SCENE

The long and proud heritage of aviation in Bedfordshire and Hertfordshire can almost be encapsulated in three names – the British Airship Company, de Havilland and Handley Page. Cardington will be forever remembered for the construction of airships and the tragic departure and loss of the ill-fated R101 in October 1930. Hatfield became synonymous with the de Havilland Aircraft Company, where, from the early 1930s, the company produced a stream of very successful civil aircraft from the tiny Moths to the sleek DH106 Comet, the world's first operational jet-airliner. The wartime feats of its DH98 Mosquitos – the 'Wooden Wonders' – ensured Hatfield and de Havilland's lasting international fame. From 1929, Colney Street near Radlett was the new aerodrome of Handley Page Ltd, which produced a number of civil aircraft, including the HP42 Hannibal airliner of Imperial Airways fame, as well as many RAF heavy bombers – the Heyford, Harrow, Hampden, and the most famous of them all, the Halifax.

For two counties situated so close to London, it is rather surprising to find that there were relatively few Service stations sited within their boundaries, at least when compared with neighbouring counties. The Airship Station at Cardington dates from 1917, and in May 1918 No 5 Eastern Area Aircraft Repair Depôt opened at Henlow some seven miles

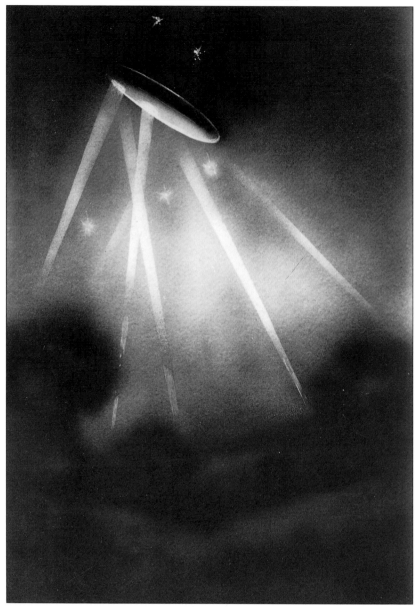

SL11 over Cuffley, 3rd September 1916.

RAF Henlow in 1918. (RAF Museum)

further south. Both sites are still in the possession of the Ministry of Defence, thus making them amongst the oldest existing Service stations. There was a Training Depôt for the Royal Flying Corps at London Colney, as well as a small advanced landing ground at Mathams Wood near Sawbridgeworth. None of these Service stations were operational, but, in March 1917, Lieutenant Cecil Lewis, MC, joined No 56 squadron at London Colney, where it was equipping with the new SE 5As prior to the squadron moving over to France. He describes the landing ground and the new aircraft in his classic book, *Sagittarius Rising*. There was no shortage of activity in the air over the two counties; indeed of the five German Zeppelin airships destroyed over England in the First World War, two were shot down over Hertfordshire. The first, SL11, came down at Cuffley on 3rd September 1916, and L31 fell to earth at Potters Bar nearly one month later.

It was not until the 1930s that there was a rapid increase in the number of aerodromes in the two counties. The term 'aerodrome' comes from the Greek words, which literally mean 'aerial racecourse', and it was used to describe aircraft landing grounds well into the Second World War before being universally replaced by the American derivative

11

R101 at its masthead.

'airfield', although the term is still used in the current *Pooley's Flight Guide*.

In June 1930 the de Havilland School of Gipsy Moths moved from Stag Lane, Edgware to 'a large green field site' at Hatfield, which by late 1934 would be greatly developed to house the company's airframe factory, paint and assembly plant. In early July the aerodrome at Colney Street, Radlett was officially opened by HRH the Duke of Kent; Handley Page Ltd had also sought greener pastures away from the encroachment of suburbia around its existing aerodrome and factory at Cricklewood. In the following month Goldington, just to the east of Bedford, opened as the temporary home of the Bedfordshire Aero Club. Towards the end of 1930 a small landing field at Broxbourne was made available for the members of the newly formed Herts & Essex Flying Club, although it was not officially opened until the following June.

Over the next few years several private aerodromes came into use. In 1932 Richard Shuttleworth opened his own airfield at Old Warden near

Biggleswade, which, of course, now houses the famous Shuttleworth Collection of old classic aircraft, attracting thousands of visitors annually. A small aerodrome at Aldenham House Country Club near Elstree was provided for those club members who could afford to own an aircraft. At the Russells' ancestral home, Woburn Abbey, a spacious landing strip had been created in the Park, and it was mainly used by the remarkable and undeniably courageous Mary, the Duchess of Bedford, DBE, who had become an avid devotee of the new 'flying craze'. She piloted her own Gipsy Moth around the country, but had also undertaken some long-distance flights to Europe, North and South Africa, and India in her relatively big and old Fokker FVII *Spider* along with her private pilot, despite being well over 60 years old! Known as the 'Flying Duchess', she sadly disappeared on a flight over the flooded Fens in May 1937. As the editor of the *Aeroplane* wrote, 'British Aviation is much poorer for losing her'.

Many of the small private aerodromes that opened during these years became recognised and approved as 'landing grounds' as a result of the active support of the Automobile Association; AA patrol men, who had been specially trained to handle aircraft, were present at most of the air shows. As the early aircraft were quite prone to mechanical failure, and also a ready supply of petrol was often rather vital, the AA produced, in late 1932, a Register of Aircraft Landing Grounds; all were 'conveniently situated close to country hotels, with petrol being readily available from nearby AA approved garages', and these landing grounds were 'guaranteed to have been tested by aircraft'! Those first listed in the two counties were Kempston, near Bedford, Lewsey Farm, situated about halfway between Dunstable and Luton, Woburn Park, and Hitchin, where the site was close to the town but it needed a special AA permit to use the landing ground.

The fast growing popularity of flying during the early 1930s owes much to the drive and enthusiasm of Sir Alan Cobham KBE, AFC, the celebrated airman famed for his pioneering long-distance flights. During this period his Air Circus travelled the length and breadth of the country with the intention of making Great Britain 'air minded'; it also brought the thrills of flying to the general public. On his National Aviation Days, as they were called, the thousands of spectators who attended were treated to aerobatic displays, spectacular stunt flying, wing-walking and parachuting; but perhaps more importantly they were given the opportunity of taking to the air for the first time on 'joy rides'. In four years almost one million people experienced the joy and thrill of flying at well over 500 different locations in Britain and Ireland. In April 1932 the Air Circus visited Luton, Royston, Bedford and Leighton Buzzard and a year later Hitchin, Elstree, Hertford and Dunstable would be the venues.

Dunstable had also become a major centre for the rapidly growing interest in gliding. The London Gliding Club had set up its headquarters on Dunstable Downs, though it was no more ambitious than a collection of small buildings with a clubhouse. Gliders or 'sailplanes' as they were then more generally called, became familiar sights in the skies over the Downs. Sadly in July 1935, George Collins, the Chief Flying Instructor of the London Gliding Club and perhaps the leading exponent of 'sailplaning' of the day, was killed whilst giving an aerobatic display at one of Cobham's Air Days held at Ramsey in Huntingdonshire. An example of the inherent dangers of any kind of flying in these still pioneering days.

Without a shadow of a doubt it was de Havilland's aerodrome at Hatfield that became the mecca of aviation enthusiasts during the 1930s. In July 1933 it was the venue for the start and finish of the country's most famous air race – the King's Cup – where the leading racing aircraft and pilots of the time could be seen performing. The finalists were required to fly nine times in a prescribed triangle from Hatfield to Broxbourne, Henlow and back, thus bringing the excitement of air racing to far more of the public than attended at the aerodrome. Rather appropriately Geoffrey de Havilland won the 1933 race in his new DH85 Leopard Moth at an average speed of 139 mph for the course of 830 miles. It is interesting to note the reason why his aircraft were called '...Moths', because of his other abiding passion – lepidoptery. Hatfield would host this prestigious Air Race for several more years before the outbreak of war effectively brought private and racing flying to a close.

In May 1934 the first Empire Air Day was celebrated at Hatfield, and over 3,000 people attended. These days were the inspiration of Air Commodore Chamier, who was the Chairman of the Air League, when RAF stations and civil aerodromes were opened to the public to view new aircraft, both Service and civil, and to be treated to RAF air

Luton aerodrome in the late 1930s. (London-Luton Airport)

displays, usually given by the aircraft and instructors of the Central Flying School. They became annual events and attracted large and enthusiastic crowds. Many wartime RAF airmen recalled that their love of flying had been first kindled by attending Empire Air Days. In 1937 the Society of British Aircraft Constructors held their annual display at Hatfield (the forerunner of the Farnborough Air Display) when visitors were able to view some of the RAF's latest aircraft, such as the Lysander, Whitley, Blenheim, Oxford and Harrow. Quite naturally de Havilland aircraft were there in profusion, including that most elegant of airliners – DH91 Albatross – which had first flown on 20th May of that year.

By 1935 there were 90 licensed civil aerodromes and landing grounds in the country, and in November another would be added to the total when Barton-in-the-Clay opened for Luton Aircraft Ltd. Of this number only 21 were operated and owned by local authorities, despite the tireless efforts of Sir Alan Cobham, during 1929, to persuade town councils to establish their own flying facilities. Luton, which became the only municipal aerodrome in the two counties, was not officially opened until July 1938, but the site had been used in April 1932 by Sir Alan

Cobham's first Air Circus tour, and then subsequently by the Luton Flying Club. Since late 1936 it had become the new home of the Percival Aircraft Company, where its splendid Gulls and Mew Gulls were produced in some numbers.

Notwithstanding the public's apparent great interest in flying there were under 3,500 licensed pilots in the country in 1934, of whom only about 6% were women, despite the intrepid and well-publicised exploits of Amy Johnson, Lady Bailey, Jean Batten, Winifred Brown, the Duchess of Bedford *et al*, and the ladies' own flying competition – the Northesk Cup. Flying was a rather exclusive and very expensive pastime, instruction fees averaged about 30 shillings per hour, and the cheapest Moth cost £595 with about another £250 to keep it flying annually. Although the London Transport Flying Club, which was based at Broxbourne, provided cheap flying for its large staff for 6d per week by subscription! However, the number of civil pilots would greatly increase in the ensuing years as more facilities for flying instruction became available. In January 1933 the Hertfordshire Flying Club started to operate from St Julians field near St Albans, and five years later the Bedford School of Flying provided instruction at Barton-in-the-Clay. In October 1938 the Civil Air Guard was launched with the intention of bringing flying instruction within the reach of the average man and woman. For about £10 a member of the Civil Air Guard could obtain a full year's flying training. The response was quite amazing, with over 34,000 applying in the first two weeks, of whom about 4,000 were enrolled. By July 1939 some 3,000–4,000 had received their pilot's licence by this means, and many of these pilots later served with the RAF or the Air Transport Auxiliary. Broxbourne was one of the many aerodromes where a unit of the Civil Air Guard was established and by the close of 1938 over 200 members were under instruction there.

The Air Ministry had decided in the mid-1930s to contract civilian flying schools to provide basic flying training for Service airmen, mainly those in the RAFVR. Thus, in August 1935, the de Havilland School of Flying opened as No 1 Elementary & Reserve Flying Training School. The aerodrome at Hatfield was already a little crowded, as the London Aero Club had moved in during September 1933 followed by the RAF Flying Club in June 1934. Soon the School was forced to use a small relief landing ground at Holwell Hyde near to Welwyn Garden City. Three

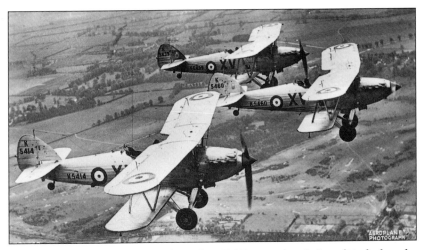

Hawker Hinds of No XV squadron; first RAF operational aircraft to be based in the two counties.

years almost to the day, another E&RFTS was formed at Luton. It was numbered 29, which shows the speed of development for this type of basic flying training, which was desperately needed for the rapidly expanding Service.

Despite the RAF's expansion during the late 1930s, there was just one new RAF airfield scheduled for completion in the two counties – Cranfield in Bedfordshire. The construction of this permanent station had commenced in 1935, and it was planned to house three operational squadrons. When it was ready for occupation in June 1937, it had been allocated to Bomber Command and within a month or so the first operational aircraft appeared. They were Hawker Hinds, the last of the Service's bi-plane light bombers, and thus they had the honour of being the first RAF operational aircraft to be based in the two counties. However, their days were severely numbered as they would soon be superseded by Fairey Battles and Bristol Blenheims.

Thus at the outbreak of the war there was just a single RAF airfield with operational aircraft, with RAF Cardington and Henlow engaged in various aspects of aircraft repair and training. Mathams Wood (later Sawbridgeworth), which had been used occasionally by Service aircraft since 1937, would not become fully occupied until the early summer of 1940. Hatfield continued its Service flying training commitment, as would Luton from the summer of 1940. De Havilland, Percival and Handley Page were engaged in producing aircraft for the RAF. An airfield site at Leavesden, to the north-west of Watford, was bought by the Ministry of Aircraft Production, and ultimately Mosquitos and Halifaxes were built and assembled there. From 31st August 1939 an Air Navigation Restriction Order forbade all civil flying without a special permit, and all the small aerodromes in the area were closed to flying. The Air Ministry quickly requisitioned them. Some like Broxbourne and Old Warden were used for the repair of Service aircraft, whilst Woburn Abbey and Beechwood Park in Bedfordshire, were used for the storage of aircraft.

It was not until the early spring of 1941 that the first wartime-built airfield opened – Hunsdon – a few miles to the north-west of Harlow, which was allocated to No 11 Group of Fighter Command as a night-fighter base. During the summer Twinwood Farm, which in the immediate pre-war years had been considered as a likely site for a possible municipal aerodrome for Bedford, began to be used by training aircraft from Cranfield. The following year there were quite major changes when six airfields opened. In the spring RAF Tempsford became operational, and would soon become renowned for its clandestine operations over occupied Europe on behalf of the Special Operations Executive. It quickly obtained a satellite airfield at Gransden Lodge, although this airfield would later be transferred to the Pathfinder Force of Bomber Command. In June the USAAF, in the guise of the Eighth Air Force, occupied Bovingdon in Hertfordshire followed shortly by installing Bomb Groups at Podington and Thurleigh. At the end of the year Little Staughton became an American Air Depôt, although in 1944 this would also pass to No 8 (PFF) Group. The final wartime airfield to open, in August 1943, was Nuthampstead in Hertfordshire, used first by USAAF fighters and later by the seemingly omnipresent B-17 heavy bombers, which appeared to dominate the daylight skies during these latter wartime years.

Royal Air Force

At the outbreak of the war the Royal Air Force had only just come of age. It had celebrated its 21st birthday on 1st April 1939, but its progress thus far had been anything but smooth and without conflict. Its saviour during the difficult 1920s had been its second Chief of Air Staff, Sir Hugh (later Viscount) Trenchard, who served in the top post for a decade from September 1919 to 1929. During his tenure he not only fought doggedly for its very survival as an independent Service in the face of severe opposition from the other two Services and politicians, but he also managed to build a Service, which although small, was nevertheless professional, well-trained and highly motivated. Viscount Trenchard certainly deserved the title of 'The Father of the RAF'.

His doctrine was that the aeroplane was 'a weapon of attack' and not to be used as 'a defence against the aeroplane'. He was utterly convinced that the future for the RAF lay in the use of heavy bombers as a strategic strike force, with fighters playing a very minor role. Trenchard's theories were deeply engrained in the peace-time Service and three of his most dedicated disciples, Sir Cyril Newall, Sir Charles Portal and Sir Arthur Harris, were in positions of such power during the war that the concept of an all-powerful bomber force prevailed within the Service. Stanley Baldwin, Lord President of the Council, memorably emphasised this doctrine in November 1932: 'the bomber will always get through. The only defence is offence, which means you have to kill more women and children more quickly than the enemy if you want to save yourselves'. Such a view was hardly a comfortable proposition for the civilian population!

It is Air Chief Marshal Sir Cyril Newall, the Chief of the Air Staff from September 1937 to October 1940, who is considered 'the prime architect of the wartime Air Force'. Like all senior RAF officers he had served with distinction in the Royal Flying Corps, when Trenchard considered him 'one of the best generals in the air service.' Newall took command of the RAF when the expansion and reorganisation of the Service was already well in hand. In July 1936 the old Air Defence of Great Britain had disappeared, being replaced by the four separate and functional Commands – Bomber, Fighter, Coastal and Training – to be followed

Air Chief Marshal Sir Cyril Newall: 'the prime architect of the wartime Air Force'.

later by Reserve, Maintenance, Balloon and Army Co-operation; each with a number of Groups. This was the basic organisation, except for minor additions, with which the RAF fought the Second World War, at least in Europe. In April 1937 recruitment for the Volunteer Reserve had commenced, and these trained aircrews would make a valuable contribution to the three operational Commands in the early war years. The only set-back experienced by the Service during this period was the loss of the operational control of the Fleet Air Arm to the Royal Navy.

During his period of command Newall presided over the RAF's most dynamic growth, in personnel, airfields and aircraft. The strength of the Service grew from 68,000 in 1937 to some 175,000 at the outbreak of the war, and over 437,000 by the time he left his post in late 1940. Many of the famous wartime aircraft came into the Service during his tenure – Hampden, Wellington, Blenheim IV, Hurricane, Spitfire, Defiant, Lysander, Hudson, Oxford, and Beaufighter. He faced the Service's early setbacks with a calm equanimity, but at least he left the top post with one major but most critical victory attained, the Battle of Britain.

Within months of taking office Newall and his Air Staff were faced with almost a complete reappraisal of the RAF's prime role in a future war. The politicians now took the view that Britain did not need the same number of long-range bombers as Germany and that the number of heavy bombers be reduced and replaced by cheaper light and medium bombers. It was argued that the role of the RAF should not be 'to deliver an early knock-out blow...but rather to prevent the Germans from knocking us out'; as a result greater emphasis and resources were diverted to fighter production. This fundamental change to the Service's long-held strategy, did mean that Fighter Command would be better equipped and prepared to face the Luftwaffe, but it also ensured that Bomber Command was far weaker in the early stages of the war than the Air Staff had hoped for and planned.

Newall was also confronted with a most dismal appraisal of the effectiveness of Bomber Command – the Service's 'sacred cow'. In November 1937 Air Chief Marshal Sir Edgar Ludlow-Hewitt, its new Commanding-in-Chief, reported, '[it] was entirely unprepared for war, unable to operate except in fair weather and extremely vulnerable both in the air and on the ground.' Even in 1939 Ludlow-Hewitt expressed grave disquiet about his crews' difficulties in identifying targets, the lack of a really efficient bomb-sight, self-sealing fuel tanks and the inadequate gun defences of the bombers. In the words of *The Official History of the RAF, 1939–45*, 'when war came in 1939 Bomber Command was not trained or equipped to penetrate into enemy territory by day or to find its target areas, let alone its targets by night.' Perhaps the best thing that could be said was that, 'Bomber Command in 1939 was above all an investment for the future'; though, in truth, such a view could be ascribed to the RAF in total. It was Bomber and Flying Training Commands that had the most impact in the two counties, and these will be examined in some detail.

Bomber Command

On 3rd September 1939 Bomber Command possessed some 900 or so aircraft in 55 squadrons. Of this number twelve squadrons would be immediately transferred to the Advanced Air Striking Force in France. Another 20 squadrons were involved in training or were non-operational for various reasons, thus leaving an effective front-line force of 23 squadrons or about 350 aircraft, of which some 70% were considered 'heavies' – Hampdens, Wellingtons and Whitleys. However, two days earlier President Roosevelt had called upon Britain, France and Germany to refrain from bombing targets that would endanger civilian lives. Britain and France readily acquiesced, with Germany following suit 18 days later only after Poland had been bombed into submission!

Thus the Air Staff found that it had no real alternative but to activate what was known as Western Air Plan 12 – to attack the German Fleet at sea. Ludlow-Hewitt had been less than pleased when this task had been given to his Command back in January 1939. The first attempt was made on 4th September and seven Blenheims and Wellingtons failed to return (24%!), ten crews had failed to locate the targets and only one vessel, the cruiser *Emden*, had sustained slight damage. Bomber Command was, however, allowed to fly over Germany to drop propaganda leaflets, and ten Whitleys of No 5 Group, the only Group that had night-flying experience, left on the first night of the war and carried over five million

'Take-Off': Interior of a Bomber Aircraft – oil painting by Dame Laura Knight, RA. (Imperial War Museum)

leaflets to Hamburg, Bremen and the Ruhr. During the so-called 'Phoney War', which really lasted until early April 1940, over 350 'Nickel' sorties (as they were code-named) were made for the loss of 6% of the aircraft, although valuable experience of night-flying and navigation was gained by the crews.

In December, the long-held tenet that a tight formation of heavy bombers operating by day would be self-defensive, was shown to be patently flawed. The two operations on the 14th and 18th when 17 out of 34 Wellingtons were shot down on shipping strikes demanded a dramatic review of bombing policy. It was reluctantly accepted that if the German war industries were to be attacked by day then the bombers would require a strong fighter escort. However, Spitfires and Hurricanes lacked the necessary range, and in any case they were desperately needed for the defence of Britain, so the only other alternative was to operate at night without fighter escort. It was readily accepted that bombing accuracy would greatly suffer, let alone the serious problem of night-navigation, a subject that had not figured high in the pre-war training of crews; indeed, during 1938 only 10% of the Command's flying hours had been flown at night. On 12th April when the largest bombing operation so far – 83 aircraft – attacked shipping in Stavanger, Norway, nine were lost. This proved to be the last time until the summer of 1944 that heavy bombers were used in a major daylight operation.

During May 1940 the air war took a dramatic turn. Whilst the Fairey Battles and Bristol Blenheims were involved in a bitter and costly battle in France, the Command made its first raids on German cities and towns. On the night of 11th/12th, Mönchengladbach was bombed, followed four nights later by targets in the Ruhr. It was estimated that 75% of Germany's industrial production was based there, and during the next five years the Ruhr was attacked so frequently that the crews dubbed it 'The Happy Valley' or perhaps more grimly 'The Land of No Return', because of the number of crews lost on such operations.

On 25th August Berlin was attacked for the first time, as a direct retaliation for the Luftwaffe's first bombing of London on the previous night. Although the German capital would be attacked again in the coming weeks, Bomber Command was not really in a position to make a major and effective strike until early 1943. Nevertheless, in September Winston Churchill told his War Cabinet and Chiefs of Staff, 'The Navy

can lose us the war, but only the Air Force can win it. Therefore our supreme effort must be to gain overwhelming mastery of the air. The fighters are our salvation, but the bombers alone provide the means of victory.' Trenchard's philosophy still held sway!

As a direct result of the Luftwaffe's heavy night-raids on London and provincial cities, the first major 'area' attack, as opposed to specific strategic targets, of a German city was authorised. On 16th/17th December 1940, Mannheim was bombed by over 130 aircraft but with no great accuracy or effect. In the New Year oil targets became the Command's first priority, quickly replaced by U-boat yards and ports as the Battle of the Atlantic was reaching critical proportions. The Command was now growing in strength and power with the first four-engined bombers – Short Stirlings and Handley Page Halifaxes – entering the fray. In the summer of 1941 the Command returned to German industrial targets with its squadrons active almost nightly. Several operations exceeded what was considered the 'tolerable' loss rate of 5%, and the daylight raids by the Blenheims of No 2 Group were also proving very costly. In just four months from early July to November over 520 bombers had been lost, almost equivalent to the Command's front-line strength.

What proved to be even more disturbing was the report compiled by D. M. Butt of the War Cabinet Secretariat for the Air Ministry. It was based on over 600 aerial photographs taken in two months of bombing operations, and it revealed that only 25% of the crews came closer than five miles of the aiming points. As far as the Ruhr was concerned, where intense flak and industrial haze hampered the bombing, the figure fell to barely 10%. The position was even more serious as the report was based largely on the performance of the most experienced crews, as they were the only ones to be provided with cameras at this stage of the war. In the face of such damning evidence and the heavy operational losses, the War Cabinet ordered Bomber Command to carry out only 'limited operations', whilst the whole future of the Command and its night-offensive was considered.

Air Chief Marshal Sir Charles F. A. Portal, who had been briefly in charge of Bomber Command in 1940, had become the Chief of Air Staff in October 1940. He was utterly dedicated to the Command's night-offensive, and he argued very persuasively for the status quo, and furthermore that the Command should pursue an outright offensive on German cities, which was virtually a mandate for area bombing with a build-up of the Command to 4,000 bombers. Portal, who was later described by Churchill as 'the accepted star of the Royal Air Force', gained Churchill's support for an all-out offensive, but not with the huge force of bombers he had proposed. Bomber Command had been given virtually the green light, and comes the hour, comes the man – Air Chief Marshal Sir Arthur Harris. On 22nd February 1942 Harris took over Bomber Command. He was Portal's personal choice, and Harris would lead the Command for the rest of the war. His name became synonymous with Bomber Command, he was a born leader, who engendered a fierce and total loyalty from his airmen, who dubbed him 'Butch'! Harris was unswerving in his commitment to outright area bombing, which he prosecuted with a grim, relentless and ruthless determination.

The new Commander quickly showed his mettle with the heavy fire-raising attack on Lubeck on 28th/29th March. This was followed by the

Avro Lancaster: the most famous RAF heavy bomber of the war. (Imperial War Museum)

three famous '1,000' bomber raids on Cologne, Essen and Bremen, which the British press heralded as 'The Greatest Air Raids in History'. Harris had the advantage of taking command when the most successful heavy bomber of the war – the Avro Lancaster – was just coming into service, the first navigational aid, GEE, would shortly be ready for operations, and then, in August 1942, the Pathfinder Force (PFF) was formed.

It must be admitted that Harris was originally firmly opposed to a 'Target Finding Force' largely on the grounds that he felt it would become a *corps d'elite*, which he considered would be detrimental to squadron morale and also rob the squadrons of the best and most experienced crews. However, on this issue he was countermanded by Portal, and despite his initial misgivings Harris managed to obtain some important changes to the original format of the Force. Rather than transferring the best crews, each Group Commander was ordered to nominate a squadron to join the Force. He altered the name to Pathfinder Force, and managed to persuade both the Air Ministry and the Treasury to concede that the PFF crews would be accorded one rank higher than they held. Considering his views on elitism, he gained the approval, by Royal Warrant, for a special PFF badge, the famous gilt hovering eagle to be worn below the medal ribbons, but strictly *not* whilst on operations.

The Pathfinders came into being on 15th August 1942 under the command of Group Captain Donald C. Bennett, DSO, later Air Vice-Marshal, a distinguished and experienced pre-war Australian pilot, and perhaps the leading navigational expert in the Service. Much of the Pathfinders' later success was due to his inspirational and firm leadership, his drive and determination. The first four pioneer squadrons, each equipped with the Command's four heavy bombers, were thrown into the offensive with high hopes of success but without any real added advantages. It was not really until 1943 that the PFF began to have an impact on the Command's operations, as its squadrons developed and refined a whole range of target marking techniques, as well as the arrival on the scene of H2S, the radar bombing aid, and Oboe, the blind bombing device, which would be used so devastatingly by the Force's Mosquitos.

The period from March 1943 to March 1944 was a time, when

according to the *Official History*, 'at last the strategic theories which for a quarter of a century had been the inspiration of the Royal Air Force were coming to operational maturity.' Harris now had over 600 heavy bombers at his disposal, the PFF had grown into a Group (No 8), and he felt that the time was ripe for a sustained and ferocious offensive against a range of targets in the Ruhr. What is now known as the Battle of the Ruhr was conducted from March to July 1943. The famous operation to the Möhne, Eder and Sorpe dams came in May, followed by devastating fire-raids over four nights on Hamburg. The successful and spectacular raid on the Peenemunde rocket research establishment in August only demonstrated the Command's growing skills and expertise in locating and accurately bombing small individual targets. In the same month the long and costly Battle of Berlin commenced, which would gain momentum through the winter when over 30,000 tons of bombs would be dropped for the loss of over 3,300 airmen. At the end of the year another new Group was formed, No 100 (Bomber Support), which would be engaged in a variety of radio-counter measures against the German night-fighter force and the radar defences.

In four years Bomber Command had advanced a very long way from its early tentative strikes against the German Fleet back in the dark days of December 1939. For example, on 15th/16th February 1944 the Command despatched nearly 900 aircraft to Berlin, the largest force so far other than the '1,000' raids, and over 2,600 tons of bombs were dropped – a record. Four nights later Leipzig was attacked by over 800 heavies with 78 failing to return (9.5%). As Harris had promised back in 1942,'They have sowed the wind, now they will reap the whirlwind.'

The winter of 1943/4 was to be a most costly time for Bomber Command. Sad to relate that just six nights after the last major operation against Berlin in March 1944, Bomber Command suffered its largest loss of the war, 95 aircraft missing whilst attacking Nuremberg on the 30th/31st. This was a major disaster with more airmen lost in one night (545) than in the whole of the Battle of Britain. Within two weeks the overall control of Bomber Command, as was that of the Eighth Air Force, passed to General Eisenhower, the Supreme Allied Commander in Europe, and much of the Command's efforts in the coming months would be directed to rail/road communications, bridges, airfields, and coastal defences as a prelude to D-Day. Before returning to German

Mosquito FBVI of No 487 squadron, February 1944.

targets, the Command was active in support of the Allied armies in Normandy, as well as attacking V1 rocket sites in Northern France.

Towards the end of August Bomber Command returned to attacking targets in the Ruhr by day, their aircraft now escorted by a strong fighter force, and losses proved to be relatively light. The PFF Mosquitos of the Light Night Strike Force wrought havoc over many German targets, but more especially Berlin. By 1945 Bomber Command was a force of quite awesome power. It had the technical equipment to operate with equal facility by day and by night, and was able to accurately bomb in all weather conditions. In the last four complete months of the war the Command dropped 181,000 tons of bombs, which was nearly one fifth of the total tonnage of the war. On the night of 25th/26th April over 100 Lancasters bombed an oil refinery in Norway; just one Lancaster failed to return, the last of more than 3,400 Lancasters lost during the war. It was left to the PFF Mosquitos to bring down the curtain on Bomber Command's long, bitter and costly war, when Kiel was attacked on 2nd/3rd May 1945.

Flying Training Command

A Training Command had been established in July 1936, which controlled all types of Service training under four Groups. However, early in 1937, due to the imminent introduction of the Volunteer Reserve, a Reserve Command was formed to take over the responsibility of the Elementary & Reserve Flying Training Schools, which would number 31 by 1939. Despite a rapid and unprecedented increase in flying training there was still a shortfall of about 1,000 pilots in early 1939. There were also certain defects in the flying training system, notably night-flying, navigation and air gunnery practice, which manifested themselves in both Bomber and Fighter Command's early operations.

Until early 1940 the student pilots were given some eight weeks' ground instruction at the Initial Training Wings, followed by up to ten weeks at the EFTS, before passing on to one of the 14 Service Flying Training Schools for advanced instruction, which could last for at least four months according to the time of the year. When they passed out of the SFTS they were in possession of their coveted 'wings', but they would now be sent to the various Commands' Group Pools to gain experience on the aircraft that they would ultimately fly operationally. This final period of conversion training could vary from four to six weeks, by which time the pilots should have logged over 160 flying hours and the whole process had taken the best part of twelve months.

Despite the fact that the whole period of flying training had been shortened, because of a desperate need for pilots and aircrews, the flow of trained personnel was still not sufficient to cope with the normal demands of the Service, let alone to replace the pilots and crews lost during the first six months of 1940. The biggest problem for Fighter Command during the Battle of Britain was not the supply of replacement aircraft but rather the trained pilots to fly them. A welcome and valuable addition to the RAF was the number of already qualified pilots from the Commonwealth and European countries. About 20% fought in the Battle of Britain, and throughout the war almost 46% of all aircrews came from the Commonwealth and Europe, making the wartime RAF a most cosmopolitan Service.

In order to try to keep pace with the ever increasing requirement for trained pilots and aircrews, in late 1939 discussions took place with the Dominion governments to set up a scheme for flying training to be undertaken in their countries. The agreement was signed in December, and in May 1940 the Empire (later British Commonwealth) Air Training Scheme (EATS) commenced, which was later described as 'one of the most brilliant pieces of imaginative organisation ever conceived.' The first flying training school under EATS, opened at Belvedere near Salisbury in Southern Rhodesia on 24th May, followed shortly by schools in Canada, and by the end of the year a number of UK based schools were transferred out to Canada. Schools were later established in Australia, New Zealand, South Africa, Southern Rhodesia and India, and by the middle of 1943 they numbered 75, offering flying training from elementary through to advanced. The pilots and crews would then return to the United Kingdom to receive their operational training. The EATS proved to be a salvation for the Service. The scheme eased the pressure on airfields and the country's crowded airspace, as well as supplying a regular and constant flow of trained airmen, with over 200,000 passing through the scheme during the war, the majority of whom were trained in Canada.

In late 1940 changes were made to the rather haphazard method by which pilots and aircrews had received their final operational training. The existing Group Pools in Bomber Command were formally organised

Pupil pilots practise formation flying with Airspeed Oxfords. (Imperial War Museum)

31

into nine Operational Training Units (OTUs) and placed under the control of No 6 Group. Fighter Command established three OTUs with a single one (then) for Coastal Command. In the following month Training Command *per se* was disbanded and replaced by two separate Commands, Flying Training and Technical Training. The former now controlled some 80 Flying Training Schools, of which 31 were devoted to pilot training. There were over 3,000 aircraft engaged in training duties from Tiger Moths, Miles Magisters and Masters, Airspeed Oxfords, Avro Ansons, Blenheims and North American Harvards to current operational aircraft. Most of the training aircraft bore yellow colourings on the underside of the fuselage, but the aircraft in OTUs were finished in the same markings as other aircraft in the Commands.

There was still an almost insatiable demand for pilots and aircrews, in late 1941 over 94,000 were said to be undergoing training. The introduction of four-engined bombers into Bomber Command resulted in an additional stage in the training programme – conversion training. Also as more Lancasters moved into the Command, an additional twelve hours or so had to be completed by crews at a Lancaster Finishing School. Air Chief Marshal Sir Arthur Harris later maintained that, 'the education of a bomber crew was the most expensive in the world; it cost some £10,000 for each man, enough to send ten men to Oxford or Cambridge for three years'!

At the end of 1943, which was the wartime peak for flying training, there were over 150 training schools in the United Kingdom without those operating overseas. No type of flying training could be undertaken without accidents, and since OTUs had been introduced over 1,700 aircraft had been lost in accidents. This figure does not include all the various training losses at Elementary and Advanced Flying Schools, where accidents tended to be far more numerous, if with somewhat less serious consequences as far as fatalities were concerned. Besides purely flying and operational training, there was a myriad of other specialised flying training courses, refresher courses on a variety of aircraft, instructors' courses, glider pilots *et al*.

By 1945 Flying Training Command had grown to seven Groups, as well as another six Groups devoted to training in the three operational Commands. The Service's commitment to flying training during the war was a massive undertaking, which ultimately produced over 307,000

The Runnymede Memorial at Cooper's Hill, Surrey.

highly trained pilots and aircrews. Furthermore it should be borne in mind that all the RAF aircrews were volunteers, at no time did the Service have to resort to conscription for flying duties. At the end of the war there were 193,000 serving aircrew, and the Service's total strength stood at over 1,079,000, including some 140,000 WAAFs, with over 55,000 aircraft.

The victory that the Service had achieved over the much vaunted Luftwaffe had been complete and utter, but at a heavy cost; 79,924 killed or missing in action. Without doubt the RAF had fully justified the confidence placed in it by HM King George VI in his message to the Service on 4th September 1939: 'you will have to shoulder far greater responsibilities than those which your Service had to shoulder in the last war...I can assure all ranks of the Air Force of my supreme confidence in their skill and courage, and their ability to meet whatever calls may be made upon them.'

It was Bomber Command that suffered the heaviest losses, over 47,268 killed in action with another 8,195 lost in flying accidents, and it is fitting that the last words should reside with Air Chief Marshal Sir Arthur

Harris: 'There are no words with which I can do justice to the aircrews who fought under my command. There is no parallel in warfare to such courage and determination...Such devotion must not be forgotten. It is unforgettable by anyone whose contacts gave them knowledge and understanding of what these young men experienced or faced.' Many of these airmen are buried in the various British War Cemeteries on the Continent, but those airmen, over 20,450, that have no known graves are commemorated in the splendid Runnymede Memorial at Cooper's Hill, Surrey.

United States Army Air Force

The arrival of the USAAF into the European air war in the late summer of 1942 was by no means a case of the US cavalry riding in to rescue the beleaguered Brits *à la* Hollywood, despite the belief of many American servicemen! Nevertheless, it must be admitted the Eighth Air Force did appear at a rather propitious time. Bomber Command was just beginning to develop into a potent strike force under its new AOC-in-C, and almost monthly it was growing in strength with more of its new heavy bomber – the Lancaster – coming into service. American brothers-in-arms to share the heavy burden of the strategic bombing offensive were more than welcome, especially as Air Chief Marshal Harris, before his appointment as Chief of Bomber Command, had served in Washington and thus was well acquainted with many senior USAAF chiefs and he fully appreciated their different operational methods, as well as being sensitive to their needs. Indeed, in his words, 'I was privileged to count all three of them [Ira Eaker, Frank Armstrong, James Doolittle] as the closest of friends'; which certainly augured well for their future working partnership.

It was Brigadier General Ira C. Eaker who was selected to prepare the way for the entry of the USAAF into the 'European Theater of Operations' (ETO). He had already spent some time in the United Kingdom during 1941 acting as an observer at Bomber Command headquarters. On 20th February, he and his right-hand man, Lieutenant Colonel Frank A. Armstrong Jr, along with five other Air Force officers

The awards of the British DFCs to Brigadier General Frank Armstrong Jr, Colonels Curtis LeMay, James Wallace and Stanley Wray. (Smithsonian Institution)

landed at Heston to begin the daunting and formidable task of establishing a large American Air Force in Great Britain. It was not until early April that they were aware that this force would be the Eighth.

The Eighth, which had originally been designated the Fifth, had only been formed in Savannah, Georgia in the previous January, specifically to provide air support for a planned invasion of North Africa – Operation Torch. However, when this operation was postponed Major General Carl A. Spaatz, the newly appointed Air Force Commander in Europe, persuaded the Pentagon in Washington that the new Air Force should move to the United Kingdom to form the nucleus of the USAAF in Europe.

The planned build-up of the Eighth Air Force was most ambitious and quite staggering in its immensity. The operational commands – Bomber, Fighter, Ground-Air Support – would comprise 60 combat groups in the region of 3,500 aircraft strong, with an Air Service Command to control all the myriad of various support services, necessary to serve and supply such a massive force. All the airmen and aircraft were planned to be in place by April 1943, which was then the target date for the invasion of Europe. Although this original blueprint was not realised, at least within the scheduled timescale, due mainly to American resources being diverted to the war in the Pacific and North Africa, it was nevertheless a quite herculean task that faced Eaker and his cadre of

Main briefing for 467th Bomb Group. (via D. Hastings)

officers. The Eighth Air Force owes a debt of deep gratitude to General Eaker for his courage, drive and determination in developing this Force into the 'Mighty' Eighth – a sobriquet that it richly deserved, not only for its sheer size, but also for the valiant and determined operations it mounted, sometimes at a great cost of men and machines.

The first and urgent need was airfields; it was estimated that at least 75 would be required. All of the operational airfields would need to be sited in Central or Eastern England (preferably the latter), and many of the RAF's airfields that were either under construction or nearing completion were allocated to the USAAF; the arrival of US Aviation Engineers in July meant that they would at least build some of the airfields that were needed by the USAAF. However, the immediate problem of airfield space was partially solved, when Bomber Command disbanded a whole new Bomber Group, No 8, which was then forming but had not yet become operational, and handed over all its alloted airfields for USAAF use.

In May 1942 the first American combat flying unit, No 15 (Light) Bomb Squadron, arrived in the United Kingdom and during the next month the first of the heavy bombers and transport aircraft began to make their way across the Atlantic. On 18th June Major General Spaatz arrived to take charge of the embryonic Air Force from his headquarters at Bushy Park, with General Eaker in command of its bomber force. Eaker's headquarters were conveniently sited at High Wycombe, close to Bomber Command's at Walter's Ash. The single US Fighter Group, the 31st, was equipped with Spitfires and operated at first under Fighter Command's tutelage. However small the Eighth Air Force was at this stage, at least it could claim that it was in business. General Eaker is reported as saying, 'We won't do much talking until we've done more flying. We hope that when we leave, you'll be glad we came.' The Eighth's first objective was stated in a Joint Directive issued in August 1942: 'American day bomber forces under British fighter protection reinforced by American Fighter forces...will attack suitable objectives within the radius of British fighter cover.'

The USAAF was completely dedicated to high-altitude precision bombing conducted by large formations of self-defensive bombers operating in daylight. For this task it considered that it had the best heavy bombers – the Boeing B-17 or Flying Fortress and the Consolidated B-24 or Liberator. Both were heavily armed, equipped with an excellent oxygen system and provided with the so-called 'wonder' Norden bomb-sight. Although the Eighth's chiefs were well

Fine formation of B-17Es of 92nd and 97th Bomb Groups. (USAF)

aware of Bomber Command's costly experience of daylight operations, as well as its brief and rather disastrous flirtation with Flying Fortresses, they were utterly convinced that their heavy bombers, which could operate at high altitudes (20,000 feet and above), would be able to defend themselves from enemy fighter attack and fly high enough to be beyond the effective range of most flak batteries. Despite heavy losses in their first year or so of operations the Eighth Air Force pursued this belief with a grim and ruthless determination, which was only rewarded when a sufficient number of long-range fighter escorts began to be available in late 1943.

On Independence Day (4th July) 1942 six USAAF crews of No 15 Bomb Squadron, in borrowed RAF Bostons, joined another six RAF crews in low-level attacks against airfields in Holland. Two of the American crews failed to return – the first of tens of thousands of American fatalities in the European air war. It was not until 17th August that the first of the heavy bombers – B-17s – were ready to be tested over enemy territory. On this historic mission just twelve left to bomb marshalling yards at Rouen in Northern France; the operation was led by Colonel Frank A. Armstrong Jr and General Eaker went along for the ride, in the rather appropriately named *Yankee Doodle*. The small force was greatly outnumbered by the escort of RAF Spitfires, and all the B-17s arrived back safely, though some suffered battle damage. Air Chief Marshal Harris sent a message of congratulations to Eaker, 'Yankee Doodle certainly went to town and you can stick another well-earned feather in his cap'! However, it would be another six months before the Eighth was able to make a significant contribution to the Allied air offensive over Germany. Towards the end of the month two Fighter Groups went into action for the first time, and in late September the three RAF 'Eagle' squadrons of Fighter Command, which had been originally formed from American volunteers, were transferred to the USAAF to form a new Fighter Group (4th).

Early in October the first B-24s were ready for operations and on 9th October the Eighth Air Force was able to despatch over 100 heavy bombers (108), no mean feat in such a short time-span. This figure would not be equalled until the following spring, mainly on account of two Bomb Groups and four Fighter Groups being transferred to serve with the Twelfth Air Force then engaged in the invasion of North Africa.

To put this into context, at this time Bomber Command regularly despatched nightly over 200 heavy bombers, even as far as targets in Northern Italy. By January 1943 the Eighth was still only about one-seventh the size of the RAF's strike force.

It was not until 27th January 1943 that the Eighth was able to launch its first operation over a German target, Wilhelmshaven, which was out of the range of fighter escorts, both RAF and USAAF. This was the first time that their self-defensive theory would be put to the test. The American Lockheed P-38s (Lightnings), which were then considered the best long-range fighters, had been diverted to the North African campaign, and they had been replaced by Republic P-47s (Thunderbolts), which were very rugged and heavily armed fighters. Although they proved to be most effective they were nevertheless

'The Mighty Eighth': B-17s fly overhead during ceremonies dedicating Nuthampstead, 17th June 1943. (National Archives & Records Administration)

restricted in range, even when equipped with special drop fuel tanks. On this day the Eighth lost three heavy bombers, which was relatively light compared with the losses that would be suffered in the months ahead. For instance when, on 17th April, the Eighth attacked the Focke-Wulf aircraft plant at Bremen, it managed once again to send out over 100 heavy bombers, but 16 were lost (14%), which was their heaviest operational loss so far.

During the coming months the Eighth Air Force would grow steadily in strength, but so too would the Luftwaffe day-fighter force that opposed it. The German High Command had not taken the early American daylight operations too seriously, it had been assumed that the Americans would be forced to change to night-bombing as indeed had both the Luftwaffe and Bomber Command. As the Eighth's operations became more regular and stronger in numbers, the Luftwaffe pulled back day-fighters from other war fronts to counter the increasing flow of B-17s and B-24s, and by the summer of 1943 its day-fighter strength had almost doubled to some 800 fighters. Their pilots had also, from combat experience, evolved new tactics to counter the concentrated fire-power of the Eighth's bomber formations. Sadly, the Eighth would suffer the full force of the strengthened Luftwaffe on 17th August, the anniversary of their first heavy raid.

The two strategic targets, a Messerschmitt factory and a major ball bearing plant, selected for this special operation – Regensburg and Schweinfurt – have now passed into American Air Force history. Out of a total force of 376 B-17s no less than 60 were lost – this was more than had been lost in almost the first six months of operations! The official booklet *Target: Germany*, which described the Eighth Bomber Command's first year of operations over Europe, reported that in 124 attacks, 16,977 bombs had been dropped for the loss of 472 bombers and 4,481 airmen killed or missing. It concluded by saying, 'clearly the battle for air supremacy is not yet won. German anti-aircraft defenses are still on the increase, their new fighters are more heavily armed. The air war in the European Theater of Operations is becoming a slugging match between offense and defense. The side with the most stamina will win by a knockout'! Thus presaging a bitter and costly war of attrition between the gunners and their 'little friends' (the fighters) and the Luftwaffe that would continue almost unabated to the final days of the

P-38s of 228th Fighter Squadron of the 55th Fighter Group. (Smithsonian Institution)

war. More immediately, in less than two months, the Eighth would have to suffer even more horrendous losses, which would shake its conviction in daylight operations to the very core.

During September 1943 there were some major changes in the command structure of the Eighth's Bomber Command, as the original Bomb Wings (1st, 2nd and 4th) became three Bomb Divisions, with a fourth added later. The Eighth Air Force now totalled over 20 Bomb Groups and six Fighter Groups. Gone was 'the piddling little force', as General Eaker had described his command in the winter of 1942. Towards the end of the month (the 27th) the Eighth launched its first Pathfinder-led operation, the leading aircraft being equipped with the RAF's radar aid, H2S, which would later be replaced by the American version, H2X. Also during the month one Bomb Squadron flew some night-missions with RAF Bomber Command to see how effective they would be, before taking a major decision to modify their aircraft for night-operations, as well as retraining their aircrews in night-flying. Just two further missions were made in October before the idea was shelved, although the Bomb Squadron in question, No 422, continued to operate by night for the rest of the war delivering propaganda leaflets.

The days of the Eighth's medium bomber force operating with B-26s

41

(Marauders) from airfields in Essex were numbered. General Eaker had never been particularly impressed with their performance, and furthermore he felt that they did not sit easily in his Command. From 16th October the four Groups were transferred to the Ninth Air Force, which had moved to Great Britain from North Africa to assist the RAF's 2nd Tactical Air Force in preparation for the Allied invasion of Europe.

The Eighth's heavy bomb crews would experience a number of torrid and costly operations over the coming six weeks. The nightmare began on 6th September over Stuttgart when 45 B-17s were lost in action and another ten in crash-landings or ditchings in the sea, many as a result of shortage of fuel. Other operations in the month brought relatively light casualties, but in just four operations from 8th to 14th October no less than 148 aircraft were lost, including another 60 on the 14th when the infamous Schweinfurt was revisited by the Eighth. For the rest of the year, somewhat mercifully, the Eighth did not suffer a repetition of the heavy losses sustained during 'Black Week', as it became known. Also P-38s began to make a reappearance as escorts, and in December the first North American P-51s started escort duties with the Eighth, although they were actually serving in the Ninth Air Force. This legendary long-range pursuit fighter was destined to make a lasting impact on the air war in Europe, where it really became the saviour of the Eighth's strategic bombing offensive.

In January 1944 the Eighth Air Force lost General Eaker, its guide and mentor, who had been in overall command since 1st December 1942. Eaker had brought it through its most testing and exacting period of growth. He was given the overall command of Allied air forces in the Mediterranean and was replaced by Lieutenant General James H. Doolittle, whose main claim to fame until then was that he had led the first bombing mission on Tokyo. Doolittle was an oustanding pilot, a very fine tactician and an excellent leader, in fact the Eighth Air Force could not have received a better replacement for Eaker. A new command had also been created, in the light of the imminent invasion – United States Strategic Air Force (USSTAF) – which brought the return of General Spaatz. He was given the operational control of the Eighth and the Fifteenth Air Forces, the latter operating from Italy. Some measure of the massive growth of the Eighth can be seen in their operations on 31st December 1943 when over 570 heavy bombers attacked a variety of airfields in France, escorted by almost 550 fighters – 25 Bomb Groups and 12 Fighter Groups. As a comparison, just two nights earlier, RAF Bomber Command had despatched over 710 bombers to Berlin; of course, they were unescorted.

Within days of General Doolittle's arrival to take over command, the Eighth suffered heavy losses at the hands of the Luftwaffe, when, on 11th January, 42 aircraft out of 291 were lost whilst attacking two important aircraft plants at Oschersleben and Halberstadt. In other operations on the same day another 18 aircraft were lost – the third time in its short existence that the Eighth had lost 60 aircraft in a day. A combined Allied air bombardment of the German aircraft industry had been planned since late 1943 under the codename 'Argument', however it was not until February that it was launched. From the 20th to 25th/26th RAF Bomber Command attacked a series of planned targets by night with the Eighth bombing by day. Three cities – Leipzig, Schweinfurt and Augsburg – suffered by day and night. Over 6,600 combined sorties were made for the loss of 330 bombers and fighters, of which the Eighth lost almost 190 aircraft. It was a costly five days for both air forces but the combined offensive did materially damage the production of German fighters.

As RAF Bomber Command's long Berlin offensive was coming to an end, the Eighth decided it was ready to tackle the ultimate target, or 'Big B' as it was known to its crews. But like their RAF comrades they found it to be a most fearsome objective. In their first major operation on 6th March 80 bombers and fighters failed to return. By the end of the month when they had bombed the German capital on three more occasions, the Eighth had lost almost 190 aircraft in action or written-off with battle damage. However, such heavy losses could now be sustained due to new aircraft and replacement crews arriving in the United Kingdom almost daily. The American war machine had gathered a tremendous momentum and was producing aircraft and replacement crews at a quite prodigious pace.

In late April (22nd) the Eighth suffered another harsh reverse. As its bomber force was returning in the dark to its bases in East Anglia after attacking Hamm, the massive railway yards in the Ruhr, the formations were infiltrated by Luftwaffe night-fighters and no less than 14 bombers were shot down almost in sight of their home airfields – almost the same number that had been lost in action over Germany earlier in the day. Many of the gunners were cleaning their guns, so convinced were they that the mission was over!

Like RAF Bomber Command, the Eighth became engaged in attacking rail/road targets, marshalling yards, bridges, coastal batteries and airfields in Northern France as a prelude to D-Day. It had been allocated 24 of the 80 specific targets laid down in the Transportation Plan. In April over 11,000 sorties were made and over 550 aircraft were lost in action with some 4,000 airmen killed or missing in action. In the following month the Eighth made their first strike against the German oil industry. On the 12th of the month Merseburg, Lutzendorf, Zwickau, Brux, Böhlen and Zeitz were attacked. These oil targets, along with many others, would figure prominently in the Eighth's operational schedules over the next six months or more. The concentrated American offensive against the German oil industry, allied with the RAF Bomber Command night-offensive, was a major contribution to the demise of the Luftwaffe as a fighting force. As Air Chief Marshal Harris later

P-51s of 361st Fighter Group prepare to take off. (Smithsonian Institution)

wrote, 'The triumph of the offensive against oil was complete and indisputable.' But it was a victory achieved at a very high cost, no single priority target in Germany brought about the loss of so many American airmen and aircraft.

By D-Day the Eighth had reached the height of its strength and power – a massive force of 40 heavy Bomb Groups of which the greater number were equipped with B-17s. This phalanx of air power was supported by 15 Fighter Groups, a huge number of fighters, which were still mainly P-47s. The appearance of the first V1 rocket meant an increased bombardment of their sites in the Pas de Calais, but before the month was over, the Eighth, like RAF Bomber Command, would return to German targets and from then until the end of the war would mount operations at a rapid rate, in great numbers and conducted on a grand scale. Several of the operations were co-ordinated with Bomber Command with many targets being bombed by day and then by night, as 'round the clock' bombing became a harsh and grim reality for many German cities. This had been the bombing philosophy that Harris and Eaker had striven to attain back in 1943, but which had all too infrequently been achieved.

Nevertheless the battle for air supremacy in the daylight skies over Germany was still being bitterly waged, despite all the Eighth's efforts, both in the air and on the ground, with the American fighter pilots becoming adept and very effective at ground-strafing. The Luftwaffe was certainly not yet a spent force, but as more and more P-51s came into operation during the autumn their pilots managed to make their presence felt on mission after mission. However, four major operations in November provided ample evidence to the Eighth's crews and fighter pilots that the Luftwaffe was far from finished. On the 2nd, when the Leuna oil refinery at Merseburg was attacked, it was estimated that over 400 enemy fighters opposed the force and 40 bombers were lost but the American fighters, which numbered 960, claimed over 100 victories. Nineteen days later (the 21st) over the same target the P-51s claimed another 70 victims, and again on two successive days, the 26th and 27th, some 200 enemy fighters were thought to have been destroyed in the air. The Luftwaffe now had the rocket-propelled Me 163s and Me 262 turbo-jet fighters, and their growing menace gave the Eighth Air Force fighter chiefs some deep concern. It is now freely acknowledged that had they appeared in greater numbers they would have posed a very serious threat to the Eighth. As it was, the final victory over the Luftwaffe was not completely achieved until April 1945.

The 'Mighty' Eighth gave a demonstration of its enormous power and strength on Christmas Eve 1944 when 'maximum effort' was the order of the day; over 2,000 heavy bombers and 850 fighters (all but 50 were P-51s) took to the air to attack a variety of airfields and communications centres in Western Germany, in support of the US ground troops, which were battling against a strong German counter-offensive in the Ardennes. This proved to be the largest air strike ever mounted by the Eighth, although it was almost equalled on 24th March 1945 in support of Operation Varsity – the Allied armies' crossing of the Rhine. Twenty-two aircraft were lost in action but another 25 were lost as a result of take-off and landing accidents due to the freezing conditions and ground fog.

In less than four complete months of the New Year the Eighth launched just under 200 operations, which was one-fifth of their total of the war; and yet their first 200 operations had taken nearly 17 months to complete! The number of heavy bombers used were frequently in excess of 800, and on 14 consecutive days from 19th February to 4th March 1945 the Eighth operated more than 1,000 bombers and 500 fighters. Most of the operations passed with minimal losses, although on 3rd February the German flak batteries still managed to bring down 24 B-17s. On 7th April the Luftwaffe mounted its last desperate fling, when it was estimated that some 250 enemy fighters were airborne, about 50 of them Me 262s. Although the Eighth lost 18 bombers, they accounted for at least 60 fighters. Three days later 20 Me 262s were destroyed, which became known as the Day of the Great Jet Massacre. The last heavy bomber mission took place on 25th April and six bombers failed to return, all were victims of flak.

In well over 900 major operations and hundreds of minor operations the Eighth Air Force had fought a bitter and costly war, with over 6,100 aircraft lost and 43,742 airmen killed or missing in action, and another 1,923 seriously injured. These young American airmen, acknowledged by Air Chief Marshal Harris as 'the bravest of the brave', made an immense contribution to the ultimate defeat of Germany. Their sacrifice is remembered on the Wall of the Missing at the American Military Cemetery and Memorial at Madingley near Cambridge, as well as at the new American Air Museum at Duxford, where the impressive memorial glass sculpture, 'Counting the Cost', records the aircraft losses of the Eighth and Ninth Air Forces. Nearer to hand are the memorials at Nuthampstead, Podington and Thurleigh, dedicated to the airmen who served there.

Airfields

The expansion of the Royal Air Force in the mid to late 1930s brought about a considerable increase in the construction of new aerodromes. In April 1933 the Service had just 27 operational stations, but over the next five years another 25 would be planned and built, along with a number of training stations, all to be ready for occupation by 1939. To this end the Air Ministry Aerodromes Board was established in 1934 especially to locate suitable sites for the new stations. The Board reported directly to the Air Ministry Works Directorate General, known colloquially as 'Works and Bricks' or more disparagingly as 'Wonders and Blunders'! The Directorate was responsible for the maintenance, improvement and construction of Service stations.

As the number of new aerodromes required was relatively small, the Aerodromes Board could afford to be rather selective in obtaining prime sites. Most 'Expansion' stations, as they became known, took about four years to complete, from taking the first legal steps to obtain the necessary land until the arrival of the first airmen. A speed of progress that appears painfully slow and pedestrian compared with the building of wartime airfields, when twelve months was the average timescale. Though in mitigation it should be noted that the Board was working under a rather cumbersome and antiquated legal procedure to obtain the land – the Defence Act of 1842 – rather than the very immediate Defence Regulations of the Emergency Powers (Defence) Act. It must also be said that these new stations were built to rigorous engineering and construction criteria, and moreover were intended for permanence. Many have survived to bear witness to these very high standards; indeed, Cranfield in Bedfordshire is a prime and fine example.

The RAF stations built in the 1930s mostly conformed to a similar

Cranfield from the air – the epitome of a pre-war 'Expansion' airfield.
(Cranfield University)

pattern and design. They were generally based around a roughly circular grassed landing ground of at least 1,100 yards diameter. The watch office (later known as the control tower) was sited along the edge of the landing ground with a number of large and imposing hangars laid out in a curve to follow the boundary of the landing ground. The various technical buildings were located behind the hangars and the airmen's quarters and dining halls were placed nearby, often adjacent to the inevitable concrete parade ground; the dispersal of accommodation blocks only came into existence during the war. The officers' and sergeants' messes were normally sited further away and closer to the station headquarters, which was invariably situated near or opposite the main entrance to the station.

The architecture of all these Expansion stations bore a very striking similarity wherever they were built, perhaps only modified slightly in respect of the facings of the buildings, which were required to be in keeping with the local surroundings. This was largely due to the architect, who was commissioned by the Directorate, Sir Edwin Lutyens. He was a fine and remarkable architect, who stamped his very distinctive style and design on so many RAF stations throughout the land. The main station buildings were imposing brick buildings with roofing tiles, usually two or three storeys high. They were well-proportioned with neo-Georgian fronts and high porched entrances or provided with imposing porticos. Even the gate houses were given a most particular style, built with formal pillars and curved arches, behind which extended a verandah. All of the buildings had the graceful lines and elegance of the period, indeed they were required to gain the formal approval of both the Royal Fine Arts Commission and the Society for the Preservation of Rural England.

The standard of comfort and the number of social and sports amenities provided were luxurious by the standards of the day, and certainly compared with later wartime stations; tennis courts, playing fields and the provision of a squash court seemed to be *de rigueur*! Most of the main buildings and barrack blocks were centrally heated, and the officers' messes especially, were most spacious; imposing entrance halls, elegant high-ceilinged rooms, which provided the ideal settings for some of the formal ceremonies that were still an important part of the pre-war Service. These stations seemed to outwardly confirm the common belief in the 1930s that the RAF was 'the best flying club in the world'. Most of the new stations were situated well away from large towns and they became virtually self-sufficient closed communities. Nevertheless they made their indelible mark. Their large brick and steel hangars, and high water towers, allied to the presence of low-flying aircraft, ensured that the countryside around the stations would never be the same again. These Expansion stations have certainly stood the test of time, 60 years later several are still operational, and many more, almost unchanged in character, are used for other purposes – notably by Cranfield University.

Despite the construction of another 16 permanent stations before the outbreak of the war (though most were not completed until 1940 at the earliest), the Air Ministry was still faced with an enormous task to accommodate the greatly expanded wartime Service, both in operational and training terms. The fact that the Ministry had requisitioned all existing private and civil aerodromes barely improved the situation. It was said that the Aerodromes Board had, by 1940, identified some 4,000 possible sites in Britain; of these perhaps just over 10% would ultimately be developed into wartime airfields.

The development of airfields during the Second World War was a monumental construction and building project conducted on a massive scale, possibly the most ambitious ever undertaken. When the programme reached its peak in 1942 over one third of the construction industry was devoted to the operation. It received top priority in the allocation of scarce manpower resources, to the detriment of the clearance of bombed buildings. Most of the well-known names in civil engineering – John Laing, George Wimpey, W. & C. French, Taylor Woodrow, Richard Costain, McAlpine, John Mowlem *et al* – were engaged in the huge enterprise, as well as hundreds upon hundreds of smaller local sub-contractors. In 1942 alone £145 million (probably equivalent to about £3½ billion in today's value!) was expended on new airfields, as well as improvements to existing ones. By the end of the war there were well in excess of 600 Service airfields, the majority of which had been hastily built during 1940 to 1943. In that year England seemed to become one vast airfield. In East Anglia, Lincolnshire and Yorkshire the average distance between airfields was less than ten miles; it is not surprising that an American pilot famously remarked that they were 'thicker than fleas on a dog's back'!

The normal procedure to locate a suitable airfield site started with a close scrutiny of the one inch Ordnance Survey maps. Ideally the land should be close to sea level, or at least not above 600 feet because of the greater incidence of hill fog and low cloud. The site should also be relatively flat, and free from obstructions, both natural and man-made. The Aerodromes Board's brief was to take careful note of any existing or planned airfield in the vicinity, with a guideline of three miles apart for quite obvious safety reasons. However, the Board invariably erred on the side of caution and worked on five miles distant as a broad rule of thumb.

Once a promising site had been identified, it was then inspected on foot field by field with notes being made of any particular construction problems that might be encountered. Trees and rising land did not greatly matter at this stage, nor indeed did the presence of the odd house or so, which might block the flight paths! If at all possible the nature of

Thurleigh airfield in October 1942. (Smithsonian Institution)

the sub-soil was determined, good drainage was considered to be essential especially as most of the early wartime airfields were only grassed. Once the site had passed all the various acid tests, steps were taken to requisition the necessary land, often in the region of about 600 acres, and the necessary planning procedures were put in motion. At this stage local objections could be raised and considered, though it must be admitted that precious few were upheld. The most frequent and vociferous opposition came from the War Agricultural Committee, who were equally hard-pressed to utilise all available agricultural land for food production. To my knowledge the only airfield site in the two counties ear-marked for development for the USAAF but not further progressed was at Dunstable.

After the various contracts had been awarded to one of the numerous construction firms, hordes of building workers would move in with their massive earth-moving equipment, heavy tractors, lorries and cement mixers; roads were closed in the area and many remained so for the whole of the war. Certainly the peace of the rural countryside was well and truly broken, especially as the construction work was often carried on by day and night, such was the urgent need for airfields. Fields were flattened, trees and hedges uprooted, ditches and hollows filled in, telephone lines removed and placed underground, water drains and sewers laid, and within weeks the whole area would either

Work on concrete runways. (John Laing plc)

become a sea of mud or disappear under thick clouds of choking dust according to the season.

The first real construction work commenced with the provision of a concrete perimeter road – 50 yards wide – right around the airfield site, which could stretch for three miles or more. This road gave access to at least 50 dispersal points for parking aircraft, generally known as hard standings. It had been decreed, in February 1939, that all aircraft should be dispersed around the perimeter of the airfield. Those airfields occupied by the USAAF from 1942 onwards had the number of hard standings increased because its Groups had a larger complement of aircraft than RAF squadrons. On the other hand most Flying Training airfields were not normally provided with such luxuries.

The next stage of construction was the laying of the three concrete runways. Most pre-war Service airfields had been grass-surfaced; tarmac, paved or concrete runways were relatively late coming onto the scene. Not until May 1939 was it decided that all future bomber stations should be provided with 'firm runways', and at the same time the Air Ministry rather grudgingly agreed that eight major Fighter Command stations should also be provided with hard runways, although only two were finished by the outbreak of the war. Flying Training airfields were quite low down on the priority list, not necessarily because of the high cost of building concrete runways but rather the Command's lack of enthusiasm on the subject. However, Cranfield, which was then solely devoted to flying training, had hard runways laid in the winter of 1939/40, and was amongst the earliest of pre-war stations to be so provided.

The prescribed lengths of the runways altered during 1940/1 but ultimately a standard specification was agreed, which became known as a Class A Standard bomber station. The main runway measured 2,000 yards by 50 yards wide, with two subsidiaries, each 1,400 yards in length but of the same width; each runway was provided with at least 100 yards of cleared land at both ends to act as an overshoot. The runways were to be as near to 60° to each other as possible, and they were invariably laid down in the shape of a letter 'A'.

The most distinctive and prominent landmarks on any airfield were the hangars. The word comes from the French to describe 'a covered space for a carriage'! In the First World War and for many years afterwards they were simply known as 'aircraft sheds'. Most of the Expansion airfields, and Cranfield was no exception, were provided with a number of 'C' type hangars, which were massive brick and steel constructions some 300 feet long, 35 feet high and with either gabled or hipped roofs. They were time-consuming and very labour intensive to erect, and therefore a simple and more easily erectable structure became essential for wartime conditions. The hangars to be seen at most wartime airfields were either Type 'T' and/or 'Blister' types. The former had been developed by Tees-Side Bridge & Engineering Works, and were of galvanised corrugated iron construction, simple and speedy to assemble. They came in various sizes, but 240 feet in length seemed to be the most prevalent, with an opening span of 113½ feet and a door height of 25 feet, quite formidable structures. These hangars were provided at Bovingdon, Gransden Lodge, Little Staughton, Nuthampstead, Podington and Thurleigh, with just a single one at Sawbridgeworth. The Blister hangars of varying types were of a far more simple construction; they were basically built of wooden arched ribs covered with curved corrugated iron sheeting. The standard span was 45 feet and they were either 25 or 45 feet long. As they did not require any flooring, they were flexible enough to be erected on uneven ground, which was a great advantage. Over 3,000 were produced by C. Miskins & Sons for the Service and examples could be seen at Hunsdon, Sawbridgeworth and Panshanger.

The wartime control tower at Little Staughton has survived.

An important building at all airfields was the watch office or control tower, which housed the air traffic control and meteorological offices, and was the nerve centre during operations. The building was fully equipped with telephone lines, radio and tele-printer apparatus and radar. By late 1941 a standardised building had evolved, which was a functional two-storey brick building rendered with concrete and provided with a railed balcony as well as railings on the flat roof. Some were also provided with an exterior steel stairway. Not many of these wartime buildings have survived, but there is a fine example, still in use, at Little Staughton, with a disused one at Twinwood Farm. However, the old control tower at Podington has been converted into a private residence.

Close to the control tower and inscribed in large white letters, was the airfield's identification code – two letters about 10 feet in size – which uniquely identified the airfield. These really date back to pre-war days when it was the practice to display the name of the aerodrome in white letters sufficiently large to be visible from an altitude of about 2,000 feet. For obvious security reasons this method was suspended during the war and the letter code was substituted. Cranfield's code was 'CX', Little Staughton 'LX' but Sawbridgeworth was allocated 'ZH' because of the number of airfields beginning with the letter 'S'. At night a mobile beacon unit (known as a 'pundit'), usually sited some way from the airfield and moved regularly, flashed in red morse signals the airfield's code, hence why the identification letters were more commonly known as the Pundit Code.

The myriad of administrative and technical buildings of wartime airfields were mostly temporary and pre-fabricated constructions. Many were made of pre-cast concrete slabs – 'Orlit' and 'Maycrete' seemed to be the most prevalent. Others were constructed from light timber materials and plasterboard sheets, of which the 'Laing' huts were the most numerous. They were produced locally by John Laing & Co at Elstree in Hertfordshire. The accommodation huts, mess halls, communal rooms, sick quarters etc, were dispersed some distance away from the airfield itself, in six or more sites in the surrounding countryside, or in some instances in nearby villages. It was in these sites that the omnipresent Nissen huts could be found, although on many airfields they were used for a variety of technical purposes, and were frequently used at the main gate as guard houses. These curved sheet constructions in differing spans of 16, 24 and 30 feet, probably epitomise wartime airfields more than any other structure. The design dated from the First World War when Colonel Peter Nissen devised their simple structure. Colonel Nissen, a Canadian by birth, settled in this country after the war and set up a company at Hoddesdon in Hertfordshire to produce the huts for military and industrial use. Nissen huts were still being used by the British forces in the Falklands conflict.

The majority of the wartime airfields have long since disappeared. Most of them returned to agriculture, others were put to a variety of uses, such as industrial estates, race tracks, prisons etc, although a number still operate for their original purpose, and are in the hands of private flying clubs. It is somewhat ironic to note that back in November 1943, when the RAF and the USAAF were deeply involved in the bitter and costly air war, the Air Ministry thought it necessary, and indeed found time, to issue a news statement, which showed that it had already recognised a future problem with the sudden and rapid demise of wartime airfields!

Old wartime building at Panshanger.

'In a country of the size of Great Britain the construction of so large a number of airfields has involved serious encroachments on land formerly available for agricultural and other purposes. It is not possible to express in terms of money what this diversion has involved, but it is very considerable. Further, a large proportion of the airfields constructed for war purposes cannot be used either for post-war military purposes or for civil aviation. Therefore, so far from representing an asset of abiding value, the British Government will, upon the termination of hostilities, be faced with a very considerable liability for the reinstatement of sites and the restoration of land to its former uses.'

One national magazine, *The Illustrated London News*, was particularly speedy to bring to the public's notice the vast number of empty airfields that were dotted throughout the countryside. In the issue of 15th September 1945 the magazine cited the example of Podington, which, 'not long since had been pulsating with energy and life…where the great

56

bombers used to thunder as they took off or landed before and after operative flights against the enemy in Europe.' It posed the question, 'What will happen to them?' Podington is now, of course, a drag-racing circuit of some fame – Santa Pod. Cranfield is the site of Cranfield University, though still an extremely busy airfield. Thurleigh has become RAE Bedford, Henlow is still in use, and Luton goes from strength to strength. Others such as Little Staughton, Little Gransden (Gransden Lodge), Nuthampstead and Panshanger are still used for private flying, but Hunsdon, Sawbridgeworth, Tempsford and Twinwood Farm have returned to farming, gone but certainly not forgotten.

2

BOVINGDON

Without doubt Bovingdon would have been an aircraft-spotter's paradise during the wartime years. No other Eighth Air Force base housed such a wide variety of American wartime aircraft. From the summer of 1942 the ubiquitous B-17s were ever present in considerable numbers, although the other major heavy bomber – B-24 – appeared there less frequently, as did the Eighth's medium B-26s. All of the American operational fighters, P-38, P-47 and P-51, were evident at various times, as well as a rare selection of small communications and liaison aircraft, such as the Beechcroft 45Fs and AT-7s, the latter used as navigational trainers. The small Fairchild UC 61As 'Forwarders', or 'Argus' as they were known in the RAF, were perhaps the most numerous as many had been provided for combat Groups. From late 1944 the two major transport aircraft of the USAAF – the Douglas C-47 and C-53 – virtually took over the airfield. Also more than the occasional RAF aircraft could be seen there, certainly from late 1942 when the ferry pilots of the Air Transport Auxiliary made training flights into Bovingdon, whilst converting to Halifaxes.

The airfield was situated about two miles to the south-west of Hemel Hempstead on the edge of the Chiltern Hills and close to the Hertfordshire and Buckinghamshire boundary. The site had been developed during 1941/2 by John Laing & Son Ltd, as the main contractor, with one runway at 1,630 yards, and two at 1,430 yards.

Fairchild UC – 61A – 'Forwarder' (RAF Museum)

Unlike most airfields that were completed during this period the runways at Bovingdon were not extended to conform with the Class A Standard bomber station.

In the spring of 1942 the new airfield was placed under the control of No 7 Group of Bomber Command, presumably with the intention of housing a new Operational Training Unit; back in July 1940 this Group had been formed to administer a number of the Command's OTUs. In fact no RAF personnel actually arrived at Bovingdon, because on 16th May it was allocated to the USAAF, although it would be the middle of August before the first American airmen arrived to take up permanent residence. However, by then the first American aircraft – B-17Fs – had already flown into Bovingdon towards the end of July; they were the harbingers of the 301st (Heavy) Bomb Group, which was scheduled to operate from Chelveston in Northamptonshire. On 9th August they departed for their permanent station although one aircraft got into some difficulties and crash-landed at RAF Church Lawford en route to Chelveston; the aircraft named *Stork* gained the dubious honour of being the first B-17F to be salvaged in England.

Ten days later the ground echelon of the 92nd (Heavy) Bomb Group, which was the oldest in the Eighth Air Force, moved into the airfield. The airmen had disembarked at Liverpool from the USS *West Point*, having taken twelve days to cross the Atlantic. Almost at the same time the first of the Group's B-17Fs began to land after making the 'short hop'

B-17 taking-off from Bovingdon. (USAF)

down from Prestwick in Scotland. The young and inexperienced crews were the first to make a direct flight across the Atlantic from Gander Lake in Newfoundland to Scotland. This was an exhausting and, no doubt, traumatic journey for them, over 2,100 miles, which took on average about eleven hours. The crews of 326th squadron had commenced their ferry flights on 15th August, followed by the 325th and 327th squadrons, and the last B-17s of the 407th squadron did not arrive at Bovingdon until the 28th of the month. For the excellent way the crews had executed the long transatlantic crossing, with no serious losses or mishaps (a single B-17 was forced to land in Northern Ireland because of bad weather) the Group received a letter of special commendation from the powers-that-be, which afforded much satisfaction to the Group's Commanding Officer, Lieutenant Colonel James S. Sutton.

The Boeing B-17 was perhaps one of the classic bomber designs of all time. It had first flown in July 1935 as 'Model 299', and was the company's response to the US Army Air Corps' requirement 5/34 for 'a high-altitude bomber to be used against fleets of vessels'! The first 13 were delivered to the Army Air Corps in March 1937. The all-metal, sleek and almost elegant four-engined monoplane was a real revolution in design, by far in advance of other contemporary bombers. Its array of armament, five gun defensive positions or twelve/thirteen .50 inch machine guns in later models, quickly gained it the rather romantic name 'Flying Fortress', which remained with it throughout its operational life.

It was a large and heavy aircraft, almost 75 feet in length with a wing span of close to 104 feet, and it proved to be most durable in combat, able to sustain heavy damage and still survive. The B-17 was universally admired by all its crews, they were utterly convinced that however battle-damaged their 'ship' (as the Americans called their heavy bombers) was, it would bring them back safely. The B-17s will forever epitomise the Eighth Air Force during its time in this country. They were operated ultimately by 26 Bomb Groups, making a massive and potent destructive force. General Ira Eaker considered it to be 'the best combat airplane ever built', though his friend and colleague Air Chief Marshal Harris thought that the Lancaster was superior! At the USAAF's peak, in March 1944, no less than 4,750 B-17s were in service and over 12,600 were produced during the Second World War, which is a quite staggering figure considering that in 1939 the US Army Air Corps had less than 30.

The model 'F' was the fifth and latest, and had only gone into production with Boeing, Douglas and Lockheed-Vega, the major B-17 manufacturers, in April 1942. Although outwardly no different to the model 'E' that it replaced, except for a slightly enlarged frameless nose transparency, it had been provided with additional wing fuel tanks to increase the aircraft's operational range enabling it to reach targets throughout the length and breadth of Germany and beyond. Some 3,400 B-17Fs were produced and they equipped most of the Eighth's Bomb Groups until late 1943. However, within days of their arrival at Bovingdon, the Group was forced to exchange their new 'F's for the older model 'E's of the 97th Bomb Group, then operating from Polebrook and Grafton Underwood in Northamptonshire. This earlier model had first flown in September 1941 and was really the first major redesign the aircraft had undergone since 1937, with over 400 changes being incorporated, many as a result of the RAF's short and unsuccessful time operating a squadron (No 90) of Flying Fortresses. It was the first B-17 model to be equipped with power-driven turrets, as well as being provided with a tail-gun position, and was the first to have the now distinctive enlarged horizontal and vertical tail-surfaces. Just over 500 B-17Es were built, and the crews of the 92nd would take them into action from Bovingdon.

The main reason for the change of aircraft was that the 92nd Group had been given the task of training new replacement crews that arrived from the States, and for this purpose it was considered that the 'E's were more than adequate. It had been back in early March that General Eaker and his small staff had quickly realised that there would be an urgent need for some form of 'Theater indoctrination', as they called it, for the hundreds of new crews that would arrive from the training schools in the States. These crews would not only be serving with the new units coming to join the Eighth but they would also replace losses; at this stage the Eighth estimated losses of bomber crews to be 5%, a figure which it had based on Bomber Command's experiences. General Eaker asked the Pentagon in Washington to authorise the establishment of two Combat Crew Replacement Centers (CCRC), one for bombers and the other for fighters, with the necessary personnel to man and service them. To say that Washington were rather dilatory on the matter would be an understatement, the Centers were not formally approved until August 1943 – almost twelve months after the 'temporary' solution devised by General Eaker had begun operating! However, it did effectively mean that the Eighth Air Force had lost two valuable operational Groups.

Despite the Group's quite heavy training commitments, it was called upon to mount some operational missions from Bovingdon. The first took place on 6th September 1942 when 24 B-17s left the airfield to join 27 B-17s of the 97th Bomb Group to attack an aircraft factory in Meaulte in France. Unfortunately two aircraft went missing and they were the first heavy bomber losses suffered by the Eighth; one crew came from the 92nd. The Group's fourth and final mission from the airfield was mounted on 9th October when over 100 B-17s and B-24s attacked the Fives/Lille steelworks; out of the 15 aircraft that left Bovingdon, four returned early with mechanical problems, and two collided over the English Channel about 20 miles west of Dunkirk. Both were badly damaged, one managed to make it back to base, but the other was forced to make an emergency landing at RAF Detling in Kent. This collision was the first of over 100 such incidents during the war, a harsh and costly penalty that had to be paid for the Eighth Air Force's dedication to close formation flying. One B-17 returning from attacking Longuenesse airfield at St Omer was badly damaged and ditched in the English Channel but sadly the crew was not rescued. The 92nd Group would not return to operations until the middle of May 1943 and they would later serve with distinction from Podington.

By now the Group had virtually lost its identity, becoming subsumed into No 11 CCRC. The new crews were instructed in flying control systems and procedures in use in the United Kingdom. Pilots were trained on the Standard Beam Approach (bad weather landings) and instrument flying, which was then a weakness in the flying training programme in the States. They were also disciplined into flight assembly procedures and close formation flying. Navigators were familiarised with British maps and the various radio and radar aids to navigation. Radio operators received instruction on the British radio frequencies and call signs, and the air gunners were given ground-to-air gunnery practice at Mousehole in Cornwall, as well as air-to-air firing over the Wash. They were also given an intensive ground course on aircraft recognition, though both RAF and USAAF fighter pilots were convinced that the gunners would fire at anything if it happened to come within range!

Parties of specialist RAF personnel were seconded to the Center to pass on their expertise and experience. The Center's crews were also used as reserves for the mere handful of heavy Bomb Groups then operating with the Eighth. Nevertheless they were still rather under-utilised despite flying a couple of diversionary flights (not counted as missions) during late October and December. It became clear that the first replacement crews would not begin to appear in the United Kingdom until the New Year, the invasion of North Africa had become the first priority for newly trained air crews. It was therefore felt that just one squadron could cope adequately with the training; early in January 1943 the 92nd moved away to Alconbury, but with just three squadrons, leaving the 326th behind to operate as the 'school's flying unit' with Major John P. Dwyer being appointed the Director of Training.

Early in 1943 as the Eighth's bomber force began to expand, there were many requests from the American news media to allow their correspondents to fly on combat missions. Eventually the USAAF acceded to the requests but only with the proviso that the reporters went through a high-altitude survival course at Bovingdon. The first civilian course was mounted in early February, and the first six American correspondents went on a combat mission on the 26th of the month; sadly Robert B. Post of the *New York Times* was lost over Wilhelmshaven. Three months later a British reporter was killed over Kiel, whilst flying with the 91st Bomb Group from Bassingbourn.

During April to mid-June 1943 the airfield became a hive of activity with a considerable number of B-17s jostling for space. On 26th April the first B-17s of 379th Bomb Group landed and they stayed for almost a month, whilst the runways at their permanent station at Kimbolton were being extended. No sooner had they departed but more B-17s arrived, again merely as 'birds in passage' as they belonged to the 381st Bomb Group, which was planned to occupy Ridgewell airfield in Essex; they left for their base on 15th June. Bovingdon was used by all manner of American aircraft – after all it was the nearest Eighth Air Force base to the various Command headquarters, as well as London, and it was also used as a major staging post for aircraft returning to the United States. For instance, on 9th June 1943, Captain K. Morgan and his crew of the *Memphis Belle*, perhaps the most famous B-17 of the war, left Bovingdon to fly back to the States to undertake a War Bond-raising tour of the country; the occasion was marked with due formal military ceremony. The aircraft's ultimate fame was ensured by William Wyler's fine documentary film of the Eighth's bombing operations, entitled *Memphis Belle*, and more recently with the successful re-make of the film in 1989. The aircraft, which has since been restored to its former glory, is now on permanent display at Memphis.

Back in the autumn of 1942 the crews of the 15th Photo Mapping Squadron of 3rd Photographic Group had been frequent visitors to the airfield before they moved to join the Twelfth Air Force in North Africa. The squadron's most famous airman was its Commanding Officer, Lt Colonel Elliott Roosevelt, one of the four sons of the US President; he would later be awarded the Distinguished Flying Cross. His mother, Eleanor, later officially visited the airfield. Indeed the men at Bovingdon would become quite used to seeing VIPs. Most of the famous film stars that came over from the States to entertain the American forces would pass through Bovingdon, for example Bob Hope, Bing Crosby, Clark Gable (who went on several missions with the Eighth), Marlene Dietrich and, of course, Glenn Miller. The airfield also housed 'A' Flight of the Eighth's Headquarters Squadron, which was used by various staff officers to visit American air bases as well as RAF airfields, so there was no shortage of the 'Top Brass'. When General Dwight Eisenhower finally arrived in the country as the Supreme Allied Commander, his personal B-17, which was piloted by Major Larry Henson, was also based at Bovingdon. There was no doubt that it was a high profile Eighth Air Force base.

Another separate unit based at Bovingdon was the Air Technical Section of the Eighth Fighter Command, which ensured that American fighters were in constant evidence around the airfield, whilst they underwent a variety of trials and tests. This Section's leading light was Lieutenant Colonel Cass H. Hough, a 36 year old technical staff officer, who had arrived in England in July 1942, along with Brigadier General Frank O'D. Hunter, the Eighth's Fighter Commander from May 1942 to August 1943.

Colonel Hough was one of those many dedicated 'backroom' officers, who did not gain the limelight and publicity accorded to the Eighth's fighter aces, but nevertheless he and his team at Bovingdon made an immense contribution to ensuring that the Eighth's fighters gained and held a technical superiority over the Luftwaffe fighters. Hough, personally, undertook tests on P-38s when their pilots were experiencing problems with their aircraft, especially in steep dives. He also trialled the P-47 when it began to appear with the Eighth in early 1943. This was followed by early experimental work on designing and developing pressurised drop fuel tanks for the fighters. His section became greatly involved in developing the potential of the P-38 as a fighter/bomber, the so-called 'Droop Snoots', which will be discussed later under Nuthampstead. The Colonel was also asked to test fly the Mustang I or P-51B, which the RAF had adapted by exchanging its original Allison engine for a Rolls-Royce Merlin. In the light of the P-51's later success, his opinion is interesting: 'it was good and very fast but I found the directional stability was poor unlike the P-47.'

When General James Doolittle took over the Eighth Air Force in early 1944, he was so impressed with the Section's work that, in February, he expanded it into a single organisation to deal with bombers as well as fighters and any other operational problems that might arise. Its express

Captain Robert K. Morgan and the crew of the 'Memphis Belle' before leaving

for the USA, 9th June 1943. (Smithsonian Institution)

Lt Colonel Cass S. Hough of Air Technical Section at Bovingdon. (USAF)

purpose was stated to be: 'Combat evaluation of existing tactics, techniques and material, and the development of new tactics, techniques and material to adjust to the tide of battle.' A wonderful catch-all to cover all eventualities! The unit was commanded by Colonel

Ben Kelsey, late of the Ninth Air Force, with Hough as his Deputy and it had almost 200 personnel working on the various projects, which by the end of the war had numbered over 350.

By August 1943 Washington had finally recognised the three major Combat Crew Replacement Centers – the others were at Cheddington in Buckinghamshire and Toome in Northern Ireland. Bovingdon was re-designated No 2900, although in practice it would still retain its original number, that is until November when it was again given a fresh number – No 1! By June of the following year the Center had only 13 B-17s on complement but it had also been engaged on training new crews for the Twelfth Air Force then operating from Italy. Three months later the Center's work was being phased out. The advanced training of crews in the United States had greatly improved with the establishment of a School of Applied Tactics, and it was decided that the individual Bomb Groups would become responsible for 'Operational Theater training'. Thus in October 1944 No 1 CCRC was disbanded and most of its personnel were assigned to the newly formed Air Disarmament Command, which had been specially established to disarm enemy aircraft units and equipment that were being captured and then arrange for their disposal. The Command's units soon moved away to two airfields in Essex – Chipping Ongar and Boreham – before leaving for the Continent.

The control of Bovingdon now passed to the US Air Transport Command with another newly-formed unit being based at the airfield. This was the US Air Transport Service (Europe), which as its name implies provided a regular air transport service to and from France, Italy and later Germany. For this service Douglas C-47s and C-53s were used, which carried a double yellow bar tail flash to identify them as the Command's aircraft. The former was the workhorse of the USAAF, and it was the military version of the most successful DC-3 civil airliner, which had first flown in 1936. It was well in advance of its time, built to a simple but robust design, which offered speed and comfort to its passengers. The military version, known as the 'Skytrain', was first ordered by the Army Air Corps in 1940 but Douglas Aircraft Company Inc did not produce C-47s in any great numbers until 1942. It was the Allied Air Forces' most commonly-used transport, known in the RAF as the 'Dakota', and it proved to be a most reliable aircraft, if somewhat

C-47 of US Air Transport Service (Europe). (Smithsonian Institution)

restricted in its operational range. The C-47 was used mainly as a cargo carrier with a capacity of two tons of stores and supplies, but it also operated as a troop carrier in all the major airborne landings of 1944/5. The aircraft would gain lasting post-war fame as a commercial airliner and freight carrier throughout the world, with over 20,000 being built, which probably made it the most remarkable and prolific aircraft in the history of aviation. The C-53 or 'Skytrooper' was another version of the C-47, it did not have quite the same cargo carrying capacity as the former, but could transport 28 fully equipped troops. The aircraft really provided an airline standard of transport for military purposes.

After VE Day Bovingdon was used as the departure point for thousands of American servicemen being transported back home to the States, and in mid-April 1946 the airfield was handed back to the RAF. Soon after, the Ministry of Civil Aviation took over Bovingdon and it was used by British Overseas Airways Corporation as a maintenance base, and at times, as a diversionary airfield for both Northolt and Heathrow. However, just over five years after the last wartime Americans had left Bovingdon, the United States Air Force returned and remained there until 1962. Then the airfield was used by a couple of film companies to make three war films, before finally closing down in 1972. Part of the airfield site now houses a HM Youth Custody Centre.

3
CARDINGTON

Although not an airfield in the strict sense, Cardington has been included because of its very special place in British aviation history; it stands as an unique memorial to the country's aeronautical past. Nevertheless Cardington also played an important, if little publicised, part in the Second World War.

Without doubt Cardington is a most contemplative place to visit, its two massive airship sheds, relics of the First World War, imposing an almost brooding presence over the rural scene. The large and impressive tomb memorial in the local churchyard bears the inscription: 'Here lies the bodies of 48 Officers and Men who perished in H.M. Airship R101 at Beauvais, France Oct 5 1930'. Indeed it is rather difficult not to associate Cardington solely with this dreadful disaster, which so deeply shocked and saddened the whole nation. As Sir Stanley Hoare, the Secretary of State for Air, wrote at the time, 'The disaster that destroyed R101 is so overwhelming in the suffering it imposed upon many families and the injury it inflicted on aeronautical science that any comment on its cause is inappropriate. Today I am thinking not of the future of airships, or the money and effort spent on a difficult experiment, but remembering those, who for eight years, were engaged upon a great adventure and have died at the moment when success of their enterprise seemed assured.' Nevertheless, the R101 disaster effectively sounded the death knell of British rigid airships.

The impressive memorial to the victims of the R101 disaster.

From 1917 when Short Brothers of Rochester opened their new 'Naval Aircraft Works/Bedford' about a mile or so to the south-west of the village of Cardington, it was at the centre of rigid airship design, development and production. The Station Headquarters building, which still stands, the various technical buildings and workshops, along with the houses built for the staff quickly became named Shortstown, as it is still known today. After a relatively brief existence the works was compulsorily purchased by the Government and renamed the Royal Airship Works. Although only four airships were built there – R31, 32, 38 and 101 – the residents of Bedford (about three miles away) and those in the surrounding countryside became quite familiar with the sight of these 'large and stately airships floating in the skies'. One local resident still remembers sighting the first airship to be built at Cardington, R31, 'sailing majestically overhead', and being told by the headmaster of her school to, 'note this moment well. You are watching history being made.' Besides the various trial flights of the R101, which began on 14th October 1929, the R100, built at Howden, cruised around Bedfordshire and nearby counties for some six hours in June 1930, prior to its historic and spectacular trip to Canada and back, leaving from Cardington on 29th July.

Just nine months later after the tragic loss of the R101 the Committee of National Expenditure effectively killed off any possibility of a revival of airship construction. Most of the permanent staff at Cardington were moved to the Royal Aircraft Establishment at Farnborough, and the Royal Airship Works was left virtually moribund, with less than 50 personnel remaining merely to prevent the site becoming derelict. In 1933 No 2 Aircraft Storage Unit was established at Cardington, which would, for the next five years, supply aircraft to the Service.

Cardington's salvation came in the shape of a barrage balloon! It was decided to resurrect a First World War defence system – the so-called 'barrage apron' – which, in 1917, had been used over London as a form of defence against the night raids of the German Gotha bombers. About 20 or so 'aprons' were suspended in an arc to the north, south and east of the city, each consisting of a line of balloons, the cables of which were linked with wires from which other wires were suspended, thus forming a curtain. The intention was to prevent low-flying attacks and to force the enemy aircraft to fly higher.

The requirements of the new barrage balloon defence system, as was envisaged in the mid-1930s, were formidable and daunting considering the number of cities, towns, and strategic targets needing such protection. Thousands of balloons would be required to be produced from high-grade rubberised fabric, which in itself was a highly skilled task. Each separate balloon site would be equipped with its own motorised winch, mobile transport, accommodation, and a number of trained operators providing a fully monitored service for 24 hours a day. Also a considerable number of repair and maintenance depôts needed to be established at convenient distances from the balloon sites. A Balloon Development Establishment, which was effectively the nucleus of the Royal Airship Works, had already undertaken considerable research into the type and shape of the balloon to be used. In 1938 this establishment became known as the Balloon Development Unit and the proud title of 'Royal Airship Works' disappeared.

Because of the proven background of research and development and the large area of open land that was needed, Cardington was selected to establish the first training courses for balloon crews. In November 1936 the station became formally known as RAF Cardington, with Group Captain A. A. Thomson, MC, AFC, appointed as its first Commanding

Officer. No 1 Balloon Training Unit was formed on 9th January 1937, and one month later the first Barrage Balloon Group, No 30, came into being, with a retired officer, Air Commodore J. G. Heaton, placed in command. The courses would instruct the part-time airmen of the Auxiliary Air Force, who had been selected to man the sites. Each crew would number ten of these airmen probably with the addition of at least one regular airman. The course comprised about 84 hours of instruction in rigging and repairs, followed by over 200 hours of practical experience in the correct handling of the balloons, and the operation of the motorised winch. In November 1938, No 30 Group was elevated into Balloon Command with Air Vice-Marshal O. T. Boyd appointed as its first Commander. However, it was still under the overall control of Fighter Command, as were the rest of the country's air defences.

Cardington had rather suddenly become an active and busy station, especially from September 1937 when No 2 RAF Recruit Centre moved up the road from nearby Henlow. From then onwards thousands upon thousands of civilians would enter the RAF at Cardington and so receive their first taste of Service life and discipline. The station would also house Aircrew Selection and Medical Boards, bringing even more airmen, albeit very briefly, to Cardington. But as the threat of war became more imminent the training of balloon handling crews accelerated and by September 1939 almost 50 squadrons had been formed, all manned by the Auxiliary Air Force, and five squadrons were controlled by one Balloon Centre. Of some 600 sites that were in operation, about two-thirds were then sited in the Greater London area. The manufacture of balloons had also been stepped up, and ultimately at its peak 26 were being produced at Cardington each week. The unit also mounted a number of training programmes for workers from outside industries to acquire the necessary manufacturing skills.

The first 24 barrage balloons appeared over London in September 1938 during the Munich crisis. The 'Blimps', as they were quickly dubbed, would become the most familiar sights in the British skies for virtually the whole of the war. The balloons, or L2s, were 62 feet long by 30 feet high with a diameter of about 25 feet. They were filled with some 20,000 cubic feet of hydrogen gas, which could cost from £25 to £45 each time they were inflated. As an aircraft defence system it was certainly not cheap, especially as there were always doubts expressed about its effectiveness.

A Balloon site 'somewhere in the North of England'. (via G. Harris)

The Women's Auxiliary Air Force was formed on 28th June 1939, and in 1940 it was proposed that WAAFs should operate the balloons, but at first it was considered that the work was too heavy and strenuous, and, at times, too dangerous for airwomen. However, as the RAF's manpower shortage became critical, WAAFs were finally trained in balloon handling with 20 of them forming a crew rather than the ten airmen, though this was later reduced to a ratio of 14 against nine, as the airwomen showed their prowess with these duties. The work of balloon operator was graded a Class II trade, and as a result the airwomen operating the barrage balloons were the highest paid WAAFs in the Service – 2s 4d to 6s 8d per day according to rank! Towards the end of 1942 the majority of the 15,700 barrage balloon sites were operated by WAAFs; in fact one of the most famous paintings of the Second World War, by Dame Laura Knight, RA, portrayed an all WAAF crew hauling up a balloon.

For those people who lived near a site, the barrage balloon became an essential part of everyday life in wartime Britain, and often the balloons were affectionately given personal family names (the writer recalls one being called 'Horace'!). However, it must be admitted that they were more generally known as 'pigs' for obvious reasons! Certainly their very presence overhead gave the public a sense of security and satisfaction, daily evidence that at least they were being defended. However, it was later proved that their defensive qualities were far, far less than the public imagined them to be. Some wartime writers could almost wax lyrical over the balloons, 'shining silver in the sun, or turning pink or golden or shades of blue in the varied lights from dawn to evening, their cable singing some kind of tune, maybe in the high wind, and just occasionally, the balloon itself, if something has gone wrong, turning over and over like a playful porpoise, or again lashing about with the fury of a wounded whale'.

The balloons were mostly placed at semi-permanent sites set at fairly equidistant points and covering a wide area to provide a more comprehensive barrage. The intention was to force the enemy aircraft to operate at about a height at which they could more accurately be engaged by the anti-aircraft batteries. They also posed a deterrent to low-flying aircraft, as well as to dive-bombing attacks. However, experiments were made, especially during the night blitz of 1940/1, of releasing a large number of free flying balloons into the path of approaching enemy aircraft, each balloon trailing a length of wire to which was attached a canister of explosives. By this method it was hoped that an aircraft hitting the cable would be destroyed. This type of balloon operation was first code-named Pegasus, though it later became known as Albino; both were less than successful, causing far more trouble and concern to the Civil Defence authorities on the ground when the balloon landed and exploded, than to the Luftwaffe crews above!

The first probable success of the balloon barrage occurred on the night of 12th/13th September 1940 at Newport, Gwent when a Heinkel III was thought to have been brought down by striking a balloon cable. A more positive kill was recorded in October and in February/March 1941 it was thought that seven enemy aircraft had been brought down by barrage balloons. After the war the Air Ministry produced figures to show that 24 enemy aircraft had been 'downed' by balloons, though it had to admit that 91 friendly aircraft had collided with cables 'causing 38 to crash'; it is now generally accepted that the latter figure was

Trainee balloon operators practise their skills at Cardington. (via A. Smith)

probably closer to over double that number. However, the barrage balloon system really came into its own during the V1 rocket onslaught, when there were well over 2,000 sites in London and the south-east. Lettice Curtis, a Air Auxiliary Transport ferry pilot recalled, 'To me the sight of those 2,000 odd silver balloons, glinting in the sunlight remains one of the most memorable of the war.' It was later reported that 233 V1 rockets had been brought down by barrage balloons.

In 1943 No 1 Balloon Training Unit was closed down; in six years over 10,000 operators and a further 12,000 operator/drivers had been trained. Cardington continued to manufacture balloons, and perhaps more importantly its gas factory still produced and supplied hydrogen cylinders to the balloon sites. Besides the recruit training and aircrew selection, several small and individual units operated from Cardington. One such was the Training Aids Development Unit, which designed and produced simulation equipment for the ground training of various aircrew catergories. The station had now been passed over to Maintenance Command, and the Barrage Command was finally disbanded in February 1945, and rather appropriately its last AOC was Air Vice-Marshal W. C. C. Gill, an ex-Auxiliary Air Force officer.

In May 1945 No 102 Personnel Despatch Centre was established at Cardington and thousands of airmen left for civilian life from the station. Indeed, many of these had joined the RAF at Cardington, so they had completed the full circle so to speak! To all those demobbed airmen and to the quarter of a million or so that had entered the Service at Cardington, this RAF station holds very special memories; to them the name 'Cardington' meant much more than the R101 disaster. The post-war story of the RAF station and the ultimate return of airships to this historic place is unfortunately not germane to this book. But at the time of writing, No 217 Maintenance Unit is still in residence at RAF Cardington, though there are plans to move away by April 2001. The RAF Museum at Hendon holds its Reserve Collection at Cardington, as well as housing its Research and Restoration Centre. These units will also have to move if the plans to develop Cardington into a housing and light industry site are finalised. However, the two large airship sheds will remain as they are listed buildings. Cardington and the surrounding countryside would not be the same without them.

4

CRANFIELD

To stroll along the roads and to have the opportunity to admire the fine buildings of Cranfield University is akin to stepping back in time. So faithfully and well preserved are they, that the experience provokes a sharp and vivid evocation of a pre-war RAF station. Indeed it is difficult to believe that over 60 years have passed since the first airmen entered the main gate at RAF Cranfield; surely a fine testimony to the craft and workmanship of the original contractors – John Laing & Sons Ltd.

The work on the airfield site commenced in 1935 but it was not until June 1937 that the new station opened under the control of No 1 Group of Bomber Command. This Group was in its infancy, it had only been formed at Abingdon in May 1936, with just ten squadrons of light bombers based at three airfields. All were equipped with Hawker Hind aircraft, so it would only be a matter of time before Hinds landed at Cranfield's large and pristine grassed airfield.

During the first week of July the Hinds of three squadrons, Nos 62, 82 and 108, duly arrived. The Hawker Hind would be the last light bomber bi-plane to operate in the Service. This aircraft, with its two-seater open cockpit, two machine guns, small bomb load (500 pounds) and relatively slow speed, seemed to belong to another age of flying and to the books of Captain W. E. Johns and his intrepid hero Biggles! And yet they had entered the Service less than two years earlier, but already were being

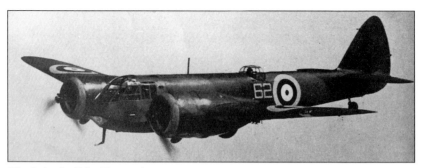

Blenheim I of No 62 squadron.

replaced by the Fairey Battles and Bristol Blenheims.

The squadrons, themselves, were also 'new', at least in the respect that they had been recently reformed, another sign of the rapidly expanding Service, but each could proudly trace its origins back to the days of the Royal Flying Corps and service in the First World War. Of the three, No 108's stay at Cranfield was rather brief, it moved away in April 1938 to another new Expansion station at Bassingbourn in Cambridgeshire. By this time the other squadrons had already begun to replace their Hinds with Blenheim Is.

No 62, also known as the Northampton squadron, received its first new aircraft in February, whereas No 82 (United Provinces) squadron did not start to re-equip until the following month. The Blenheim was the military version of the Bristol Type 142 or 'Britain First', as it was named; an aircraft that had been developed as a private venture and presented to the Nation by Lord Rothermere after the Air Ministry had requested its retention for a period of development in order to evaluate its potential as a light bomber. The design of the military version had so impressed the Air Ministry that they ordered 150 aircraft straight from the drawing board – quite a rare occurrence in those peacetime days.

The military prototype was produced by the Bristol Aeroplane Company in June 1936. It was the first stretched skin metal monoplane with a retractable undercarriage to be built in Britain. Designed as a light bomber with a three-man crew, the aircraft was found to be some 30 mph faster that the RAF's most recent fighter. The Blenheim was powered by two Bristol Mercury engines, which gave it a maximum speed of 260 mph at 15,000 feet with a range of some 900 miles. It was armed with one .303 inch Browning machine gun in its port wing, and a Vickers K gun in a power-assisted dorsal turret, with a bomb load double that of the Hind. Although production was switched in late 1938 to the improved 'long nosed' Mark IV, some of the almost 900 Mark Is that were still on the RAF's complement at the outset of war, were hastily modified to become Fighter Command's first and stop-gap night-fighters.

The Blenheims presented their crews with quite a radical change, as they were the first monoplanes they had encountered so far in their flying careers. As they were slowly gaining experience and coming to terms with their new charges, the station was transferred, in July 1938, to No 2 Group of Bomber Command. The Air Ministry planned to concentrate all the Blenheim squadrons into this Group. From the Munich crisis in September, the crews' training intensified and became more war-like in intent, with long cross-country flights, several large special air exercises, extra bombing practices, range estimation and fuel consumption trials as well as so-called publicity flights over France. However, in August 1939, No 62 squadron received orders to mobilise for service in the Far East. The ground crews left by sea on the 12th and three flights of Blenheims started their long journey to Singapore in the third week of the month. In December 1941 one of its airmen, Squadron Leader Arthur Scarfe, would be posthumously awarded the Victoria Cross. The other squadron also moved away from Cranfield towards the end of August, to Watton in Norfolk, where it would suffer horrendous losses during the summer of 1940. In November 1953 No 82 would be the last squadron in Bomber Command to operate Lancasters.

Once again RAF Cranfield was transferred to another of the Command's Groups – No 6 – which had originally been formed in April 1936 to administer the Auxiliary Air Force units, but from 1st January had begun to build up into an operational Group. In the months leading up to the war a critical and far-reaching decision was taken – to withdraw a number of front-line squadrons from operations for the express purpose of acting as 'advanced or operational training units'. Although this resulted in a considerable reduction in the Command's strike force, it was later described by the *Official History* as, 'a clear, courageous and ultimately justified decision'. Thus, in September 1939,

No 6 (Training) Group became responsible for the eight 'Group Pool' units, as they were known, which comprised no fewer than 14 squadrons. Two of these squadrons, No 35 (Madras Presidency) and No 207 (Leicester) arrived at Cranfield towards the end of August to form one of No 1 Group Pools.

This decision heralded the arrival of yet another light bomber – the Fairey Battle. It was in March 1936 that the prototype Battle first flew, and in those days the aircraft promised great things. The Battle was a rather sleek, well-designed monoplane with a maximum speed of 240 mph and a bomb load of 1,000 pounds. However, it was only lightly armed with one .303 inch Browning machine gun forward in the right wing and a single Vickers gun aft. The first Battles entered the service in May 1937 but two years later they were virtually obsolete because of the under-powered engine and sad lack of fire power. The Advanced Air Striking Force, which had moved over to France after the outbreak of war, was totally equipped with Fairey Battles and the aircraft's woeful inadequacies were harshly and grievously exposed during May 1940, when they seemed to be sitting ducks for the modern Luftwaffe fighters. Before the year was out the Battles were withdrawn from front-line service, and were then mainly used for training or as target towers.

The two squadrons at Cranfield undertook the operational training of replacement crews (pilot and air gunner/observer) for the AASF, and plenty were needed! Each course was scheduled to last six weeks, at least depending on the weather, with a normal intake of 30 airmen. However, the training programme had hardly got into its stride before more changes were planned for Cranfield. It had been decided to lay 'firm' runways, and Cranfield became one of the first pre-war Expansion stations to be so modernised. Towards the end of December both squadrons left Cranfield, though in the case of No 35 its Servicing Flight remained because it was thought that the move would be just temporary.

The harsh winter of 1939/40, one of the worst of the century so far, did little to help the contractors and fairly soon they fell behind schedule. No 35's Servicing Flight left, which was more than a hint that the squadron would not return. The squadron was ultimately re-formed to introduce the Halifax into the Service, and was a pioneer Pathfinder squadron.

By the spring of 1940 Cranfield could be said to be a prime RAF station with excellent buildings, fine accommodation blocks, four large 'C' type hangars and now possessing three immaculate tarmac runways. It would seem a perfect operational airfield for one of the Command's heavy bomber squadrons, but perhaps situated a shade too far west of 'bomber country'. Nevertheless it is still rather surprising that in April, a Service Flying Training School moved in to occupy the airfield; No 14 SFTS came down from Kinloss in Scotland, when that station had been required for detachments of heavy bombers for the Norway campaign.

RAF Cranfield now changed Commands, into Training Command, although in May it would become part of the new Flying Training Command. A Service Flying School, of which there were twelve at the time, was the second and most important stage along an airman's progress to become a trained pilot. He would have spent eight weeks at one of the 19 Elementary Flying Schools where he would have gained experience flying either Tiger Moths or Miles Magisters, mostly the former. Although these schools were now in the Service, they had retained their fairly relaxed and relatively easy-going atmosphere of civilian days, but from now on the student pilot faced something completely different.

The regime and discipline of a SFTS were far stricter and more rigorous. The training programme, both on the ground and in the air, was really quite demanding with extra and more complex theoretical subjects to study and exacting tests to pass throughout the 20 week course, which had only recently been increased from 16 weeks. Some of the subjects covered, according to an Air Ministry press release, were, 'airmanship, armaments, signals, navigation, meteorology, mathematics, map reading, as well as Service law and discipline, and leadership'. Certainly there was a far greater emphasis placed on the students' physical fitness mainly because the training aircraft were faster, heavier and more complicated to control. The course would prove to be an intense period of mental and physical exertion, with a failure rate of about 25%. The ultimate goal of all the students was the award of their coveted 'wings'. No 14 School provided pilots for either Bomber, Coastal or Transport Commands, hence why the students would train on the twin-engined Airspeed Oxfords (which will be discussed under Luton), rather than single-engined training aircraft.

Oxfords of No 14 SFTS lined up at Cranfield, 1940. (RAF Museum)

With the number of students averaging about 160 per course the pressure on the runways at Cranfield was quite considerable. By early January 1941 the School began to use a small airfield at Sibson, about seven miles from Peterborough, as a relief landing ground, where portable flares were used for night landings and take-offs; also during the summer Twinwood Farm to the north of Bedford was used. During 1941/2 when there was considerable debate taking place within the Air Ministry on the subject of concrete runways for training airfields, the Station Commander at Cranfield was asked for his opinion; after all he could speak from first-hand experience. He was greatly in favour and reported, 'their experience during the winter of 1940/1 showed that there was a very distinct advantage in having proper runways... In the first three months of 1941 all flying had been done from runways, with only one accident when the aircraft overshot onto the grassed area.' He also remarked that neither the pupils nor the training staff had experienced any problems operating from the runways at night. However, the Air Ministry did not appear to be particularly impressed with the strong arguments in favour of concrete runways, as it was slow in providing them for flying training stations.

During May 1941 there were rumours circulating around the airfield that a newly formed Operational Training Unit for Coastal Command crews (perhaps No 5 or 6?) would be based at Cranfield, but the proposal was shelved because of the airfield's distance from the Command's operational stations. In the event No 14 SFTS left for Lyneham in Wiltshire in early August, and in its place came another new OTU, which had already begun to form at Debden in Essex. It was No 51 and would be solely devoted to the operational training of night-fighter crews for Fighter Command. The Unit's first Blenheim Ifs arrived during the first week of August, followed about ten days later by Douglas Havoc Is, thus enabling the Unit to start its first course on 25th August. No 51 OTU was destined to remain at Cranfield for the rest of the war.

The heavy and concentrated night bombing offensive by the Luftwaffe from September 1940 had found Fighter Command at a grave disadvantage with the lack of a specialist night-fighter. The Blenheim Is had been modified for the role, mainly because they were almost redundant, having been superseded by the Mark IVs, and moreover they were the only fighters then capable of carrying the first heavy and cumbersome AI (Airborne Interception) radar sets. The arrival of a small number of Bristol Beaufighters in the autumn of 1940, and the formation of the first night-fighter OTU in December, at least held the promise of

Bristol Beaufighter Mk 1F.

better things to come. By the middle of 1941 there were 18 night-fighter squadrons in operation with more planned to be formed in the next six months. Therefore No 51 OTU became an essential part of the maintenance of the Command's night-fighter force.

The training was largely conducted with the Blenheims and Havocs, because the Unit did not receive its first Beaufighters until 1942. This heavy, pugnacious and very reliable fighter fully proved its worth in the night skies during 1941/2. It was heavily armed with four 20mm cannons, six .303 machine guns and one Vickers K gun in the dorsal turret. Although it had only first flown in July 1939, the performance was so impressive that it was rushed into production and entered the Service to fly operationally just 14 months later; one of the swiftest introductions for any wartime aircraft. The first Beaufighter IF was powered by two Bristol Hercules radial engines, and equipped with the much improved AI Mk IV radar. However, it was the slightly improved Mk IIFs, equipped with Rolls-Royce Merlin XX engines, that made inroads into the Luftwaffe night-bombers. The Beaufighter was described by one of its pilots – the legendary Guy Gibson – as 'sturdy, powerful and fearsome'. The various marks of Beaufighters would operate in quite a variety of attacking roles but perhaps none more successfully than as a night-fighter, and they were only replaced by the remarkable de Havilland Mosquito night-fighters.

By July 1943 the Unit at Cranfield had well over 70 Beaufighters on its complement, along with about ten Blenheim Vs, now adapted to dual control. There was yet another Bristol Aeroplane Company aircraft operating in the Unit – the Beaufort. This aircraft had been originally designed, back in 1937, as a derivation of the Blenheim, and at the request of the Air Ministry for 'a general reconnaissance bomber and land-based torpedo bomber to carry a crew of four'. The Beaufort had first flown in October 1938 but it did not enter the Service until December 1939 with Coastal Command, though Beauforts did drop the RAF's first 2,000 pound bomb in May 1940. The Beauforts served very successfully with Coastal Command and especially in the Pacific with the Royal Australian Air Force. The Mark II version of the aircraft, of which 415 were produced, was powered with Pratt & Whitney Twin Wasp engines; many had been completed as purpose built trainers with dual control and with the two-gun dorsal turret omitted. The Unit also had on hand some smaller aircraft, such as Westland Lysanders and Miles Martinets, both used as target-towers for gunnery practice, with just the odd de Havilland Dominie, which was used for navigational and radio training. This military version of the company's successful Dragon Rapide small airliner could accommodate up to five pupils plus an instructor.

Besides mounting the bread and butter operational training courses, the Unit also operated an instructor's course, refresher Beaufighter courses, and during mid-1943 became engaged in the training of Mosquito crews of No 100 (Bomber Support) Group of Bomber Command. This Group was involved in a variety of radio and radar counter-measures to negate the German flak defences and its night-fighters. For this rather specialised training the Unit used a number of Vickers Wellington XIs, which were normally used by Coastal Command, but those flown by the Unit had been provided with special equipment for night-fighter training. Largely as a result of the Unit's increased training commitments, Twinwood Farm was brought into regular use as Cranfield's satellite airfield.

Like all OTUs, whether they served Bomber, Fighter or Coastal Commands, No 51 suffered from an acute shortage of trained and experienced instructors. This was especially so in 1941 when there was a relatively small number of crews experienced on AI. It was an axiom of wartime service that tour-expired aircrews, after a welcome spell of leave, were then sent on an instructor's course, which could last about four to five weeks, before being inevitably posted to an OTU. The turnover of instructors was quite considerable, many only stayed for a few months before returning to operations as they found life at the Units a trifle dull and monotonous after operational service! Some of the instructors stayed far longer, of course, perhaps they found that they had a hidden skill for instruction. But all those who instructed at Cranfield were, without exception, well experienced in night-fighting techniques, having flown operationally in either Blenheim, Beaufighter, Defiant/Hurricane or Havoc squadrons.

Just to pick out at random a few of the instructors who served with the Unit will illustrate the wealth of experience and expertise that was available to the trainee crews at Cranfield. One of the earliest instructors was Sergeant Colin Pyne, a New Zealander, who had started his Service

Bristol Beaufort II modified for use as a trainer. (via J. Adams)

career as an air gunner but retrained as a radio operator flying in Beaufighters with No 219 squadron. He was placed on the first instructor's course at Cranfield in September 1941, and then remained with the Unit until the following January before returning to operations with his old squadron. In early 1942 Flying Officer Henry Jacobs, DFC, arrived at Cranfield to become the Unit's Chief AI instructor. Another Beaufighter man, but with No 600 squadron, he had crewed with J. R. D. Braham, one of the most successful fighter pilots of the war, and together they had claimed five night victories. Jacobs stayed with the Unit until August 1943 when he left to join Braham's squadron, No 141. Another ex-600 squadron airman became the Wing Commander Flying at Cranfield. He was Squadron Leader C. A. Pritchard, DFC, RAAF, who had commanded the squadron back in November 1940 – the pioneering days of AI and GCI (Ground Control Interception). The Chief Technical Officer for the Unit was Wing Commander C.A.L. Holland, a RAF regular officer, who had received his early flying training at Hatfield, and he later completed a two year engineering course at RAF Henlow. In the summer of 1940 Holland returned to operational flying and commanded a famous Spitfire squadron, No 65, during the Battle of Britain.

Cranfield was certainly no different from all Service airfields when the months running up to D-Day proved to be its busiest period of the war. A new Unit had been formed there – No 3501 Servicing Unit – especially to facilitate and hasten the servicing and repair of fighters operating

Aerial view of Cranfield airfield. (Cranfield University)

with the 2nd Tactical Air Force. It also undertook any modifications that were necessary to the aircraft, and seemed to specialise in the fitting of Malcolm cockpit hoods to North American Mustang IIIs. There had been considerable criticism of the pilots' rear vision on Mustangs, and a British firm, Malcolm Company, had designed a special domed and sliding canopy for the aircraft. These Malcolm canopies were found to be so successful that they were later fitted by the Eighth and Ninth Air Forces to its P-51s. There was no shortage of pilots at Cranfield to test-fly the aircraft because No 3501 Pilot Replacement Unit was also based there. Just before D-Day the airfield was crowded with an amazing number of RAF fighters – Mustangs, Typhoons, and a bewildering array of Spitfires of various Marks. To this phalanx of fighter power could be added the Mosquito NFIIs of No 51 Unit, which had been the first night-fighter version of this quite remarkable aircraft.

No 51 OTU was finally disbanded on 14th June 1945, and the following day Group Captain Harold S. Darley, DSO, arrived to take command of the station. He was a pre-war regular officer, who had commanded No 609 squadron almost throughout the Battle of Britain, and had recently been in charge of No 62 OTU at Ouston. For a few months an Aircrew Holding Unit was stationed at Cranfield, which was engaged in the processing of Canadian and Australian airmen back to their home countries until it closed down in mid-September. Then for just a few brief months the airfield was strangely quiet. However, the Empire Test Pilots School moved in from Boscombe Down, and its first course at Cranfield commenced on 2nd January 1946. All the students were highly experienced wartime pilots, and they had a very wide choice of aircraft to test their flying skills – Lancasters, Bostons, Tempests, Mosquitos, Spitfires, Harvards, and even the jet-propelled Gloster Meteors. The School finally moved away to Farnborough in August 1947.

Since the previous October the School had shared the facilities at Cranfield with Britain's first College of Aeronautics, which was often referred to as 'The University of the Air'. The Cranfield College of Technology, as it later became known, received university status in December 1969. Today the airfield is an integral and very active part of Cranfield University; in 1997 there were 100,000 aircraft movements – what a vast change in 60 years of aviation from this quiet corner of Bedfordshire.

5

GRANSDEN LODGE

For the last three years of the war this airfield was a very active RAF operational station, and for much of that time it was an integral part of No 8 (PFF) Group. Situated on the western edge of what became known as 'Pathfinder Country', it had been built during 1941/2 by John Laing & Son Ltd as a Class A Standard bomber airfield, to act as a satellite for RAF Tempsford, which itself was only in its infancy.

The first aircraft to use the new concrete runways, in early 1942, were Vickers Wellington IIIs of No 1418 (Experimental) Flight. These famous twin-engined bombers, which had been designed by Barnes Wallis (later to gain fame for his 'bouncing bomb'), had entered the Service in October 1938, and they formed the backbone of Bomber Command during the early war years. The aircraft's unique geodetic design, metal lattices covered with fabric, proved to be immensely strong and durable, able to sustain considerable damage. The Wellingtons were also most reliable aircraft, inspiring confidence in their six-man crews, who fondly named them 'Wimpys', a name derived from J. Wellington Wimpy of the *Popeye* strip cartoon fame. It was the Mark III that was the main variant, with over 1,500 being produced. Wellingtons survived as front-line bombers until October 1943, though they did also operate very successfully as trainers, anti-submarine and torpedo bombers, cargo

Vickers Wellingtons were the first aircraft to use Gransden Lodge.

carriers, troop transports and air ambulances.

No 1418 Flight had only been formed a few months earlier, and had been tasked with trialling TR1335, otherwise better known as GEE. This was a new radio navigational aid, which had been developed, particularly by R. J. Dippy, at the Telecommunications Research Establishment in Dorset. The system involved sending synchronised pulses from three ground stations (one 'master' and two 'slaves') and from the differences in the arrival times of the radio pulses at the aircraft, the navigator was able to accurately determine the aircraft's position. GEE was relatively simple to operate and proved to be very reliable. Although it did have a range limitation of about 350 miles, this was sufficient to cover the many and various strategic targets, which were centred in the Ruhr valley. The new equipment was first tested operationally on 12th/13th August 1941 over Hanover, but it was not until early March 1942 that GEE was used on a major bombing operation. Although the German defences later found the means to jam the signals, GEE proved invaluable in getting aircraft to a target area and also aiding the crews on their return flights, especially in bad weather.

During the first week of July, Wellington ICs on No 1474 (Wireless Investigation) Flight moved in. This unit had been formed out of a Flight of No 109 squadron, and was also engaged on special duties – the development of various radio-counter measures as well as certain radar aids. Then just two weeks later a new Unit was formed at the airfield – No 1 Bombing Development Unit – which effectively absorbed No 1418 Flight and became engaged on a series of trials and tests of a number of bombing aids and techniques. The Unit would ultimately be equipped with the four major heavy bombers – Wellington, Stirling, Halifax and Lancaster.

In January 1943 another new Special Duties squadron was formed at Gransden Lodge, No 192, and it was also equipped with Wellingtons. The crews became involved in the investigation, monitoring and gathering of information on the enemy's radio and radar air defences; its operations were known as 'Elint', which was derived from ELectronic INTelligence. The squadron would later be transferred to No 100 (Bomber Support) Group of Bomber Command, formed to co-ordinate all the different squadrons engaged in the very patient 'battle of wits' with the German night-fighters and ground defences. Sadly, on 25th January, one of the squadron's Wellington Xs crashed whilst being air tested on its first flight. There was an engine failure and the aircraft came down near Papworth in Huntingdon killing four of the five-man crew.

The nature of the station changed quite dramatically in April 1943 from experimental and test flying to being fully operational. The airfield was transferred out of No 3 Group of Bomber Command and into No 8 (PFF) Group. For just a brief period it became a satellite of Oakington but in June Gransden Lodge became a full station in its own right. The two resident units moved out and they were replaced by the Pathfinder Navigation Training Unit, which as its name implies was dedicated to the final navigation training of all new crews posted into the various PFF squadrons. The Unit was commanded by Wing Commander R. P. Elliott, DSO, DFC, and it was planned to train six crews every three days.

However, it was a Royal Canadian Air Force squadron that was destined to make Gransden Lodge its home for the duration of the war. No 405 (Vancouver) squadron arrived from Leeming in Yorkshire on 19th April. It had been the first RCAF squadron to enter Bomber Command when it was formed in this country back in April 1941. The squadron's motto 'Decimus' or 'We Lead' recognised its pioneering role, and it would be the only RCAF squadron to serve in the Pathfinder

Force. The crews had only recently returned from a six month secondment with Coastal Command, where they had been engaged on anti-submarine patrols over the Bay of Biscay. Air Vice-Marshal D. C. T. Bennett, the AOC of the PFF, felt that the squadron was a very welcome addition to his Force, at least 'when they had been whipped into shape'!

The squadron's transfer into the Pathfinders had brought the return of its most experienced airman, Group Captain J. E. 'Johnnie' Fauquier, DSO 2 Bars, DFC, as its Commanding Officer. He had previously led the squadron from February to August 1942. Fauquier was an outstanding pilot, with a flair for leadership, although he was a very stern taskmaster and demanded the highest standard from his crews. It is said that one night a crew that were on probation to the Pathfinders returned early from an operation because one of their engines had failed. The CO was not best pleased with them and Fauquier refused permission for the crew to land, telling them to return to their old squadron as they were not up to the standard he expected from Pathfinders! Fauquier ultimately earned the nickname 'The King of the Pathfinders'. He remained at Gransden Lodge until June 1944, and later he would command the famous No 617 (Dambusters) squadron.

The Canadian crews, along with the Navigation Unit, were equipped with Halifax IIs and the early development of this famous bomber will be noted later under Radlett. The Mark IIs were powered by Merlin 22 and 24 engines, which had improved the aircraft's maximum and cruising speeds by some 10%. The aircraft had also been supplied with a Boulton & Paul dorsal turret, which housed four rather than two guns. The squadron had first been equipped with Halifax IIs in April 1942, and they had proved to be extremely durable, being universally known as 'Halibags'! However, Air Chief Marshal Harris was not particularly enamoured with the Halifax, he considered its performance greatly inferior to his much beloved Lancaster, and he freely admitted that he would have gladly traded them in for more and more Lancasters. Nevertheless over 82,000 Halifax bombing sorties were made for the loss of 1,884 aircraft or 2.8% compared with the Lancaster loss rate of 2.2%.

The Canadian crews had their baptism of fire with the PFF on 26th/27th April 1943 over Duisburg. They returned convinced that the marking of the target had been successful, but photographic evidence later revealed that the majority of the bombing had fallen outside the

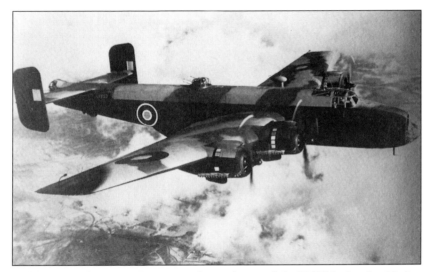

Halifax II: Both No 405 (Vancouver) squadron and the PFF Navigation Unit operated these aircraft.

target area mainly on the approach path. This was known as 'creep back', a problem that bedevilled both Bomber Command and the Eighth Air Force for much of the war. Losses on this particular night were relatively slight, 17 aircraft (3%), but No 405 lost one Halifax – with all eight airmen killed.

This Duisburg operation was just part of the Command's massive five month long Battle of the Ruhr. The squadron had entered the fray whilst operating from Leeming and had lost four out of 15 aircraft on 12th/13th March over the Krupps munitions complex at Essen. From now until the end of July the crews would be fully engaged in the Battle, losing eleven aircraft over Essen, Dortmund, Bochum, Krefeld and Wuppertal. However, on the night of 13th/14th July they were in action over Aachen, only the second time this ancient city had been bombed; severe damage was inflicted with over 3,000 buildings destroyed. The German authorities described the operation as a 'Terrorangriffe [Terror raid] of the severe scale.' Most of the civilian population left the city and even two months later many still did not feel it safe to return; Aachen was described as a 'ghost city'. One Halifax was lost, shot down by a

Halifax BII – W7710 LQ – R 'Ruhr Valley Express', first used 30th/31st May 1942. (Canadian Aviation Museum)

night-fighter over Holland. Six of the crew were killed, including Squadron Leader D. L. Wolfe, DFC, a Canadian pilot who had entered the RAF prior to the outbreak of the war.

The three major Hamburg raids during July 1943 passed without any major incidents, but on the fourth (2nd/3rd August) out of the squadron's 14 crews taking part, only five reached the target. Three bombed alternative targets, three were forced to jettison their bombs, and three failed to return, one of which was abandoned over Sweden, where the crew was interned for six months.

The airfield was now the sole preserve of the Canadians because, in June, the PFF Navigation Unit had moved out to Upwood; although briefly towards the end of August the squadron would share the airfield's facilities with a Flight of No 97 squadron, whilst the runways at Bourn were being repaired.

During July/August the crews began to exchange their Halifaxes for Lancaster IIIs, and the first of the new aircraft was lost in rather bizarre

Lancasters at dusk. (Imperial War Museum)

circumstances. The aircraft having landed safely from a mission to Nuremberg on 10th/11th August, the pilot was taxiing to a dispersal point when the aircraft ran into a ditch and was so severely damaged that it was written-off. The unfortunate pilot on this occasion was none other than Group Captain Fauquier. One wonders how long it took him to live down this incident, considering the high standards he expected from his airmen! Somewhat appropriately, No 405 were supplied with the first Lancasters to be produced in Canada by the Victory Aircraft Company. Designated Mark Xs, they were powered by Packard-built

Merlin engines. The first one of these, KB7000 'Q' – named *Ruhr Express* – completed just two operations with No 405 before being transferred to another Canadian squadron, No 419 (Moose), at the end of the year.

On two successive nights in August, 16th/17th and 17th/18th, the crews were involved in particularly long and arduous operations. The first was to the Fiat motor works in Turin, which turned out to be the Command's last Italian raid. The enemy night-fighters were very active over France on both the outward and homeward flights, although only four aircraft were lost, one from No 405. On the following night the rocket research establishment at Peenemunde was the target for a major operation, when one of the squadron's crews strayed south of the planned route and the Halifax was shot down over Flensburg; the first of 40 aircraft to be lost on this operation.

In the first of the 19 raids mounted to Berlin between August 1943 and March 1944 – the long, harrowing and costly Battle of Berlin – Group Captain Fauquier was acting as Master Bomber, though the quaint term 'Master of Ceremonies' was still being used. The plan was that Fauquier would fly above the main force to control, direct and co-ordinate the bombing for the duration of the operation. This was a technique that had been first used by Group Captain Guy Gibson on the Dambusters raid. Fauquier's first Berlin mission had been back in November 1941, such was his vast operational experience. The Berlin operation on 23rd/24th August was the first time that a Master Bomber had been used over a major German city, although from 1944 onwards the technique became an essential part of the Command's operations. It must be admitted that this Berlin raid was not a conspicuous success, most of the bombing fell outside the city, and 56 aircraft were lost, the highest single total of the war so far. Two came from Fauquier's squadron, one of which crashed in Sweden after being heavily damaged from night-fighter attacks. It was rather unusual for one squadron to have two crews interned in Sweden within a month of each other.

All of the Berlin operations were rugged and torrid affairs and none more so than on the night of 16th/17th December 1943. The weather forecasters had suggested that the German night-fighter bases would be closed in with fog, though there was also a risk that fog could descend over England during the night. Nevertheless, Air Chief Marshal Harris ordered the operation to go ahead, and 483 Lancasters were despatched along with just ten Mosquitos. The German fighter controllers plotted the course of the bomber formations with great accuracy. A strong force of enemy fighters first attacked over Holland and the onslaught continued all the way to the target. So much for the forecast of fog. Twenty-five Lancasters went missing in action (5.2%) but on the crews' return to England many of the airfields were covered with low cloud. Of the 14 crews that left Gransden Lodge, only six managed to land on return. Five were diverted to other airfields and three crashed killing 14 airmen. In total 29 Lancasters crashed or were abandoned, bringing the overall losses on the night to 54 aircraft (11%), hence it became known in Bomber Command as 'Black Thursday'.

For the first fortnight in February 1944 Bomber Command did not mount any major bombing operations, and during this period their Majesties, the King and Queen, took the opportunity to visit some of the Pathfinder stations. King George VI took a particular interest in the work of the Pathfinders and was aware of the important role they were playing in Bomber Command; on 8th February they visited Warboys, Graveley and Gransden Lodge airfields. These visits were informal affairs with the officers and airmen that were on parade being presented wearing the normal working battledress. A week later the same crews were engaged over Berlin, before taking part in the four heavy raids later in the month to Leipzig, Stuttgart, Schweinfurt and Augsburg – part of the Allied combined offensive against the German aircraft industry.

For the final Berlin operation on 24th/25th March, the squadron again supplied one of the Master Bombers – Wing Commander R. J. Lane, DSO, DFC Bar – who, in June, would replace Fauquier as Commanding Officer. This raid has entered RAF folklore as 'The Night of the Big Winds' when ferocious winds of over 100 mph, that had not been forecast, caused havoc with the target marking and bomber formations. It was said that Lane's strong Canadian accent (his call-sign was 'Redskin') could be clearly heard exhorting the crews, 'Those bastards wanted a war, now show them what war is like!' Seventy-two aircraft (9%) were lost on the night mainly on the return journey over central Germany and Holland; quite remarkably No 405 escaped without any casualties. Throughout the Berlin operations the squadron sustained the lowest losses of all the Pathfinder squadrons – eleven crews missing in action. As one of its pilots, Squadron Leader H. W. Trilsbach, later recalled, 'The Battle of Berlin was the worst part of my operational flying. It involved the worst weather, the most flak, most searchlights, and by far the greatest fighter opposition. Oh, but what a terrible price the young Bomber Command crews had to pay.'

Like all squadrons, No 405 was heavily engaged in the months leading up to D-Day. In April only two crews were lost; one on 22nd/23rd over the railway yards at Laon when quite severe damage was inflicted by 'just' 180 heavy bombers. This operation was one of the many mounted by Bomber Command under the Transportation Plan. Five nights later railway yards at Monzen near Aachen were the target in an operation that was conducted in two waves, the second of which suffered heavy and concentrated attacks from the Luftwaffe. Fifteen aircraft (10½%) were shot down, with only one coming from the squadron. It was piloted by Squadron Leader E. M. Blenkinsopp, DFC, who was acting as a Deputy Master Bomber. Blenkinsopp managed to evade capture and worked with a Belgian Resistance group until captured in December. He was taken to Hamburg to work as a forced labourer, but he later died in Belsen concentration camp of 'heart failure'.

During May and early June 1944 the squadron continued to lose experienced pilots and crews. On 6th/7th May Pilot Officer R. D. Burrows, DFC, was killed whilst attacking railway installations at Mantes-La-Jolie, when he had completed over 44 operations. Towards the end of the month Squadron Leader G. Bennett, DSO, DFC, was the only fatality when his Lancaster was shot down over Holland; he, like others in his crew, had already completed one operational tour with another Canadian squadron, No 408. During late July through to September, No 405 lost in action two Wing Commanders, with another, H. A. Morrison, DSO, DFC, being shot down over Le Havre on 8th September. The aircraft crashed just inside the enemy lines, but Morrison and his crew all successfully evaded capture and returned to Gransden. Morrison would command the squadron from 27th September when Wing Commander C. W. Palmer, DSO, DFC, was killed whilst attacking enemy strong points at Cap Gris Nez. Palmer had commanded the squadron for a little over one month. This steady and persistent drain of highly experienced leaders and crews was a problem

100

faced by all the Pathfinder squadrons, which by the very nature of their role suffered heavier losses than the main force squadrons. However, despite that fact, I have no doubt that the opinion expressed by one of the squadron's survivors that, 'The only time during my operational flying (63 ops) when I felt I was doing something worthwhile was with the Pathfinders', was a view generally held by the majority of Pathfinder airmen.

On 27th October 1944 the first Mosquitos landed at Gransden Lodge, and perhaps rather appropriately they were Canadian-built coming from de Havilland's factory in Toronto. These Canadian-built Mosquitos were Mark BXXVs, similiar to the earlier BXXs, except that they were powered by American Packard Merlin 225 engines and only 400 BXXVs were produced. Neither of the two Marks were able to carry the 4,000-pound 'Cookie' bombs. These 'spanking little' aircraft, as they were once described, belonged to No 142 squadron, which had only re-formed two days earlier after a somewhat varied wartime existence so far. It had served in France during 1940 with the ill-fated Fairey Battles, then returned to England to operate Wellingtons, before being transferred to the Middle East. The squadron now became the latest addition to the Pathfinder's Light Night Striking Force or LNSF.

This quite amazing Striking Force was solely the concept of Air Vice-Marshal Donald Bennett, such was his boundless and abiding faith in what he considered was 'a master aircraft'. The LNSF caused untold damage and mayhem to German cities, towns and strategic targets, completely out of all proportion to its size and to the infinitesimal losses it sustained in action. From May 1943 until the end of the war over 27,000 sorties were flown for the loss of 108 aircraft missing in action and another 88 written-off due to battle damage. The Force raided Berlin on no less than 170 occasions and from 20th February until 27th March 1945 the German capital was bombed on 36 consecutive nights – the 'Berlin Express', or more commonly known as the 'Milk Run'! It could be argued that the LNSF was the RAF's most successful force of the war.

Just two of the squadron's crews went out on 29th October to join a force of 57 Mosquitos attacking Cologne, followed the next night by another two making the squadron's first raid on Berlin. This would be the start of countless operations the squadron would make to the 'Big B'. During its time at Gransden Lodge 1,100 Mosquito sorties were made in

116 separate raids and all for the loss of two aircraft missing in action, although several more were damaged beyond repair due to crashes or forced-landings. For example on 5th/6th December whilst bound for Nuremberg, one Mosquito had persistent engine trouble and Squadron Leader B. S. Jones was forced to make an emergency landing at Melsbrock airfield in Belgium, after jettisoning the bombs; although the Mosquito was a write-off, both crewmen survived. There was a familiar RAF wartime saying, 'It's a good landing if you can walk away from it'! Sadly this could not be said for the damaged Mosquito that returned from Sieburg on 23rd/24th December. The aircraft crashed on landing and burst into flames; both airmen, Flying Officers A. S. Keogh, RNZAF and C. A. Lynde, RCAF, were badly burned. They were the first serious injuries to be suffered by the squadron.

During 1944 No 405 squadron had lost 38 aircraft in action. The last one went missing on the penultimate night of the year when the oil refinery at Scholven was bombed in difficult conditions with heavy cloud over the target area. However, the Oboe-led force bombed very accurately for the loss of four aircraft; the squadron's missing Lancaster with an all Canadian crew probably crashed into the North Sea, as no trace was found. The squadron was now commanded by Wing Commander W. F. M. Newson, DSO, DFC Bar, who would remain in charge for the duration of the war.

In February 1945 a new Station Commander was appointed, Group Captain G. H. Womersley, DSO, DFC Bar. He was a Pathfinder through and through, having been a Flight Commander with No 156, a pioneer PFF squadron. He then served on the Pathfinder headquarters staff, before commanding a PFF Mosquito squadron, No 139; such was the operational experience and expertise to be found within the Pathfinder Force.

The month of February proved to be No 142 squadron's busiest month so far, with over 120 sorties flown and 156 tons of bombs dropped. The crews' targets ranged over Dresden, Bonn, Berlin (of course!), Frankfurt, Darmstadt, Böhlen, and Cologne. It was on the night of 20th/21st April that Berlin was bombed for the final time by the RAF when 76 Mosquitos in six separate waves attacked. Eight of the squadron's crews were in the first wave, followed some 20 minutes later by another four crews. Their last Mosquito sorties went out from Gransden Lodge on 2nd/3rd May to attack Kiel. By then the Canadian airmen had finished

Bombing up a Mosquito. (RAF Museum)

their bombing offensive – four crews had attacked gun positions on the Island of Wangerooge on 25th April, whilst another nine crews went to Berchtesgaden and Hitler's 'Eagle's Nest'; all returned safely.

During its time in the Pathfinders No 405 had completed 288 operations for the loss of 62 aircraft, although throughout the war 167 aircraft had been lost in 450 raids with over 750 airmen killed in action – a massive contribution to Bomber Command. Air Vice-Marshal Bennett's victory message to all his personnel acknowledged the vital role his airmen had played: 'Bomber Command's share in this great effort has been a major one. You, each one of you, have made that possible. The Pathfinder Force has shouldered a grave responsibility. It has led Bomber Command, the greatest striking force ever known. That we have been successful can be seen in the far-reaching results which the bomber offensive has achieved. That is the greatest reward the Pathfinder Force ever hopes to receive, for those results have benefited all law-abiding peoples.'

Stained glass window in Great Gransden church.

104

The Canadians flew back home in June for a further period of training prior to joining the RAF's 'Tiger Force' as its Pacific strike force was known. The sudden end of hostilities resulted in No 405 being disbanded in September, the same month as the Mosquito squadron disbanded at Gransden Lodge. Although some Liberators arrived at the airfield at the end of the year, they stayed for barely two months. What remains of the old wartime airfield is at present used by the Cambridge Gliding Club. The exploits and sacrifices of the brave Canadian airmen have not been forgotten. An imposing stained glass window in Great Gransden church commemorates No 405 (Vancouver) squadron; beneath the window there is a plaque, which bears the message: 'The people of these villages cared for the airmen, who flew from RAF Gransden Lodge. They watched for them and prayed for them.'

6

HATFIELD

On the morning of 3rd October 1940 the Second World War suddenly became a dread reality for the de Havilland workers at Hatfield. A solitary Junkers 88 came low over the airfield, and from about 100 feet, four high explosive bombs were dropped and people were machine-gunned as they ran to the air-raid shelters. One of the bombs fell directly onto the sheet metal shop, destroying most of the aircraft construction work in progress, including the mock-up of the AS (Airspeed) 49, a single-seat fighter trainer along with all the drawings and design calculations; this project was not resuscitated. Sadly 21 workers were killed and another 70 injured, but the enemy aircraft, damaged by the airfield's anti-aircraft defences, later crashed at nearby Hertingfordbury.

In September 1939 Hatfield airfield had quickly assumed a war footing. De Havilland's factory was fully engaged in producing their famous Tiger Moth trainers, and the very successful DH 98A Dragon Rapide civil aircraft, which had now been converted into a military version to operate as a 'flying classroom' for both radio and navigational training. It was known as a Dominie in military circles, over 520 being produced, of which about 180 were constructed at Hatfield before pressure of other work decreed that the Dominies would be built by a sub-contractor – Brush Coachworks Ltd of Loughborough.

Some Moth Minors and Queen Bees were also being built, along with

Fine shot of de Havilland Tiger Moth.

Airspeed Oxfords. In 1940 de Havilland would acquire control of Airspeed (1934) Ltd based at Portsmouth and Christchurch. That company had originally been founded in 1931 by N. S. Norway, who was involved with the design of the R100 airship but is perhaps more famous as the novelist Nevil Shute. The Hatfield factory was also undertaking repair work on Hurricanes, but at this time the company's most famous wartime aircraft – the Mosquito – mainly resided in the minds of its design team, and its only tangible presence was in the outline plans and designs on the drawing boards.

The Flying Training School had been taken into the Service's fold, and was now known as No 1 Elementary Flying Training School with its civilian instructors being seconded into the RAF and given appropriate ranks. The School's Moths would slowly lose their civil identification numbers, with their upper surfaces being camouflaged, RAF roundels and serial numbers applied, and their wing undersides and tips painted in training yellow. The initial training course still lasted two months, it would not be until the summer of 1940 that the course was reduced to five weeks, largely because of pilot losses in France and the Battle of Britain, as well as the formation of new squadrons. This cutback in the training programme imposed far greater pressure on the instructors, the ground crews in the servicing and maintenance of the training aircraft, and the proper utilisation of airfield space.

The student pilots arrived from one of the four Initial Training Wings, where they would be introduced into the discipline of Service life. Besides the purely practical aspects of the course – flying tuition – they were also given a thorough grounding in the theories of navigation, armaments, radio signals, aircraft rigging and photography, as well as more general subjects such as mathematics, Service organisation and law. Throughout the short course their progress was closely monitored, and their aptitude for either single-engined or multi-engined flying would be noted. This would determine which Service Flying Training School they would proceed to and their ultimate employment in either Fighter, Bomber or Coastal Command. The students would spend many hours 'flying' in the covered cockpit of the Link trainer, which fairly accurately simulated flying whilst firmly staying on the ground. They would be required to respond to instructions given by the Link instructor, and the apparatus' automatic recorder, known as the 'crab', would faithfully record all their reactions and errors! As the Air Ministry stated, 'The Link trainer saves valuable hours of instruction in the air, as well as saving lives and aircraft.'

The most memorable part of the course for all students was that special moment when they were considered ready to fly solo for the first time; on average most reached this stage after some ten hours of dual instruction. If the instructors were satisfied with their pupils' progress, it now became a matter of improving and refining their newly acquired skills, both by day and night. This stage of training covered forced landings with some 'pretty' flying thrown in for good measure, which was said to promote self-confidence in the air. Those students that had satisfied all the necessary criteria – the failure rate was about 30% – passed on to the second and most important stage of their training at one of the 17 SFTSs then still situated in the United Kingdom.

It is perhaps a little invidious to select just a few of the hundreds upon hundreds of student pilots that passed through No 1 School at Hatfield, but three airmen do stand out because of their subsequent successful Service careers; by a strange coincidence two were New Zealand airmen, although a considerable number of NZ airmen were initially trained at Hatfield. Patrick G. Jameson arrived at Hatfield in March 1936 for his *ab initio* flying training, and by the outbreak of the war he was a Flight commander with No 266 squadron. He was one of the first pilots to land a Hurricane on an aircraft carrier, and survived the tragic sinking of HMS *Glorious* in May 1940. Jameson then fought in the Battle of Britain before becoming a successful night-fighter pilot. He led fighter Wings at Wittering, North Weald and in Normandy, and survived the war with eleven victories to his name, being decorated with DSO, DFC Bar, MiD. He retired from the RAF in 1960 as an Air Commodore. The other New Zealander was Colin F. Gray, who arrived at Hatfield in January 1939. Gray proved to be an exceptional Spitfire pilot, who became one of the most successful fighter pilots of the war with 27 $\frac{1}{2}$ victories and the DSO, DFC 2 Bars added to his name. He fought throughout the Battle of Britain and commanded several Spitfire Wings both in this country and the Middle East. Gray retired as a Group Captain in 1961 and died in August 1995 aged 80 years. A. Ken Gatward had entered the RAFVR in 1937 and completed his early flying training at Hatfield in the same year. By August 1940 he had been commissioned and after flying Blenheims, he became one of the famous Beaufighter pilots of the war, operating with distinction with Coastal Command's strike wings. He retired from the Service as a Group Captain with a DSO, DFC Bar and died in December 1998.

In January 1940 Hatfield airfield became the permanent base of a small and exclusive group of women ferry pilots, and as a result it unwittingly became the centre of considerable press attention. This unusual situation came about because of the proposal in the summer of 1939 to establish a pool of civilian pilots to assist the existing two RAF ferry pools to move aircraft from factories to reserve stores and operational stations. At first it is fair to say that the Air Ministry were less than enthusiastic about the idea, they considered that the RAF had sufficient resources to cope with all their requirements. However, with the outbreak of the war the Air Ministry changed its mind and Gerald d'Erlanger, a banker, peacetime pilot and Director of British Airways, was given the task of selecting about 30 male pilots, between the ages of

Avro Anson – N5060 – of ATA: the 'taxi' aircraft for the ferry pilots. (RAF Museum)

28 and 50 years and with at least 250 flying hours, to form the first pool of civilian ferry pilots. Ultimately 28 pilots were placed under contract and thus the Air Transport Auxiliary was born.

The ATA was placed under the direction of Commodore d'Erlanger (known to his pilots as 'Pops') and controlled jointly by British Overseas Airways Corporation, Lord Beaverbrook as the first Minister of Aircraft Production and No 41 Group of RAF Maintenance Command; this rather cumbersome chain of command did create certain problems in the early days. Its headquarters was based at White Waltham, a small airfield near Maidenhead in Berkshire, and ultimately there would be no fewer than 16 Ferry Pools dotted around the country, usually placed close to either major aircraft factories or large RAF Maintenance Units.

After much heated discussion and debate the Air Ministry, who originally utterly opposed the use of women pilots, relented and conceded that a small Pool of women pilots could be formed to ferry Tiger Moths only, a job that the RAF was only too pleased to relinquish. It was for this reason that Hatfield was selected to be the permanent base for the first all-female Ferry Pool. On 1st December 1939 Miss Pauline

Gower, a well-known and very experienced pilot, was appointed to select just eight women pilots. These eight ladies, all highly experienced pilots and fully-qualified flying instructors, signed contracts on 1st January 1940. They were provided with navy-blue service type tunics, and were ranked either first or second officer. Their salary was set at £230 per annum with an additional £8 a month flying pay, which was, not surprisingly, about 20% less than their male colleagues! Although the original formation of the ATA had largely passed unnoticed, the appointment of women ferry pilots received extensive press and radio coverage, and it certainly engendered considerable comment from the public, most of it quite unfavourable: 'Women who are anxious to serve their country should take on work more befitting their sex instead of encroaching on a man's occupation', and also, 'someone has erred grievously in allowing a handful of women to ferry toy trainers from A to B at the magnificent salary of £6 a week. When women are capable of flying fast and/or heavy service aircraft to their destination in all weathers, by all means pay them for the trouble'!

No 5 Ferry Pool at Hatfield was initially employed to ferry the completed Tiger Moths to reserve storage sites mainly at Lossiemouth, Kinloss and Perth in all weather conditions, no mean feat in itself as the women pilots had to make the long and tiring journey back to Hatfield by the crowded and irregular wartime trains, as there were an insufficient number of 'taxi' aircraft to ferry them back by air. Later in the year the 'Faithful Annie' or Avro Anson was used by the ATA as a flying 'taxi', with some 180,000 flying hours completed in Ansons by the ferry pilots.

During the summer of 1940 Hatfield airfield was becoming a little congested, as the production aircraft from de Havilland's vied for space with the School's Tiger Moths. Then, on 8th June, three Flights of Westland Lysanders arrived from Bekesbourne in Kent; they belonged to No 2 (Army Co-operation) squadron, which had recently been withdrawn from France. Their sudden appearance caused a rift between the RAF and the Ministry of Aircraft Production, who felt that so many Lysanders operating from the airfield would have a serious effect on aircraft production, and perhaps attract even more attention from the Luftwaffe. The Ministry won this particular battle (as indeed they would prevail in many similar disputes!) and the RAF was forced to find an alternative airfield for the Lysanders, although one Flight would remain until the autumn.

In that brilliant summer of 1940, the appointment of a number of extra women pilots was approved, as well as extending their duties to include all training aircraft – mainly Oxfords and Miles Masters. It was at this time that Lettice Curtis joined the ATA at Hatfield and her excellent book, *The Forgotten Pilots*, faithfully traces the little known story of this admirable and valuable wartime air service.

Perhaps the most famous woman ATA pilot to serve at Hatfield was Amy Mollinson (nee Johnson), who had about 2,300 flying hours in her log when she was accepted as a ferry pilot, though like all other candidates she had to undergo a stringent flying test! On 3rd February 1941 Amy Johnson set off from Hatfield to ferry an Oxford to Prestwick, and once there she was required to transport another Oxford down to Kidlington near Oxford. For some reason she stopped overnight at Squires Gate, Blackpool, and set out on Sunday the 5th, which was a bleak day of snow and low cloud. Unable to land at Kidlington because of the weather, she flew east to locate an airfield clear for landing. It would appear that she lost her direction above the thick cloud, and her aircraft ran out of fuel over the Thames Estuary. She parachuted out and was spotted by the crew of a Naval trawler, *Haslemere*. Sadly, a Naval officer lost his life whilst unsuccessfully attempting to rescue her from the sea. Her body was never recovered but some of her effects were found – a sad end for a very popular and courageous airwoman.

On 10th May 1941 Lieutenant Colonel Moore-Brabazon, who had only recently taken over as Minister of Aircraft Production, visited de Havilland's factory at Hatfield, and took the opportunity to meet his women ferry pilots, who within a couple of months would number 50 or so. It was an ideal opportunity for the national press and photographs appeared the following day wherein the ladies were dubbed 'Brabazon's beauties'! By now the women ferry pilots were delivering operational aircraft, mainly Spitfires and Hurricanes, and by 1942 a number of them would qualify to fly the heavy four-engined bombers such as the Stirlings and Halifaxes. Indeed, Lettice Curtis was one of the first to fly Halifaxes, normally from Radlett. Ultimately many achieved their ambition, qualification to fly the top Class of aircraft – No 6 – the massive Short Sunderland flying boat. So much for all the earlier criticism!

No 5 Ferry Pool remained at Hatfield until the spring of 1942, but by now the majority of Tiger Moths were being built by Morris Motors at Cowley, and the production of Oxfords at Hatfield had ceased. The Pool moved away to a new home at Luton. Hatfield was fully engaged in the production and testing of Mosquitos, with the result that No 1 EFTS had been forced to use Holwell Hyde near Welwyn Garden City as a relief airfield, and they moved there in April 1943.

Despite the increasing pressure on airfield space, a new squadron, No 116, was formed at Hatfield in February 1941. This was basically the RAF's original radio calibration squadron, a natural growth out of No 1 Anti-Aircraft Calibration Flight, which had been operating from the airfield. The arrival of radar had brought an entirely new task for the RAF, which only added to the complexity of radio calibration duties already undertaken by a number of small and specialised units. There was an urgent need for the air calibration of the various defence radars around the country with aircraft checking the accuracy of the systems on a regular basis. These special units' duties were also extended to cover other radio and radar systems, such as blind-landing and homing devices. The squadron was equipped with Westland Lysander IIs and IIIs, but it was also forced out of Hatfield, and in April 1941 the squadron moved to Hendon.

To have progressed thus far in describing wartime Hatfield with merely passing references to the Mosquito is tantamount to heresy! From late 1940 until the end of the war and beyond, Hatfield and the Mosquito were synonymous, but the story of this most famous aircraft goes back to 1938. It was then that Sir Geoffrey de Havilland and his fellow director and Chief Engineer, C. C. Walker, attempted to interest the Air Ministry in their idea of a twin-engined, high-speed and unarmed bomber constructed of wood, which would be capable of carrying 1,000 pounds of bombs over a range of 1,500 miles at a speed in the region of 400 mph, which was then faster than any known fighter. The Air Ministry was less than impressed with the project, after all military aircraft were now mainly constructed of metal, and it was common knowledge that the Luftwaffe had experimented with laminated wood for aircraft construction but had all too quickly dropped the idea; as for a bomber being unarmed, such a thought was far too fanciful. In any case it was considered that it was far too late to

Prototype Mosquito – W4050 – racing across Hatfield's grass airfield. (British Aerospace plc)

think about such a revolutionary design, especially as war seemed all too imminent – this was the time of the Munich crisis of Autumn 1938!

To the RAF's and the country's everlasting thanks, de Havilland's decided to continue the Mosquito project on their own, but it was not really until the outbreak of the war that the project was taken up in earnest. Sir Geoffrey knew that it was essential to move his Chief Designer, Ronald E. Bishop and his small design team, to a quiet place away from the daily pressures of Hatfield, in order that they could concentrate on the project in peace. Hence Salisbury Hall, a fine moated manor house surrounded by trees at London Colney and not far from St Albans, was acquired and it became the birthplace of not only the Mosquito but later the Vampire and Hornet. It also saw the creation of the AS 51 Horsa troop carrying glider; Airspeed's design project team moved into the Hall in late 1940.

There was at least one dedicated supporter of the Mosquito project on the Air Council. He was Air Marshal Sir Wilfred R. Freeman, who was the Air Member for Development and Production. By Christmas 1939 the first Mosquito mock-up had been produced and from this model and the design drawings, Freeman ordered 50 'high-speed wooden reconnaissance bombers' for the RAF under Air Ministry Specification B1/40 dated 1st March. A Service order from the drawing board was a most rare concession, but it proved to be a momentous decision. It is reported that de Havilland had said, 'This is the fastest bomber in the world. It must be useful.' Certainly Freeman had put his reputation at risk, although his colleagues in the Air Ministry should have shown greater faith in his judgement, because since 1936 he had strenuously helped progress the production of Spitfires and Hurricanes, among others. Nevertheless his decision to back the Mosquito so whole-heartedly, resulted in the aircraft becoming known in Service circles as 'Freeman's Folly' during its early stages of development!

In May 1940 the Mosquito project received a serious set-back when Lord Beaverbrook ordered the work to stop in favour of more current development but two months later after certain pressure was applied, he relented. The initial Mosquitos were constructed from the finest balsa wood from Ecuador, though as supplies became scarce, English ash and Canadian yellow birch were later used. Not only did G-Plan, the famous furniture manufacturer, become involved in the construction work, but many other smaller furniture makers were also engaged. De Havilland's also established a thriving cottage industry of local men and women coming to Salisbury Hall, as well as many making wooden parts and assembling electrical items for the aircraft either in their own homes or back gardens! On 3rd November 1940 the first prototype Mosquito was removed from the hangar adjacent to Salisbury Hall, where it had been built; it was carefully dismantled and removed to Hatfield by road. By a strange coincidence on the very same day, Freeman moved from his post, in which he had been so influential in approving the Mosquito, to become Deputy to the RAF's new Chief of the Air Staff, Lord Portal.

It was on 25th November 1940 that Geoffrey de Havilland Jr, along with John E. Walker, the company's Chief Engine Installation Engineer, took off from Hatfield on the aircraft's first flight, which lasted about 45 minutes. The performance of the aircraft was impressive, as the company had expected, and its twin Rolls-Royce Merlin 21 engines had behaved perfectly. Before the aircraft was taken to the Armament Experimental Establishment at Boscombe Down in February 1941 for the Service's handling tests and acceptance trials, the young Geoffrey de Havilland, and his brother John gave further flying displays of the

Production of Mosquitos at Hatfield, late 1943. (Imperial War Museum)

aircraft's manoeuvrability and performance to a rapidly growing number of official visitors to Hatfield, including the chiefs of the USAAF. Without doubt the Mosquito was an out-and-out winner, its range, speed and high-altitude performance put it far ahead of anything flying at the time. The prototype, W4050, was regularly flying at speeds in excess of 380 mph, or about 20 mph faster than the current Spitfire, and John de Havilland did manage to achieve 437 mph. Sadly he would be killed in a tragic head-on Mosquito collision over Hatfield in 1943. The night-fighter prototype was somewhat boldly flown by Geoffrey de Havilland Jr from a field near Salisbury Hall on 15th May 1941. He explained that it was 'to save time dismantling it'! This was followed in early June by the photo/reconnaissance prototype, leaving just two Mosquitos out of the five that were built at the Hall. Salisbury Hall now houses the Mosquito Aircraft Museum, including the prototype W4050. The museum, which is operated by the de Havilland Aircraft Museum Trust, is a fascinating place to visit, and it does justice to this remarkable aircraft.

The original Service order had been amended to read 19 photo/

Perhaps the most famous Mosquito photograph – BXVI ML963 8K-K – of No 571 squadron, September 1944. (RAF Museum)

reconnaissance aircraft and 20 fighters, though some of the latter were converted to dual-control T MkIIIs to help with the pilot conversion training. From now on matters moved at some pace. A Mosquito PR Mk1 was delivered to No 1 Photographic Reconnaissance Unit in July 1941 and Squadron Leader Rupert Clerke flew the initial Mosquito operational sortie on 17th September. This became the first de Havilland designed and constructed aircraft to be flown regularly in a RAF operational squadron since the DH 9A back in 1917. By the middle of November a B MkIV had been delivered to No 105 squadron at Swanton Morley in Norfolk. It was capable of carrying four 500 pound bombs (double its original planned bomb load) and the first Mosquito bombing mission took place on 31st May 1942. The initial NF MkII had been delivered to No 157 squadron at Castle Camps in January 1942 and the Mosquito night-fighters went into action in late April. Major Hereward de Havilland, who visited the early Mosquito squadrons, was able to report back to his father, 'The machine is being accepted by aircrew as something outstanding…in a few months it has achieved a popularity which I think must be almost unique in that its praises are sung, not only by the pilots, but also by maintenance staffs. Even engineer officers have been known to walk up and pat its fuselage.'

The rest is now history, a quite brilliant chapter of British aviation: 7,781 Mosquitos were ultimately produced, of which 6,710 were built during the war, and almost half of these wartime aircraft came from the factory at Hatfield. Numbers rose from just 21 completed during 1941, to 389 in the following year when de Havilland's No 2 factory at Leavesden near Watford began to build the aircraft, as indeed did the Standard Motor Company at Anstey. In 1943 Hatfield constructed 806 and in that year their factory in Canada started production, as well as another plant in Australia. During 1944/5 over 1,800 Mosquitos were built at Hatfield, such was the almost unsatiable demand for this most versatile of aircraft. The last Mosquito was completed in November 1950. Without doubt the Mosquito was one of the most outstanding and successful Allied aircraft of the war – so much for Freeman's Folly! Reichsmarshal Herman Goering is reported as saying, 'I turn green with envy when I see the Mosquito. The British knock together a beautiful wooden aircraft that every piano factory there is building. There is nothing the British do not have.'

The de Havilland design team did not rest on their laurels, there was continual development work on the Mosquito. Sir Geoffrey de Havilland in his book *Sky Fever*, put the number of Mosquito marks at 43! From 1941 onwards the design team was also working on the DH 100, code-named Spidercrab, a new jet-fighter later to be called the Vampire. This aircraft was powered by de Havilland's own developed turbo-jet engine – the H1 or Goblin – which was running on a test-bed at Hatfield in 1942. On 29th September 1943 Geoffrey de Havilland Jr made the initial test flight of the Vampire from Hatfield and he achieved a top speed of 540 mph, the first British aircraft to exceed 500 mph in level flight. Also the company developed the DH 103 Hornet, which was effectively a scaled down single-seat version of the Mosquito, designed specifically as a long-range fighter to combat the Japanese aircraft in the Pacific. The Hornet made its first flight on 28th July 1944, and the first deliveries to the RAF came in the following year. However, neither aircraft saw service during the Second World War.

DH 100 Vampire jet-propelled fighter.

The story of Hatfield and de Havilland's in the years following the war is not relevant to this account, but suffice it to say the company still continued to produce a number of fine civil and military aircraft at Hatfield. Geoffrey de Havilland Jr, who had been so involved in the Mosquito's early development, was tragically killed in August 1946 whilst piloting the DH 108, a tail-less research aircraft. Only two weeks previously he had flown the aircraft in excess of 616 mph in level flight, which was then a world record. Sir Geoffrey lived on until 1965, he was 83 years old at his death. He had built his first aircraft in 1908 and had lived to witness the world's first jet-airliner service started by BOAC in May 1962 with de Havilland Comets. The airfield at Hatfield finally closed in April 1994 thus bringing to a close a most glorious period of aviation history.

7

HENLOW

There are precious few current RAF stations that can boast a longer lineage than Henlow – over 80 years of continuous service – almost, but not quite, as old as the Royal Air Force itself. It is no mean feat for a RAF station to have survived thus far, despite the stringent reductions in the Service and its stations and squadrons that followed two World Wars and more recently the seemingly endless succession of defence reviews and cuts. The station's badge, which has as its motto 'Labor Arma Ministrat' or 'Hard Work Supplies Arms' captures Henlow's early and lasting existence as an aircraft repair and supply depôt. However, over its long history Henlow has been the home of various specialist units, as well as a number of training establishments, one of which, the RAF School of Aeronautical Engineering, made the name of 'Henlow' famous, not only within Service circles but also far beyond.

It all started back in 1917 in the days of the Royal Flying Corps when a site of about 220 acres to the south of the village of Henlow, was acquired to function as an Aircraft Repair Depôt. The pre-conditions for such depôts were that they should be situated on relatively flat terrain, as near as possible to an existing main line railway and/or a major road route, as well as being close to an industrial town; given such parameters the selected site at Henlow appeared to be ideal.

The Station badge of RAF Henlow. (Crown Copyright)

On 10th May 1918 Lieutenant Colonel Stapleton Cotton, along with 40 airmen, arrived from Farnborough, which was then the Service's main repair depôt, to establish the nucleus of the new depôt, which was numbered No 5 Eastern Area, intended to service the numerous flying squadrons and units within the 'Eastern Area'. Henlow was the first new station to be opened under the aegis of the Royal Air Force, which had only been formed on 1st April 1918. By the end of the year the depôt had overhauled and repaired a considerable number of aircraft, mainly Bristol F2B fighters and de Havilland DH4s. Already some 300 local women were employed, either in the fabric repair shops or on clerical duties. One of the features of RAF Henlow in the coming decades would be the relatively large number of civilians that were employed there. This, plus its proximity to the village, made the station an important and

Parachutists drop from Vickers Vimy bombers over Henlow, May 1929.
(Bedfordshire & Luton Archives & Records Services)

integral part of the local community, perhaps more so than many other RAF stations. Indeed, it is difficult to think of this part of the county without associating it with RAF Henlow.

Henlow's first moment of truth came during 1919/20 when so many active stations were closed and their squadrons and training units disbanded; hundreds of surplus aircraft were sold at nominal values and even more were scrapped. However, the station's immediate future seemed fairly secure when, in February 1920, another 160 acres of land was purchased to provide a large grassed landing ground, mainly for the purposes of test flying. In the following month Henlow became the Aircraft Depôt for the 'Inland Area'. For a brief period, less than two years, Henlow was also an operational fighter station when Nos 23 and 43 squadrons reformed there with Snipes, soon to be replaced by Gamecocks. However, by February 1927 the squadrons had moved out to Kenley and Tangmere respectively. Like Henlow, both squadrons have miraculously survived, and at the time of writing, No 23 is serving at RAF Waddington with No 43 at RAF Leuchars.

Some three years earlier (April 1924) the Officers' Engineering School had moved in from Farnborough, and for the next 40 or so years the School would provide a constant stream of well trained aeronautical engineers for the Service. The School, which would later be known as the RAF School of Aeronautical Engineering, and then the RAF Technical College, was a vital part of the small but very professional pre-war RAF. Those officers that graduated were entitled to use the annotation '(e)' after their rank, which proved to be highly esteemed as the School's reputation and standing gained in stature, especially during the 1930s. The School fitted in well with the Air Staff's general policy, which was substantially Lord Trenchard's rationale, that pilots should, after about five years' flying duties, spend at least two years employed in a ground trade.

Without doubt the School's most illustrious student was Frank Whittle, the 'Father of the Jet Engine'. This brilliant young officer was one of the few Service apprentices to graduate through the RAF College at Cranwell. He entered the School at Henlow in August 1932, and very quickly passed out towards the end of 1933. Whittle then spent some six months at Henlow in charge of the Aero Engine tests, before being sent to Peterhouse College, Cambridge for a two-year engineering course, which he passed with First Class honours. His subsequent RAF career was spent developing his jet-engine, which ultimately revolutionised the aviation industry. When, in January 1944, his jet-propulsion achievement was announced to the world, Group Captain Whittle became a household name. Whittle retired in April 1948 on the grounds of ill health at the rank of Air Commodore, though he lived until August 1996 and was aged 89 years at his death.

In the 1930s the College was also opened to non-Service personnel by way of an open competitive examination, and the successful graduates, once they had satisfactorily completed the Henlow course, were ensured a permanent commission. The normal intake of students at that time was about 50 or so per course, most of them serving officers. By the end of 1965 the RAF Technical College had been amalgamated with the RAF College at Cranwell, and it had developed into a Headquarters Section and four Wings – Basic Studies, Mechanical Engineering, Electrical

Weapons Systems and Engineering and Cadet.

The immediate pre-war years saw a variety of other training courses being conducted at Henlow – air frame riggers and fitters, flight mechanics, machine tool operators, motor transport drivers, and cooks as well as initial Service recruits: the latter Unit moved out to nearby Cardington in September 1937. In April 1938 Maintenance Command was formed with Air Vice-Marshal J.S.T. Bradley appointed as its AOC-in-C, and the Home Aircraft Depôt, as it had become known since 1926, had its name changed to No 13 Maintenance Unit and was placed under the control of No 43 Group. The Unit was mainly engaged in the repair and modification of aircraft, the manufacture and fitting of replacement parts, and many other tasks relating to the armament of aircraft. By June 1940 most of the training units had left the station, leaving over 3,000 officers and airmen stationed there, although this figure would double before the year was out, and additionally some 900 civilians were employed in various capacities.

It was quite clear that the Luftwaffe considered that Henlow was of some strategic importance because in the afternoon of 26th September 1940 eight high explosive bombs fell on the camp, damaging two hangars. The hangars at Henlow were large targets to hit, some dated from 1918 and were known as 'Handley Page Storage Sheds' – over 540 feet long, 170 feet wide and at least 30 feet high! In November (26th) some incendiaries were dropped close to the station and there were a few isolated raids in February 1941 and July 1942 but none had any serious consequences.

One specialised and rather unusual unit, the PAS or Pilotless Aircraft Section, had left Henlow for Hawkinge in Kent in February 1940. It had been stationed at Henlow since October 1936 and maintained a small flight of radio-controlled aircraft used by fighter squadrons for aerial gunnery practice. The pilotless aircraft were de Havilland Queen Bees, which were a variant of the Tiger Moths. But because the Queen Bees were considered rather too slow for contemporary fighters – a little over 100 mph – Airspeed (1934) Ltd had developed their AS30 or Queen Wasp, which was a single-engined monoplane that could also be flown independently of its radio-control system, and had a top speed of about 175 mph.

The most familiar aircraft to be seen at Henlow during the early war

Hawker Hurricane of No 87 squadron: this classic aircraft was very evident at Henlow during the early war years.

years was the Hawker Hurricane. This classic fighter had been designed by Sidney Camm, the chief designer of Hawker Aircraft Ltd, as a development of his successful Fury bi-plane. The prototype first flew at Brooklands on 6th November 1935, and it was six months later that the Air Ministry placed an order for the 'Fury Interceptor Monoplane', as the aircraft was known until Camm suggested the name 'Hurricane' in June 1936. The early Hurricanes were powered by Rolls-Royce Merlin II engines, armed with eight .303 inch machine guns, four in each wing, and the aircraft was capable of a top speed of 325/330 mph, although one was flown from Edinburgh to Northolt in February 1938 at an average speed of almost 409 mph. When the Hurricanes entered the Service with No 111 squadron in December 1937 they became the RAF's first monoplane fighter. The Hurricane squadrons were the mainstay of Fighter Command's strength throughout 1939 and 1940, and they destroyed more enemy aircraft during the Battle of Britain than all the other defences, both land and air, combined. The 'Hurry' was admired and trusted by all who flew it, inspiring in its pilots an immense and deep loyalty. The Hurricane was an outstanding combat aircraft, operating in all theatres of war, and in so many different roles – day or night fighter, fighter/bomber, and 'tank buster'. They could also operate from aircraft carriers as well as being catapulted from merchant vessels, and some Canadian Hurricanes were even fitted with skis!

Somewhat wisely the Air Ministry had, in January 1939, arranged for Hurricanes to be built under licence in Canada by the Canadian Car and Foundry Company. The first aircraft left the Canadian production lines in January 1940 and was delivered to the United Kingdom the following month. No 13 Maintenance Unit was given the task of assembling these Canadian Hurricanes and testing the aircraft before their being delivered to operational squadrons. Towards the end of 1941 the Canadian company began to use the American-produced Packard Merlin 28 engines as well as different propellors, these Hurricanes were designated Mark Xs. Over 1,400 Canadian Hurricanes were produced (Marks X to XII) and they made up about 10% of the total production. The Unit had its own small group of test pilots; one of those who served with the Unit from September 1941 was Sergeant E. H. Adams, who may have been a local man. He had joined the RAFVR in 1937 and completed his initial flying training at No 29 E&RFTS at Luton. During the Battle of Britain Adams had flown with No 236 squadron.

The Parachute Test and Training Section was an old Henlow resident; the Test Section had been formed in September 1925 with the Training Section moving in twelve months later. The PTS was the obvious place to seek parachute instructors when the Airborne Forces Experimental Establishment and its School of Parachute Training was being formed in the early summer of 1941 (ultimately sited at Ringway airfield near Manchester in the following July). Although parachutes had been used by the crews of observation balloons in the First World War, they did not become standard equipment for pilots and aircrews until 1927. Right up until 1941 the Section had used Vickers Virginias or 'Ginnies' for its parachute testing. These lumbering bi-planes were relics of days long past (they had first flown in 1922) which for 13 years had served as a major heavy bomber, and in fact had introduced the 'tail-end Charlie' rear turret into the Service. The Section's 'Ginnies' began to be replaced by Armstrong Whitworth Whitleys, another rather cumbersome and

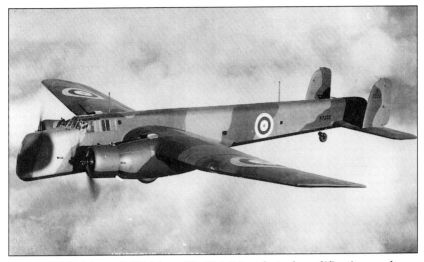

Armstrong Whitworth Whitley – No 13 MU undertook modification work on these aircraft.

inelegant aircraft, which was commonly called the 'Flying Barn Door'!

The Whitley had first flown in March 1936 and its name was taken from the district of Coventry where the factory was situated. The aircraft had a cruising speed of about 190 mph and carried a maximum bomb load of 7,000 pounds. Whitleys were the first aircraft to bomb German targets in March 1940 and Italian targets in the following June. They were also the first to be used for the training of paratroops, and later acted as glider towers as well as troop carriers. Certainly from 1941 onwards Whitleys were very evident at the airfield and No 13 MU undertook modification work on them as well as Dakotas and Halifaxes.

Henlow's large grassed airfield was also used by the Whitleys, Halifaxes and Hudsons of Nos 138 and 161 (Special Duties) squadrons, which were operating from nearby RAF Tempsford; the crews would practise and perfect their techniques of dropping supply containers. Both squadrons used these aircraft in their clandestine operations over enemy occupied territories. Sadly, on 19th December 1943, a Halifax II of No 138 squadron crashed into a tall factory chimney on the site of Arlesey brickworks, about a mile south-east of Henlow. The crew had just completed its practice runs and all eight of them were killed. In March of the following year a Hudson IIIA of No 161 squadron crashed into the ground to the south side of the airfield, whilst on a training flight, and four of the crew were killed.

By late 1944 most of the Hurricanes had disappeared from Henlow; the last Hurricane, appropriately named *The Last of the Many* was produced in September 1944 – over 14,500 in total had been built. Their place at Henlow had been taken by the ubiquitous Mosquitos and a number of Hawker Typhoons. No 13 MU had become the main receiving airfield for those Mosquitos manufactured in Toronto, and they were flown over the Atlantic via Greenland. Some 90 Canadian Mosquitos had been produced in 1943, increasing to over 400 in 1944, and ultimately over 1,100 were built in Canada.

The station, although still nominally in No 43 Maintenance Group, was in fact operationally controlled by the Ministry of Aircraft Production, which gives more than a hint of its prime role and purpose. At the end of 1944 No 13 MU was still the main occupant but No 6 Repairable Equipment Unit was based there, as well as a number of mobile Dental Units. The School of Aeronautical Engineering was still very much alive and active, although it was controlled by No 24 Group of Technical Training Command.

In 1968, on its fiftieth anniversary, RAF Henlow was given the freedom of the town of Bedford, 38 years after airmen from Henlow had lined its streets during the funeral of the victims of the R101 disaster. In June 1953 RAF Henlow was raised to Group status and was commanded by an Air Commodore. The Radio Engineering Unit, which had arrived at Henlow in 1950, now shares the station with the Land Registry. Although the name 'Henlow' may not capture the imagination so readily as some operational stations, or perhaps does not have the cachet of, say, Wittering, Marham or Coltishall, it has, over its long history, given inestimable service to the Royal Air Force, and it is held in special affection by the thousands upon thousands of airmen that either served or trained there in the last 80 years.

8

HUNSDON

It was in March 1941 that RAF Hunsdon, situated in a quiet corner of the Hertfordshire countryside, opened as a night-fighter station within No 11 Group of Fighter Command. During the next four years the airfield would play host to over 20 squadrons, and to virtually all the famous RAF fighters of the Second World War. But of all the squadrons that operated from Hunsdon, none were more illustrious than the first two to serve there – Nos 85 and 3.

On 4th May 1941 the two flights of No 85 squadron landed at Hunsdon after a short flight of some 30 miles from Debden in Essex. This squadron had a long and proud history, which dated back to the First World War, when it had been commanded by no less than two Victoria Cross 'aces' – Majors Bishop and Mannock. During May 1940 its pilots had served valiantly in France, and then fought with distinction in the Battle of Britain; indeed, the Station Commander at Debden maintained, 'to my mind [85] will always be the First fighter squadron in the RAF.' Additionally the squadron was commanded by a celebrated fighter pilot, Squadron Leader Peter Townsend, DSO, DFC Bar. Townsend would later rise to the rank of Group Captain, and in the 1950s become a household name because of his friendship with HRH the Princess Margaret; he died in June 1995 aged 80 years.

Townsend later recalled his arrival at Hunsdon, with particular notice for 'the long brand-new asphalt runways still smelling of fresh tar.'

Havoc of No 85 squadron, early 1941.

These two runways, 1,750 and 1,450 yards long, had been put down by George Wimpey & Co Ltd during the winter of 1940/1. The construction of the airfield had been relatively swift, work had only commenced in the previous October, with a fairly local firm – H. C. Janes Ltd of Luton – being awarded the contract to erect the temporary hutted accommodation in eight sites dispersed around the countryside well away from the main airfield.

Since the previous autumn, the squadron had been operating totally at night with their all-black Hurricanes, one of the several 'cats-eyes' night-fighter squadrons, so called because their aircraft were not equipped with AI (Airborne Interception) radar sets, so the pilots had to rely on their night-vision to make contact with the enemy aircraft. Despite their numerous and exhausting night-patrols the pilots had gained scant success, in fact the squadron's solitary night-victory came on 27th February 1941 when their CO had destroyed a Dornier 17.

By the following month the pilots had begun to exchange their Hurricanes for Douglas Havoc 1s. This American twin-engined aircraft – DB-7 – had orginally been designed and built for the French Air Force as a light bomber, but after the fall of France, the British Government took up the residue of aircraft, with the first 40 being delivered to the RAF in December 1940. Some of these were modified into stopgap night-fighters at Burtonwood Air Depôt, with the provision of eight .303 Browning machine guns in the nose, as well being equipped with AI sets. No 85 would be the first squadron to operate Havocs as night-fighters. The squadron experienced a period of technical problems with the aircraft, which at least allowed the pilots time to familiarise themselves with the Havocs, as they had not previously flown twin-engined aircraft. They also had to team up with radio operators. The first night-sorties with Havocs were made on 7th April, and Townsend was rather impressed with the new aircraft and its performance. It had a top speed of just under 300 mph, and he found 'the cockpit was most commodious, laid with green carpet and the different levers were all variously coloured'! But perhaps the most striking feature was the additional nose wheel, which in effect gave it a tricycle undercarriage. In his opinion the Havoc was, 'a powerful yet docile aircraft, which proved easy to handle.'

There was precious little time for the crews to settle in at their new station, indeed barely time for them to catch their breath because for the rest of the month they would be operating nightly and, according to Townsend, 'averaging four combats per night'. The squadron's Ground Control Interception station was at Foulness in Essex, which used the call-sign 'Cranford'. These GCI stations were able to plot both the enemy aircraft and the night-fighters, thus enabling more accurate fixes to be reported to the crews. Also they were able to identify enemy aircraft and so obviated the need for the crews to establish visual contact. The squadron's first success came on 10th/11th May, the night when London suffered its most devastating raid of the war; of the eleven aircraft destroyed on the night, two Heinkel 111s fell to the squadron. One was claimed by Flight Lieutenant Gordon K. Raphael, DFC, RCAF, and his operator Sergeant Addison; Raphael would command the squadron in 1942. In June 1941 Townsend was given a well earned rest from operational flying, having commanded the squadron since May 1940. He was promoted and given a desk job at Group headquarters. His replacement, Squadron Leader A. T. D. 'Scruffy' Sanders, DFC, was sadly killed in action at the end of August.

In the early summer orders were received to form a Turbinlite Flight at Hunsdon, which would be commanded by a recent arrival to No 85, Flight Lieutenant Paul Rabone, RNZAF, who had already gained considerable night-fighting experience with No 422 Flight (later No 92 squadron) in the defence of Liverpool and Manchester. On 16th June, No

1451 (Turbinlite) Flight was duly formed. The concept of these Flights was that the Havocs would be equipped with a large Helmore searchlight (the originator was Group Captain Helmore), which was capable of throwing a wide beam of light for a distance of about a mile. The Turbinlite would be guided onto an enemy contact by GCI and its own AI radar, and at a distance of about 3,000 feet its crew would pass the code-word 'Hot' to its following 'parasite' fighter. Once the target was firmly locked on, the code-word 'Boiling' would be passed and when the fighter was within about 900 feet of the enemy aircraft, the 'Turbinlite' Havoc would illuminate the target, for the 'parasite' fighter to move in to destroy it. This rather bizarre idea is said to have originated with Winston Churchill, and it was because of his enthusiasm for the project that the Flights were quickly formed. Indeed, a second Flight (No 1459) was formed at Hunsdon, only to move away in September. Although No 85's Havocs acted as the 'parasite' or supporting fighters, the intention was to use Hurricanes in this role, and largely to this end No 3 squadron arrived from Stapleford Tawney in early August.

The squadron's motto was 'The Third Shall Be First', which more than hinted at its long lineage dating back to May 1912! The squadron was equipped with Hurricane IIBs and Cs, the Series 2 aircraft, which were the first to have the newly developed and interchangeable wings housing twelve .303 inch machine guns or four 20mm cannons, and with the provision to carry two 250 or 500 pound bombs. The Mark IIs were supplied with Rolls-Royce Merlin XX engines, which gave a maximum speed of 340 mph or a cruising speed of just under 300 mph. The squadron's operations with the Turbinlite Flight were completely unsuccessful despite considerable efforts by all concerned and furthermore they were not free from accidents, with several of them proving fatal. This was not unusual as the other nine Turbinlite Flights also gained scant reward and suffered a higher rate of accidents. It was thought that in total the Turbinlites accounted for only one enemy aircraft destroyed, a couple of probables and maybe half a dozen or so damaged. Despite this all the Flights were upgraded to squadrons in September 1942, No 1451 becoming No 530, but all were disbanded about four months later. With the benefit of hindsight this experiment can be seen as an utter waste of valuable resources, both in aircraft and men.

Hurricanes of No 3 squadron, September 1941. (via T. Matthews)

From early 1942, No 85 squadron became more engaged in patrols over the North Sea, as well as acting as escort for shipping convoys. Whereas No 3 squadron became increasingly engaged in 'Intruder' operations over the near Continent, frequently using airfields close to the south coast as forward landing grounds. In the middle of August Squadron Leader A. E. 'Alex' Berry, DFC, who had been with the squadron since September 1940, led his pilots to Shoreham in Sussex for a special operation, code-named 'Jubilee', which involved the very costly landings of Canadian troops at Dieppe on 19th August. A massive air battle took place over Dieppe on that day, which was one of the greatest of the war in terms of aircraft in action and lost by both sides, all in the space of about 16 hours. The RAF flew almost 3,000 sorties with 56 squadrons taking part, and 106 aircraft were lost, 88 of them fighters with 71 pilots missing or killed in action. The Air Ministry claimed over 270 enemy aircraft destroyed or damaged, and it was, at the time, hailed as a great victory. However, when the true figures were known after the end of the war, it was found that the Luftwaffe had actually lost only 48 aircraft, in effect a heavy defeat for the RAF. No 3 squadron flew four missions on the day and lost two pilots – Sergeant S. D. Banks and Squadron Leader Berry, who was killed on his fourth sortie.

Back at Hunsdon the crews of No 85 squadron were finding that their Havocs were now somewhat lacking in speed and performance, and pressure was being applied to No 11 Group for the squadron to be re-equipped with the new de Havilland NFIIs. The first Mosquitos appeared at the airfield on 15th August 1942. 'These beautiful, graceful, little grey machines', as they were once described, never failed to cause interest and excitement whenever and wherever they operated. The NFIIs proved to be merely the precursors of literally hundreds of Mosquitos that would grace Hunsdon over the next two and a half years. The first night-fighter version was fitted with AI Mark V sets and armed with four 20mm cannons and four .303 inch Browning machine guns, and they would begin to alter the whole balance of the German night-bombing offensive.

Early in January 1943 the most famous night-fighter 'ace' of the war, Wing Commander John 'Cat's Eyes' Cunningham, DSO, DFC Bar, arrived to take command of No 85 squadron. It was his second tour of operations, which he completed in March 1944 with 20 night-victories to

Wing Commander John Cunningham, DSO, DFC Bar, CO of No 85 squadron from January 1943. (via Robin J. Brooks)

his name. He brought with him his trusty operator, Flight Lieutenant C. F. 'Jimmie' Rawnsley, DSO, DFC, DFM, who would also act as the squadron's Navigation Leader. Rawnsley later recalled Hunsdon at this time: 'there were comfortable brick crew-rooms, well dispersed parking pens for the aircraft and small blister hangars and concrete perimeter track and runways... The officers' mess was an old country house

135

named Bonningtons, which sat squat and comfortable among its iron-railed meadows.' This house had originally been owned by the Brooke Bond Tea Company and had been used for office staff dispersed from London. No 85's long sojourn at the airfield was fast coming to a close, and the pilots finally moved to West Malling in Kent on 13th May, where they would be re-united with their old Commanding Officer, now Wing Commander Townsend, who was the Station Commander.

On the following day No 3 squadron also bade farewell to the airfield that had been their home for almost two years, the pilots also moving to West Malling. They had only recently become operational on their new aircraft, Hawker Typhoons. These aircraft had managed to survive an unpromising and difficult introduction into the Service, when they were bedevilled with endless technical problems, but ultimately the Typhoon developed into a splendid fighter/bomber, which found its true métier as a low-level strike aircraft of devastating power and strength. It was certainly very quick at low-level, just in excess of 400 mph, and there was a current Service joke that you could tell 'Tiffy' pilots because they were, 'always blue in the face from the speed'! No 3 squadron has survived all the defence cuts of recent years and, at the time of writing, is currently serving at RAF Laarbruch in Germany.

From being the sole preserve of just two fighter squadrons, Hunsdon would now be the home of a proliferation of squadrons for varying periods of occupation, and pressure of space here dictates that not all will be noted individually. The first of these many squadrons, however, was No 157, which had been the first night-fighter unit to introduce the Mosquito into Fighter Command, whilst stationed at Castle Camps in Cambridgeshire. On the night of 14th/15th May 1943, Flight Lieutenant H. Tappin, DFC, (an ex-member of No 3 squadron) shot down a FW190, although the squadron's crews were more often engaged on 'Intruder' operations over Northern France, and in the process had gained something of a reputation for destroying locomotives or 'train-busting'. They also flew what were known as 'Insteps', that is providing air cover for Coastal Command aircraft patrolling the Bay of Biscay. In November the squadron moved to Predannack in Cornwall to continue such operations.

From the end of May the crews had shared the airfield with No 515 squadron, which had been equipped with a mixture of Defiants and

Beaufighters. The former aircraft were now certainly out-of-date, and steps were taken to make it into an all Beaufighter squadron. It ultimately moved into No 100 (Bomber Support) Group of Bomber Command in the middle of December. It is interesting to note that even in February 1944 the squadron was still not operational at its new airfield, Little Snoring in Norfolk. The main reason given for this state of affairs was that, 'On taking over the squadron from Fighter Command...the training of the crews was found to be woefully inadequate. The squadron's aircraft had been standing in the open for two years and the state of serviceability was grave'! Finally the Beaufighters were scrapped and Mosquitos were supplied.

Early in November 1943 a Canadian night-fighter squadron, No 410, arrived from West Malling, and inevitably it was equipped with Mosquitos. Since the squadron's formation in June 1941 it had also been equipped with Defiants and Beaufighters, and was now under the command of Wing Commander G. H. Elms. No 410 was the first Commonwealth squadron to operate from Hunsdon, but from now on Canadian, Australian and New Zealand airmen would become frequent visitors to the airfield, evidence of the very cosmopolitan nature of the wartime RAF. The squadron gained instant success, when on the night of 11th/12th November, one of its pilots, Flying Officer Schultz, shot down three Dornier 217s during a raid on Chelmsford. The squadron left Hunsdon on 30th December, but it would return a couple of times more over the next ten months.

Hunsdon now passed into the control of No 85 Group, and was about to enter a period of excitement and action with the arrival, on 31st December, of about 70 Mosquito FBVIs of No 140 Wing. This Wing had been formed at Sculthorpe in Norfolk, and comprised three squadrons, Nos 21, 464 (RAAF), and 487 (RNZAF). The crews had been trained and developed at Sculthorpe under the guidance and control of Group Captain P. C. Pickard, DSO Bar, DFC, who was the Station Commander. Pickard was a truly amazing airman, and more about him will be noted under Tempsford. Since October the Wing had gained no mean reputation for its daring low-level operations, and it owed much to the strong support and enthusiasm of the Commander of No 2 Group of Bomber Command, Air Vice-Marshal Sir Basil Embry, DSO 3 Bars, DFC, AFC. He was probably the most dedicated supporter and admirer of the

Mosquito in Bomber Command; in his view the Mosquito, 'was the finest aeroplane, without exception, that has ever been built in this country.'

The Mosquito Wing had been mainly engaged in attacking V1 rocket sites in Northern France, and indeed the flight to their new airfield had been routed via a rocket site at Le Ploy. Nevertheless, the Wing will be forever remembered for a daring low-level operation from Hunsdon on 18th February 1944 code-named 'Jericho'. This operation was planned, 'with the intention of breaking the walls of the prison [at Amiens in Northern France] to assist the escape of 120 French Resistance workers that had been condemned to death for helping the Allies. In the event of failure they had requested that the whole of the building be bombed.' Operation Jericho had been meticulously planned using a scale-model of Amiens prison, and Group Captain Pickard would lead the Wing flying with No 464 squadron, although originally Air Vice-Marshal Embry had wanted to lead the operation but had been expressly forbidden to do so by his C-in-C, Air Chief Marshal Sir Trafford Leigh-Mallory. The 18 Mosquitos (six from each squadron) would attack in three waves, with No 487's new Commanding Officer, Wing Commander Irvine S. Smith, DFC Bar, leading the first wave. Wing Commander Smith of the RNZAF was a most experienced pilot, having served and commanded No 151 squadron mainly from Wittering. There would be one additional Mosquito from the Operational Film Production Unit, to film the whole operation.

The Mosquito force left Hunsdon in quite atrocious weather, thick cloud and snow, and four of the original twelve Typhoons of No 198 squadron acting as escorts became detached and were forced to return to base. One of the leading Mosquitos had engine trouble close to the target and had to abort. The first three Mosquitos of No 487 made the first bombing run and dropped their bombs, which had an eleven-second time fuse; at the same time the remaining two of the squadron's Mosquitos made a diversionary attack on Amiens railway station. The second wave of Mosquitos from No 464 squadron with Wing Commander Bob Iredale in the lead attacked the prison walls, followed by Group Captain Pickard. He then circled the target to assess the damage, and decided that the walls had been sufficiently breached. The third wave (No 21 squadron) was ordered to withdraw and return to

Hunsdon. The whole operation had lasted no more than five minutes, with just one casualty. However, Pickard's Mosquito had been damaged by enemy flak and about five miles from Amiens, it was shot down by FW190s, and he and his operator, Flight Lieutenant Peter Broadley, DSO, DFC, DFM, were killed.

It is thought that 258 out of the total 700 prisoners managed to make their escape, although many were later recaptured; also 94 people were killed in the attack with another 92 injured. The rights and wrongs of this historic operation have been debated many times, and the details of the raid were not made public until October 1944. It has since been argued that Group Captain Pickard should have been posthumously awarded the Victoria Cross. In fact on the cross above his grave in Saint-Pierre cemetery at Amiens, the French had added 'VC' to his other decorations, and later his widow, Dorothy, requested that the 'VC' should be removed. According to Sir Basil Embry, Pickard was, 'in courage, devotion to duty, fighting spirit and powers of leadership...one of the great airmen of the war'.

Until the Wing left Hunsdon during March/April 1944, the three squadrons mainly concentrated on V1 rocket site targets – part of the so-called 'Crossbow' operations. It should be noted that by later interpretation of photographs it was estimated that it would take almost a hundred Mosquitos to destroy just one small V1 site because of the weight of bombs they could carry; one of the reasons why the heavy bombers of both Bomber Command and the Eighth Air Force were increasingly used against the sites.

Towards the end of April No 410 squadron returned to Hunsdon, followed two days later (30th) by No 409 (RCAF) squadron. Both would be involved in providing air support for the D-Day landings and the armada of supply vessels that went back and forth across the English Channel. Each squadron would operate from advanced bases in Wiltshire, and ultimately move over to France. The squadrons were joined on 19th June, by what might be considered Hunsdon's last 'permanent' squadron, No 29, which would remain at the airfield until late February 1945. It operated Mosquito NFXIIIs, which were provided with the latest Mk VIII AI radar, and was commanded by Wing Commander Paul W. Arbon, a pre-war airman, who had served with No 85 during the Battle of Britain. The crews' main activity was 'Intruder' raids over Northern France;

Mosquito Mk XIII of No 39 squadron.

although as the land battle moved further east, by the end of the year the front-line areas would be effectively beyond the range of most Mosquitos operating from Hunsdon. During the autumn the crews also flew 'anti-diver' patrols, attempting to intercept and destroy the V1 rockets that appeared almost daily across south-east England and the London area.

In late August another Canadian Mosquito squadron arrived, No 418 (City of Vancouver). It was equipped with FBVIs, which when fitted with two 50 gallon drop-fuel tanks extended their operational range. One of the Canadian navigators, Sergeant Dave McIntosh, DFC, has given an amusing description of Hunsdon in his very readable book, *Terror in the Starboard Seat*: 'a small village with one pub (there had been two but some dumbbell had landed on the other one!) only 30 miles from London. The main railway line to London was only two miles from the field…there was a brewery only ten miles away. With such amenities and proximity to London, who would ever need to leave?' He vividly recalls attacking a number of airfields along the Dutch/German border, as well as other targets in Germany itself, and also 'Big Ben' sites, the code-name for the V2 rockets.

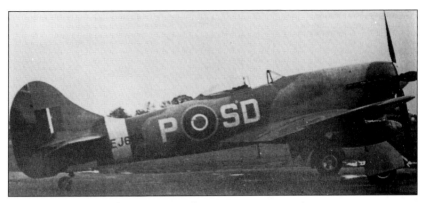

Hawker Tempest V of No 501 squadron.

Hunsdon was a premier Mosquito station with three squadrons – the third, No 488(RNZAF), arrived in early October but only stayed for about five weeks. When the Canadian airmen left for Hartford Bridge towards the end of November, they were replaced by a famous night-fighter squadron, No 151, which now had the Mosquito NFXXXs that had given the aircraft a much improved high-altitude performance due to its modified Merlin 76 engine. The squadron remained at Hunsdon until March 1945 and its departure brought a sad and final farewell, as far as the airfield was concerned, to this amazing aircraft.

During the final months of the war a number of squadrons came and went, and all but one of them were equipped with North American Mustang IVs, the superb long-range escort fighter. The one exception was No 501 (County of Gloucester) – an Auxiliary Air Force squadron – that had been formed back in June 1929. Until 1944 it had been a Spitfire squadron but it was now equipped with Hawker Tempests, which have been described as, 'a superb combat aircraft...and a pleasure to fly.' It was yet another classic fighter to be designed by Sidney Camm, and owed much to the Typhoon. The Tempest was very fast, over 425 mph, sturdy and powerful, which really made its name against the V1 rockets; over one third of those shot down by the RAF fell to Tempest pilots, of which the squadron had claimed in excess of 100. No 501 was disbanded at the end of April, although it was reformed again just twelve months later, and survived until March 1957.

Perhaps it was rather fitting, considering the number of Commonwealth squadrons that had served at Hunsdon, that two RCAF squadrons, Nos 441 (Silver Fox) and 442, should bring the airfield's wartime existence to a conclusion. When they left about a week after VE Day, the airfield was placed on a care and maintenance basis, but it was not officially closed until July 1947. The 'airfield' is still referred to as such by the local residents, though there is precious little left to remind one of those days, well over 50 years ago, when the countryside echoed to the rich and vibrant sounds of the Rolls-Royce Merlin engines of the Mosquito squadrons.

9

LITTLE STAUGHTON

For its relatively short wartime existence – less than three years – Little Staughton airfield saw plenty of action; from starting out as an American base crammed full of B-17s to becoming a Pathfinder station housing two of the finest aircraft of the Second World War – the Lancaster and Mosquito. For added measure two airmen from its squadrons were posthumously awarded the Victoria Cross, a rare distinction for an RAF station. Even today Little Staughton has probably one of the best preserved examples of a wartime control tower in the whole of the country.

The airfield was built during 1942, a little to the south-east of the village that bears its name, and situated on an enclave of land surrounded on three sides by the present Cambridgeshire and Bedfordshire boundary. It was a standard bomber station but was unusual in that eight Robin hangars had been supplied, in addition to the three more normal T2 type hangars. The Robin hangars were much smaller, produced to a Ministry of Aircraft Production design and were more usually found at smaller satellite landing grounds. The probable reason for their existence at the airfield was to provide additional and valuable workshop space for the American air depôt. The site had been first allocated to the USAAF in November 1941, confirmed the following

B-17 of 379th Bomb Group crashed at Little Staughton, 29th May 1943. (USAF via M. Harris)

May, and planned as a temporary Advanced Air Depôt four months later.

It was not until early December 1942 that some 500 or so American airmen arrived at Little Staughton to set up Strategic Air Depôt No 2 for the 1st Bombardment Wing of the Eighth Air Force, whose Bomb Groups were operating from bases in Bedfordshire and the neighbouring counties. The Depôt would be responsible for the maintenance and repair of damaged B-17s operated by those Groups, as well as undertaking major overhauls and any necessary B-17 modifications. Also new B-17s arrived at the airfield for general inspections and checks before being allocated to the different Groups.

The Depôt was also used on occasions as an emergency landing ground when damaged B-17s limping back to their home bases were diverted to land at Little Staughton. Presumably it saved the time of delivering the damaged aircraft there later! This inevitably led to a number of spectacular crash-landings at the airfield. One such incident occurred on 29th May 1943 when a B-17 from the 379th Group, which had been heavily damaged on the Group's first mission to St Nazaire, was diverted to Little Staughton. The pilot managed on this occasion to make a successful emergency landing with no fatalities, but subsequently the repaired aircraft crashed near Bozeat in February 1944. During January 1944 at least three B-17s made forced-landings at the airfield, and in each case the aircraft was written off.

There was also a Reclamation Unit stationed there, which visited American bases in the area to identify serviceable items for repair at the Depôt. This Unit established a close working relationship with Morris Motors at Cowley near Oxford, which received scrap metal for melting down and recycling for fresh aircraft production. Quite often the Unit was called out to remove crashed B-17s. On 5th January 1943 a B-17 of the 306th Group at Thurleigh crashed shortly after taking-off for Kiel, coming down at Sharnbrook, almost due west of Thurleigh. Three hours later a nine-man team from the Unit arrived on the scene and they worked until 10th January clearing the site, with most of the remains of the aircraft being transported to Cowley.

During the latter months of 1943 the American airmen knew that their days at Little Staughton were fast coming to a close, as a specially constructed depôt was being built at Abbots Ripton adjacent to Alconbury. The move took place on 29th February 1944 and the USAAF officially handed back the airfield to the RAF on the next day. Little Staughton was now allocated to No 8 (PFF) Group and it became an operational station for the first time.

The first RAF aircraft to be permanently based at the airfield began to arrive during late March; they were a mixture of Avro Lancaster Is and IIIs originally on the complement of 'B' Flight of No 7 squadron based at Oakington and 'C' Flight of No 156 squadron, which had recently moved to Upwood. Both squadrons were long experienced in PFF techniques, as each had served with the Pathfinders since its inception in August 1942. It had been decided that heavy bomber squadrons would now only comprise two Flights, so these two became the nucleus of a new Lancaster squadron, No 582, which was officially formed on 1st April 1944.

The Lancaster had come into being almost by accident; its immediate predecessor, the twin-engined Manchester, failed to live up to expectations. The Manchester had been A. V. Roe's response to an Air

145

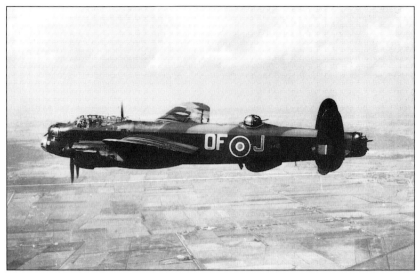

No 582 squadron operated Lancasters IIIs; although this aircraft flew with No 97 squadron. (RAF Museum)

Ministry specification, B13/36, which called for a bomber to be powered by two Rolls-Royce Vulture engines. The prototype first flew in July 1939 but because of delays with the production of the Vulture engines, Roy Chadwick designed a four-engined version of the Manchester equipped with four Rolls-Royce Merlin engines. This prototype was first known as the Manchester III, only later to be renamed the Lancaster. However, Manchesters did fly operationally, although only 202 were built with almost half of them being either lost in action or in crashes.

Without a shadow of doubt the Lancaster was the finest British heavy bomber of the war. Air Chief Marshal Harris could hardly find adequate words to praise the aircraft enough: 'it was easy to handle...lowest accident rate...the casualty rate of Lancasters was consistently below that of other types...Its efficiency was almost incredible – in performance and bomb capacity...I continually pressed for its production at the expense of other types'! The first prototype, Avro 683, powered by four Merlin X engines flew on 9th January 1941, followed five months later (13th May) by the second. The aircraft was sent for

Service trials in September, and the first production aircraft took to the air at the end of October, and began to enter the Service with No 44 (Rhodesia) squadron towards the end of the year. On 10th/11th March 1942 just two Lancasters were used over Essen – another 156,190 Lancaster sorties would be made by the end of the war, of which 3,431 were lost in action, or 2.2%.

The Mark Is were equipped with either Merlin XX or XXII engines, which gave the aircraft a maximum speed of about 285 mph, a cruising rate of some 210 mph. The aircraft was originally designed to carry 4,000 pounds of bombs but this figure steadily rose up to the 12,000 pound (Tallboy) bomb, and ultimately to the massive 22,000 pound (Grand Slam) bomb. It was the only Allied bomber capable of carrying these two bombs. The Lancaster had three gun turrets – nose, dorsal and tail. The Mark IIIs were virtually identical except for an enlarged bomb-aimer's 'bubble' in the nose, and they were supplied with American-built Packard Merlin engines. Over 7,370 Lancasters were built by four different UK manufacturers, and one in Canada. The Mark Is and IIIs were the most numerous accounting for over 87% of the production, and the last Lancaster was delivered in February 1946.

The Lancaster crews were joined, on 2nd April 1944, by the Mosquito crews of No 109 squadron, who flew in from Marham. This was no ordinary Mosquito unit, it had originally been involved in the trialling of 'Oboe' with Wellingtons, and had pioneered its operational use back in December 1942. Oboe or Type 9,000 Precision Bombing System, to give it the name it was known by during its development, was the brain child of the Telecommunications Research Establishment, and was, according to Professor R. V. Jones, the Head of the wartime Scientific Intelligence Unit, 'the most accurate radio bombing system produced by either side.' Basically it operated from two ground stations set some 100 miles apart; the first station (Cat) would accurately direct an aircraft towards the target by radio pulses, which sounded very similar to those produced by the musical instrument, hence the code-name, and the second station (Mouse) transmitted a second signal as the aircraft approached the target in the sounds of a series of dashes and then dots, when these ceased the bomb aimer immediately released the bombs. The system was said 'to be as simple and easy as that'! Perhaps the only major weakness of Oboe was its limited range (some 270 miles) because

'Oboe' Mosquito BIX LR504 – of No 109 squadron. (RAF Museum)

of the curvature of the earth, but the development of the high-altitude Mosquitos minimised this disadvantage to some extent.

No 109 squadron was mainly equipped with BIXs, but had recently received its first BXVIs. The former had been provided with more powerful two-stage Merlin engines, which had increased their ceiling height and cruising speed, and in addition to its normal bomb load (2,000 pounds) it could carry two 500 pound bombs under the wings or drop tanks if extra fuel was required. The BXVIs were the pressurised version of the BIXs with little difference in performance; their flat-out speed was 400 mph. Both marks could be converted to carry a 4,000 pound (Cookie) bomb. This required the provision of a special 'bulged' bomb bay, which gave the aircraft a somewhat pregnant appearance, at least when placed alongside normal Mosquitos. In total some 1,200 BXVIs were produced.

On 4th/5th April 1944 the Mosquito crews went into action over Cologne, and four nights later one crew failed to return from Essen, crash-landing at Bradwell Bay airfield in Essex. During the month the squadron launched 190 sorties mainly to targets in the Ruhr valley. In the following month the figure increased to 320, but unfortunately on

6th/7th May when five Mosquitos left to bomb the large I. G. Farben factory at Leverkusen, one Mosquito IX was shot down by a night-fighter over Holland – a rare occurrence; the pilot, Squadron Leader H. B. Stevens, DFC, had previously flown in excess of 86 sorties. This important target would claim another two crews in the coming months.

For Bomber Command the first three months of 1944 had been a torrid time – the costly Berlin raids, the offensive against the German aircraft industry and finally the disastrous Nuremberg operation, had all taken a heavy toll of aircraft and crews. Now the Command turned its endeavours to railway targets, military camps, ammunition depôts and armament factories in France and Belgium, as a prelude to the Normandy invasion. Thus No 582 entered the air war as this new phase of bombing was already in progress. The crews' first operation was mounted on 9th/10th April when just seven joined a force of 230 Lancasters attacking the Deliverance railway yards at Lille. It was an intensive attack, but sadly over 450 French civilians were killed in the raid – the very reason why the Allies' Transportation Plan had been so hotly debated by the Allied Air Chiefs. It was not until the 22nd/23rd of the month when the marshalling yards at Laon were attacked for the second time in a fortnight that the squadron lost their first aircraft in action; it was shot down by a night-fighter, and the seven-man crew were all killed. During May four aircraft were lost in action, over a Luftwaffe airfield at Montdidier, railway yards at Aachen and Rennes airfield; the latter Lancaster was piloted by Squadron Leader H. W. Heney, DSO, RNZAF, who was a very experienced PFF airman, having completed 60 sorties when he was killed.

Both squadrons were very active in June. On the eve of D-Day (5th/6th) the Command launched Operation Flashlight – the bombing of ten gun batteries around the Seine Bay. Crews from No 109 squadron Oboe-marked the targets for each separate attack and all 25 crews taking part returned safely to Little Staughton. Eleven of the Lancaster crews were detailed to bomb Longues near Arromanches where the Mulberry harbour would later be assembled. Sadly, No 582 lost one of three aircraft that failed to return from the night's total operations. Once again the aircraft had a very senior and experienced crew. The pilot, Squadron Leader A. W. Raybould, DSO, DFC had already completed 78 operations. All but two of the ten targets had been covered with cloud, so most of the bombing was entirely based on Oboe marking; well over 5,000 tons of bombs were dropped, which was the highest total for a single night, and 1,012 aircraft had taken part, which was another record.

For the rest of the month road and rail junctions, airfields and enemy troop positions were attacked. From the middle of the month (16th/17th) the Command renewed their offensive against V1 rocket sites, with the 'Oboe' Mosquitos coming into their own for marking and bombing such relatively small targets. The Lancaster crews were engaged mainly over rail targets, and four were lost over Etampes, Douai, Lens and Blainville. During July the two squadrons mounted over 360 sorties in total. What became known as 'controlled Oboe' was used more and more frequently. This involved at least one Lancaster being fitted with Oboe; this aircraft would then lead the operation, when it dropped its bombs the rest of the aircraft would follow suit. This method allowed a greater tonnage of bombs to be dropped on the Oboe signals. It also meant that crews from 109 squadron would operate in No 582's Lancasters, because they were highly experienced with Oboe.

On a daylight raid on 11th July 1944 to a V1 rocket site at Gappenes, Wing Commander George F. Grant, DSO, DFC, the Commander of 109 squadron, led in a Lancaster. It was a very successful operation with all the 33 aircraft returning safely. The same could not be said nine days later (20th) when 20 Lancasters attacked another V1 rocket site at Fôret-de-Croc. The Lancaster 'Oboe' leader on this occasion was Squadron Leader L. J. Foulsham, DFC, AFC, of 109 squadron, accompanied by three Mosquito navigators, one acting as Flight Engineer and Air Bomber. On the run-in to the target the 'Oboe' Lancaster was directly hit by flak, and it exploded with great force; all eight airmen were killed.

Bomber Command mounted its first major operation on a German city for over two months when, on 23rd/24th July, Kiel was attacked; the bombing lasted for just 25 minutes with the city suffering its heaviest damage of the war. Only four Lancasters were lost but one of these came from Little Staughton; a second one, piloted by Lieutenant E. Swales, SAAF (more of him later) ran short of fuel and crashed whilst making an emergency landing at Radlett. During the month Stuttgart was attacked three times in five nights. The third raid on the 28th/29th proved rather costly with 39 aircraft lost, most of them victims of night-fighters on the outward leg over France. Once again the squadron lost a Lancaster. All of the crew were killed except for the pilot, Squadron Leader V. G. Coleman, who was blown clear of the aircraft and survived the terrific blast, ending up as a prisoner of war. One member of his crew, Flight Sergeant R. C. L. Lewis, was, at the age of 39 years, one of the oldest airmen flying with Bomber Command.

The month of August proved to be the busiest of the war for the Mosquito crews with over 500 sorties mounted against V1 rocket sites, oil plants, airfields, enemy troop positions and fuel dumps. On the 27th, Bomber Command launched their first major daylight operation against a German target since August 1941, with the Rheinpreussen synthetic oil refinery near Homberg being the target. The operation was escorted by a strong force of Spitfires. The bombing was based on Oboe marking but heavy cloud cover made the marking difficult, and eight Mosquitos from 109 squadron were in action. Although intense and accurate flak was encountered over the target area, not a single aircraft was lost. On the last night of the month the Mosquito crews were active over Cologne, Düsseldorf and Leverkusen and three failed to return. Two aircraft came down over the Continent and in both cases the crews managed to evade capture; the third had to make an emergency landing at Woodbridge in Suffolk. It proved to be the squadron's worst night of the war for losses.

One of the most successful missions to be undertaken from Little Staughton came on 3rd October 1944 when it was decided to attack the sea walls at Walcheren Island as the coastal batteries sited there dominated the approach to the port of Antwerp, which was needed to supply the Allied armies in Holland. The intention of the operation was to breach the walls and flood the island, which was below sea level. The raid was directed by a Master Bomber – Group Captain P. H. Cribb, DFC, flying a Lancaster from No 582 squadron. The attack was planned in eight waves, with the specific target being Westkapelle, the most westerly point of the island. After the fifth wave had bombed, the wall was breached with a gap some 100 yards wide being made, and as a result virtually all the batteries were submerged. The Lancasters of No 617 (Dambusters) squadron carrying 12,000 pound (Tallboy) bombs, who were being held in reserve, were not needed. It was a most successful operation with not a single aircraft lost.

On the night of 27th/28th November five Mosquito crews marked the target for over 300 Lancasters at Freiburg. It had no industrial targets to speak of, and the town had never been bombed before, but intelligence sources had revealed that there were heavy concentrations of enemy troops in the town, which was a railway junction. The Oboe marking was directed from mobile caravan stations situated in France, and it proved to be deadly accurate with quite devastating bombing, almost 2,000 tons of bombs dropped in only 25 minutes – an example of the awesome power of Bomber Command at this stage of the war. The operation was considered 'the most outstanding attack of the year.'

The month of December proved to be a costly time for both squadrons. On the 4th/5th when No 109 squadron was in action over Karlsruhe, two Mosquitos collided at a height of 30,000 feet. One crashed but the crew escaped and managed to return to Little Staughton in the New Year; the other aircraft, although heavily damaged, struggled back to the airfield. Another four were lost towards the end of the month. Only one crew made it back to England but their Mosquito finally crashed near Saxmundham in Suffolk and both airmen were killed. On the 12th/13th of the month No 582 was engaged in the last heavy night raid on the Krupps munitions factories at Essen, which had been a major target for most of the war; six Lancasters were lost, one of which came from Little Staughton.

Then just two days before Christmas 30 PFF Lancasters and Mosquitos were detailed to attack the Gremberg railway yards at Cologne. The force was split into three formations, each led by an 'Oboe' Lancaster with an 'Oboe' Mosquito in reserve. The Master Bomber on this occasion was Squadron Leader Robert A. M. Palmer, DFC Bar, of 109 squadron, who was on his third operational tour and flying his 111th sortie in a Lancaster from No 582. The operation made an unfortunate start with two Lancasters colliding over the French coast. On reaching the target area, where heavy cloud had been forecast, visibility was found to be clear, so a message was sent for the formations to break and bomb visually. This signal did not reach Squadron Leader Palmer and he continued his measured and careful run onto the target, despite the fact that the Lancaster had already been hit by flak (one of the essential features of Oboe marking was that the final approach had to be completely straight and steady). Palmer's Lancaster began to fill with

*Squadron Leader R.A.M. Palmer, VC, DFC, Bar, of No 109 squadron.
(Imperial War Museum)*

*Captain Edwin Swales, VC, DFC, SAAF, and his crew, November 1944.
(RAF Museum)*

smoke but he kept going doggedly on, making an exact and perfect
Oboe approach, with the bombs accurately hitting the target. His
Lancaster was last seen spiralling to earth in flames, and only one
member of the crew managed to escape. Palmer was posthumously
awarded the Victoria Cross for 'his record of prolonged and heroic
endeavour is beyond praise'. He was the first 'Oboe' pilot to receive the
ultimate award, as well as becoming the first Pathfinder VC. It was a
costly operation – five Lancasters and one Mosquito did not return to
Little Staughton. One of the Lancaster pilots, Captain E. Swales, SAAF,
was awarded the DFC for his part in the raid. Air Vice-Marshal Bennett,
the legendary leader of the Pathfinders, had predicted that should any
of his airmen be awarded the VC, it would be posthumously, such were
the dangers they faced every time they flew.

Captain Swales, DFC, of No 582 squadron was the only South African

The simple memorial stone to Nos 109 and 582 squadrons.

airman to serve with the Pathfinders, and on the 23rd/24th February 1945, he was chosen to be the Master Bomber on a raid to Pforzheim, to the north-west of Stuttgart. Three hundred and eighty Lancasters and Mosquitos were involved in the first heavy operation to this town. Although Swales' Lancaster was hit twice by night-fighters over the target area, he continued to direct the bombing (1,825 tons in 22 minutes!). It was thought that about 80% of the town was destroyed with a heavy loss of civilian lives, third only to Dresden and Hamburg. Only when Captain Swales was completely satisfied that the attack had achieved its objectives, did he turn for home. By now the Lancaster was so severely damaged that it was very difficult to control, only with considerable skill and strength did Swales manage to keep it sufficiently steady for his crew to bale out. However, before he could make his escape the aircraft plunged to the ground and Swales was found dead at the controls. This brave South African airman was also awarded the Victoria Cross and his citation read: 'Intrepid in the attack, courageous in the face of danger, he did his duty to the last, giving his life that his comrades might live.'

In April 1945 the 'Oboe' Mosquito crews finally achieved their ambition, when the ground stations had moved forward sufficiently to bring Berlin within Oboe range. On the 8th/9th three crews from 109 squadron attacked the city for the first time, and continued to do so until the RAF's final raid on Berlin on the 20th/21st. It fell to a Mosquito XVI of the squadron, crewed by Flying Officers A. C. Austin and P. Moorehead to drop the last bombs – four 500 pounders – at 02.14 am. The RAF dropped over 45,500 tons on Berlin and every third house in the city was destroyed.

The squadron's operational sorties ceased on 7th May 1945 when ten crews marked five different aiming points for aircraft dropping urgent food supplies for the starving Dutch people at the Hague, Gouda, Rotterdam and Leiden. The contribution of the 'Oboe' squadrons to the Command's bombing offensive was really immeasurable, out of all proportion to the small number of crews engaged in their operations. No 109 squadron had mounted 522 bombing raids or 5,421 sorties for the loss of 18 aircraft (0.3%).

Four Lancaster crews were also active on the same day, although their brief wartime offensive had been completed almost two weeks earlier, when 16 Lancasters bombed the gun batteries at Wangerooge. In just over twelve months No 582 had mounted over 2,100 sorties in 165 raids, losing 28 aircraft in action. The squadron disbanded on 10th September and at the end of the month so did No 109; although another bomber squadron, No 627, was renumbered 109, thus ensuring the continuity of this famous squadron.

At the end of 1945 the airfield was placed under care and maintenance, but it was effectively closed to Service flying. Nowadays the odd private aircraft can be seen taking off past the old control tower but not with quite the same throaty roar as the Rolls-Royce Merlin engines of yesteryear! In the village church is a tablet and Book of Remembrance to commemorate more than 200 airmen lost from the airfield. A small and very simple roadside marker records the fact that Little Staughton was a Pathfinder station.

10

LUTON

The very words 'Luton Airport' conjure up images of package-tour charter flights and the famous Campari television advertisements of 1979 with Lorraine Chase maintaining that she came 'from Luton Airport'! But the airport has a far longer lineage – back to the mid-1930s – when municipal airports were quite a rarity. It was at that time that Edgar F. Percival brought his nascent aircraft company to the small grassed airfield, which was perched on a plateau of land about 500 feet above sea level and some two miles to the south-east of the centre of the town. Although Luton Flying Club was already using the airfield and its rather primitive facilities, it would be Captain Percival and his company that would bring the airfield its early fame.

Captain Percival was a well-known figure in aviation circles. He had been a successful racing pilot/owner, and, in 1932, began to produce his first distinctive and most attractive aircraft – the Percival Gull – at Gravesend airfield in Kent. By the time he decided to move his production to Luton in late 1936, he had already built 22 Gulls and, according to the editor of *The Aeroplane* magazine, 'had a flourishing business from very small beginnings. It has sprung from the sale of civil machines and has never had to depend on military orders.' His company's very successful, fast and elegant range of aircraft from the original Gull, to the Mew Gull and on to the Vega Gull, were flown by many famous pre-war aviators, amongst them Jean Batten, Amy Johnson, Alex Henshaw and Sir Charles Kingsford-Smith. Indeed, no King's Cup air race in the 1930s would have been complete without a number of Gulls taking part.

The airfield was not officially opened until 16th July 1938 when Sir Kingsley Wood, the Secretary of State for Aviation, performed the ceremony, and for the special occasion there was a variety of both civil and military aircraft on display. Just 16 days later (1st August) No 29 Elementary & Reserve Flying Training School opened its doors for trainee pilots, operated by Birkett's Air Services under contract to the Air Ministry. The Mew and Vega Gulls of Percival Aircraft Ltd (as it had become in 1937) had to vie for airfield space with the ubiquitous Tiger Moths of No 29 School. Percival's premises sited at the far northern edge were always an integral part of the airfield.

It proved to be quite an important year for Percival Aircraft Ltd. For the first time they received Air Ministry approval, under Specification 20/38, to convert their Vega Gull into a communications and radio trainer for the RAF, and the military version would be known as the Proctor. In the previous year the company had responded to several Air Ministry specifications with a number of aircraft designs but without any tangible success or orders. Also in the same year the company had been appointed as one of a number of sub-contractors to build another new Service trainer – the Airspeed Oxford.

The Vega Gull had first flown in December 1935 and had become the company's most successful light sporting/racing and touring aircraft. Besides its obvious attraction to many private pilots, it was also used by several Air Attaches abroad, and by 1939 the RAF had eleven Vega Gulls on their charge. The prototype Proctor P28 (P5998) made its first flight on 8th October 1939. It was of wooden construction covered with plywood and fabric, and was powered by a single de Havilland Gipsy Queen II engine, which produced a top speed of 160 mph with a cruising speed of about 20 mph less.

The Proctor I was a three-seat aircraft provided with dual controls. Ultimately four marks of Proctors were built during the war, with a fifth being produced post-war. The Mark IIs and IIIs were radio trainers without dual-controls, the latter being the most numerous with over 430

Proctor IV – LA589 – second prototype, August 1943. (RAF Museum)

being produced. The Mark IV was originally called the Preceptor and was a four-seat radio trainer and communication aircraft. It had been completely redesigned and structurally strengthened, having a longer and deeper fuselage. It first flew in 1943 and over 250 were produced, some of which were still operating with the RAF in 1955. In total over 1,140 Proctors were built, but because of Percival's wartime commitment to the production of Oxfords and later Mosquitos, most of the Proctor IIs, IIIs and IVs were built by a sub-contractor, F. Hills & Sons Ltd of Manchester.

There was just one other Percival aircraft to see war service – the Q6 or Petrel, as it was known in the Service. This twin-engined four/six seat communication aircraft had first flown at Luton on 14th September 1937, entering production the following year. It was ordered for the Service under Specification 25/38 and just eight Petrels were delivered by March 1940, although the Service had requisitioned at least another twelve civil Q6s. It is interesting to note that about one quarter of the country's total aircraft production during the war, was given over to training and communications aircraft.

At the outbreak of war all civilian flying ceased and No 29 E&RFTS was closed down, so the airfield now became the sole preserve of Percival Aircraft Ltd. The company would soon become engaged in the production of Proctor Is and some IIs for the RAF, but it was also

Percival Q 6 or Petrel. (via M. Butcher)

involved with the building of Oxfords; the Airspeed factory at Portsmouth could not cope with the large Service demand for this excellent training aircraft.

The Oxford, or 'Ox-box' as it was known to all airmen, had flown for the first time in June 1937, and was the military version of the company's small 'airliner' – the AS6 Envoy. It had entered the Service with the Central Flying School in November 1937 as the RAF's first twin-engined monoplane trainer, and from then the aircraft really never looked back. The original Mark Is were intended for all aspects of aircrew training and an Armstrong Whitworth dorsal turret had been fitted, which disappeared on the Mark IIs, as they were mainly used for pilot training. Perhaps every bomber pilot of the Second World War underwent a spell of training on this small but sturdy aircraft; its handling qualities were specifically designed to match those of the far larger and heavier bombers.

The aircraft was powered by two Cheetah radial engines and flat out it could be nursed to over 185 mph, but cruised more leisurely at about 140 mph. The Oxford had dual-controls as standard equipment and it

Airspeed Oxford: 1,356 were built by Percival's at Luton.

became a sturdy and reliable advanced flying trainer, although it was also used as an air ambulance, and for radar calibration and beam approach training. By the end of the war over 8,580 had been built, of which 1,356 were produced by Percival's at Luton. The Oxfords operated also in Canada, Australia, New Zealand, Southern Rhodesia and the Middle East – they seemed to go on and on, and were not finally withdrawn from Service training until 1954.

The airfield was not allowed to stay relatively quiet for very long, because on 22nd July 1940 No 24 Elementary Flying Training School moved in from Sydenham, near Belfast, where Short Brothers operated. The Tiger Moths and Miles Magisters soon took over the small airfield and in May 1941 the School was forced to use nearby Barton-in-the-Clay as a Relief Landing Ground. Even this extra airfield was not sufficient to cope with all the training flights, so in the following August the airfield adjacent to the Technical School at Halton in Buckinghamshire was also used by the School. During August and September 1940 the Luftwaffe found that Luton was a promising target, what with the Vauxhall factory, Percival's and the flying training school. In the event although the airfield was attacked on several occasions, very little damage was sustained, except to the flare-path in September.

In early February 1942 the School was forced to move once again, this time even further north – to Sealand in Cheshire. Its place was taken by

Aerial view of London Luton Airport, August 1998. (London Luton Airport)

No 5 Ferry Pool of the Air Transport Auxiliary, which had also been forced to move out of Hatfield in April. This was the only all female Ferry Pool, but on its move to Luton it became a 'mixed' pool with about two dozen or so female pilots. Luton also became the new home of ATA's Training Unit and its Cross-Country Flight, both of which had previously been based at White Waltham. The Ferry Pool and the Unit were under the command of Captain O. M. Mills, with ten flying instructors and about 70 aircraft – Ansons, Harvards, Masters, Magisters, Moths and Oxfords. Lecture and rest rooms were planned to cope with about 100 pupils, and the course was designed to last for about two months and included a fair amount of ground technical instruction. By the summer the initial flying training unit had taken up residence at Barton-in-the-Clay.

By 1943 the ATA had a strength in excess of 600 pilots and since the spring of 1942 a number of experienced American women pilots had been recruited, and had passed through the Training Unit; as early as

August 1940 there were also a number of American male pilots flying with ATA. However, in late 1943 the Ministry of Aircraft Production requested that the Ferry Pool and the Training Unit vacate Luton, because Percival Aircraft Ltd was now becoming involved in the assembly of Mosquitos. The Pool moved up to Cosford, where it would be close to a Spitfire factory; it was renumbered to No 12 and reverted to an all-female pilot Pool. The Training Unit departed to a small airfield at Haddenham near Thame.

The Air Transport Auxiliary was probably the most unrenowned air service of the war, despite the fact that in January 1942 a propaganda film *Ferry Pilot*, about the daily work of an ATA ferry pilot, was first shown and well received – although it must be said it did not feature any women pilots! The service, at its peak, employed some 700 pilots, and on just one day, 21st February 1945, it ferried 570 aircraft! Winston Churchill's letter to Commodore D'Erlanger in May 1944 shows the important part the ATA played during the war.

'I am much impressed by the achievement of the Organization under your command in making more than 200,000 aircraft ferryings on behalf of the Royal Navy and Royal Air Force during the past four years; this is indeed a wonderful record.

That this formidable task should have been performed with so low an accident record redounds greatly to the credit of both your pilots and ground staff. It was not to be expected that operations of this magnitude could have been undertaken without incurring casualties, and I note with regret and sympathy that 113 pilots have lost their lives in the course of their ferrying duties.

The time may come when many of your pilots will be delivering aircraft to the RAF bases that are to be established on the Continent [which ATA did from September 1944], and I am confident that this important task, which is being entrusted to the Organization under your command, will be carried out with the same efficiency and devotion to duty as has been shown by the personnel of the Air Transport Auxiliary since its inception.

Please convey to all my thanks for, and appreciation of, their past services, and my best wishes in the task that lies before them.'

The Air Transport Auxiliary was finally disbanded at the end of November 1945, and five years later a memorial plaque was unveiled in St Paul's Cathedral to all who served in the ATA, and to those who lost their lives whilst on ferrying duties.

From 1943 onwards until the end of the war Percival Aircraft Ltd continued to produce Oxfords and also a greater number of Mosquitos – 245 in total. After the war the company, now part of the Hunting Group, produced the famous Prentice training aircraft, which had first flown from Luton in March 1946. The Proctor became the RAF's navigational trainer from 1948 to 1953. This aircraft was followed by the equally successful Provost trainer. The development and growth of the airfield from the late 1950s to a major passenger airport, now known as London Luton Airport, is yet another story.

11

NUTHAMPSTEAD

There are many fine memorials to Eighth Air Force Groups dotted throughout the country, but one of the most splendid and dramatic can be seen on a small neat plot of land adjacent to the Woodman inn at Nuthampstead. It is constructed of black granite and below the legend 'Hell From Heaven' is an outline of a B-17G flying through fiery skies with the Group's badge and the badges of its four squadrons in each corner. On the white plinth are details of 398th (Heavy) Bomb Group, to which the memorial is commemorated; there is also a verse:

> 'Their wings of silver touched the passing clouds,
> Made soft white lines across the azure blue.
> But not for them this life we share on earth,
> They sacrificed that for me and you.'

The airfield was sited due east of the village on land known as Scales Park and owned by Baron Dimsdale. The construction work commenced in 1942 by the 814th and 830th US Engineer (Aviation) Battalions, who had been given a completion target date of 1st April 1943. This was the only wartime airfield in the two counties to be built by American engineers. Like so many other wartime airfields in East Anglia and Eastern England, much of the hardcore that was laid down for the concrete roads and runways came from the blitzed areas of London and Coventry. Nuthampstead was a Standard A bomber airfield in all respects, and was first allocated to the USAAF in August 1942 whilst under construction. It was occupied by the Eighth Air Force some twelve months later, but it was not formally dedicated until 17th June 1943. It was then known as 'Station 131'; all American air bases were so numbered and their number appeared on official reports and correspondence. The airmen serving there were also actively encouraged to use the station number rather than its more usual local name, for obvious security reasons.

The first American airmen arrived at Nuthampstead on 16th September 1943, after leaving New York on the SS *Orion* some eleven days earlier. They were serving with the 55th Fighter Group, which would operate in the Eighth's 66th Fighter Wing, which had its headquarters at Sawston Grange near Cambridge. The Group's three squadrons – 38th, 338th and 343rd – were equipped with Lockheed P-38Hs (or Lightnings). This fighter/bomber was quite a *rara avis* in British skies at least, the first P-38s had made a somewhat fleeting appearance with the Eighth during the late summer of 1942, but had then been transferred to serve with the Twelfth Air Force in North Africa. The RAF, which had trialled and tested some Lightnings, were rather dismissive of the aircraft: 'not likely to be of any use except for convoy escort and against the occasional unescorted bomber'! Though it must be said that this opinion related to an earlier model of the aircraft, rather than the much improved P-38Hs.

Without doubt the P-38 was a brilliant aircraft both in design and concept, and at the time of its design was quite in advance of other contemporary fighters. The large twin-boom and twin-engined fighter was really revolutionary back in 1937. It was the first time that the Lockheed Aircraft Corporation had developed a military aircraft, and it first flew in January 1939 under the name 'Atlanta', though this was soon changed to 'Lightning', which was considered to be more appropriate for a fast pursuit fighter. The aircraft's early trials were so impressive that the US Army Air Corps placed an initial order, but because of certain development problems at Lockheeds, the P-38s were not received in the Service until March 1941.

The aircraft's most immediate attraction for the Eighth's Fighter

P-38s of 38th Fighter Squadron coming in to land after an escort mission, 15th October 1943. (National Archives & Records Administration)

Command was its operational range, about 450 miles without the use of drop fuel tanks; the P-38 would appear to offer a solution to the Eighth's mounting heavy bomber losses, by providing a long-range escort capability. The aircraft was certainly fast, just in excess of 400 mph at 25,000 feet, and it was well-armed with four .50 inch machine guns and two .20mm cannons grouped in the nose. However, its Allison engines, which were provided with turbo-chargers, proved to be rather temperamental and somewhat unreliable in the cold and damp air of a Northern European winter, also the cockpit heating was less than satisfactory, making combat flying decidedly uncomfortable and

A fine aerial shot of a P-38 of 55th Fighter Group. (Smithsonian Institute)

somewhat painful for its pilots. Although the P-38 was a formidable fighter, it did not quite make the same impact in Europe as it did in both North Africa and the Pacific.

Almost one month after the Group's arrival at Nuthampstead, 36 P-38s made a rather uneventful sweep of the Dutch coast. Three days later (18th October) 33 pilots left for their first bomber escort duties, but because of bad weather they were unable to make contact with the bomber formations. Sadly one P-38 failed to return, and it was thought that mechanical failure rather than enemy action had been the cause. The Group's ground engineers were wrestling with considerable problems with the P-38s, often one third or even more of the Group's aircraft were unserviceable for one reason or another. On each mission a number of pilots had to return early because of engine malfunctions.

It was not until 3rd November 1943 that the pilots chalked up their first victories over the Luftwaffe, when five enemy aircraft were downed whilst escorting bombers to Wilhelmshaven, and two days later another four were claimed over Gelsenkirchen without a single loss on either day. The Group's Commanding Officer, Lieutenant Colonel Frank B. James, reported, 'Morale is sky high and the mechanics are going wild!' Unfortunately these initial successes proved to be a false dawn because the Group would suffer a hard time during the winter, mainly due to the unreliability of the aircraft, and more especially when operating at high-altitudes. On several occasions in November they were joined by a squadron of No 20th Fighter Group, another P-38 unit stationed at King's Cliffe in Northamptonshire, which was busily working towards full operational readiness. By the end of the year 28 missions had been completed, 27 enemy aircraft had been shot down for the loss of the same number of P-38s, but another five had been written-off in crashes. Not a particularly inspiring performance.

In January 1944 ten missions were flown with 13 victories claimed against the loss of nine pilots in action. The Group was now almost completely re-equipped with the improved P-38Js, which had been provided with extra fuel tanks in the wings; in theory they could reach about 640 miles from the airfield, when using 150 gallon fuel tanks, but because they were required to give fighter support for about 15 minutes over the target area, realistically the range was closer to 380 miles or so. Nevertheless this was a considerable and distinct advantage over the other American fighter – the P-47 (Thunderbolt).

The two models had virtually the same performance, and the later 'J's were only distinguished by a flat panel windscreen and deeper radiator intake to improve the engine cooling, but alas the inherent problems with the Allison engine had not been cured. For example, on the last day of the month, 47 aircraft took off for a sweep over Holland, and although seven victories were claimed, six pilots went missing. At least two of the losses were thought to be due to engine failure, with another aircraft

Colonel Jack S. Jenkins, CO of 55th Fighter Group. (USAF)

crash-landing on return to the airfield. The Group's report on the day's operation concludes, 'With renewed vigor every pilot of the fighting 55th really resolved determinedly to hunt out the Hun and annihilate him.'

During February the Group mounted 15 missions operating as far afield as Leipzig, Schweinfurt, Regensburg and Frankfurt; eight victories were made for the loss of seven P-38s either in action or crashes. On the 7th of the month the Group's Executive Officer,

Lieutenant Colonel Jack S. Jenkins, took over as Commanding Officer. Colonel Jenkins had, on 3rd March, the honour of being the first American airman to fly over Berlin, in his P-38 named *Texas Ranger IV*. The Eighth's first operation to Berlin was abandoned because of the heavy cloud formations, at times up to 28,000 feet, but the recall signal failed to reach Colonel Jenkins and most of his pilots. When they arrived over Berlin they flew around and could not understand where all the bombers were! Three days later it was an entirely different story, on this Berlin mission the Colonel was forced to order his pilots back to base because of the excessive number of engine failures. However, on the 8th and 9th the Group did manage to make Berlin, but it lost four aircraft into the bargain without being able to record a single 'kill'. Indeed, March was not a good month for the Group with twelve aircraft lost, and all for just three enemy aircraft destroyed.

During the previous winter Colonel Cass Hough and Colonel Don Ostrander, an armaments expert, had been conducting a series of experiments into developing the capabilities of the P38 as a fighter/bomber. This involved modifying a number of P-38s with the installation of a special plexiglass nose section to provide a cabin for a bombardier and space for a Norden bomb-sight. These specially modified P-38s became known as 'Droop Snoots', and it was planned to use them as the sighting aircraft for following P-38s acting as bombers.

The first operational use of 'Droop Snoots' was made by the Group on 10th April with St Dizier airfield in France being selected as the target. Because this airfield was found to be cloud covered, Colonel Jenkins led his force to Coulommiers airfield, and the two 'Droop Snoots' landed their 1,000 bombs accurately with another 17 tons of bombs being dropped by the following P-38s. Colonel Jenkins then led his third squadron, which had been acting as a fighter escort, into a ground-strafe of the airfield. Two P-38s – Jenkins and his wingman – were shot down; however, the Colonel managed to make a forced landing and he was taken prisoner.

The Group and its new Commanding Officer, Colonel George T. Cromell, had little time left at Nuthampstead, as just four more missions were mounted before the 55th left for Wormingford in Essex. Their last operation from Nuthampstead took place on 15th April 1944, which was a ground-strafe of targets in Central and Western Germany, and they

Lt Holsted and his crew of 398th Bomb Group, April 1944. (National Archives & Records Administration)

returned home with five victories for the loss of three pilots. The Group would remain at Wormingford for the duration of the war, and in the summer the pilots converted to P-51s, with which they would become experts in the art of ground-strafing, ultimately receiving two Distinguished Unit Citations for these operations. Unfortunately the 55th also had the unenviable record of having the second highest loss of aircraft in the Eighth Fighter Command, no less than 181, this figure mainly being made up of the losses it suffered whilst flying P-38s.

Within days the P-38s were replaced by the B-17Gs of the 398th (Heavy) Bomb Group, which became one of the last Bomb Groups to join the Eighth Air Force. The Group had been activated back in March 1943, but after the completion of its training, it was used as a Replacement Training Unit and prepared over 300 crews for combat service. It was only in the New Year that the 398th was ordered into operations, and the personnel left the United States in April 1944. The four squadrons, 600th to 603rd, began to arrive at Nuthampstead from the 22nd of the month onwards, and within two weeks the crews were considered ready for their first operation.

The B-17G was the latest model of this famous aircraft; the major change was the provision of a Bendix twin-gun 'chin' turret in the nose of the aircraft. This modification had been made by Boeing at the express request of the Eighth Air Force, as an attempt to counter the Luftwaffe's head-on frontal attacks to which the older B-17Fs had proved to be most vulnerable. The Group had been assigned 60 aircraft, on account of the fact that the squadron complement had been increased to 15 aircraft. The model 'G's proved to be the most numerous mark with over 8,600 finally being produced.

The 398th Group had been placed in the 1st Bomb (later Air) Division and in the 1st Combat Bomb Wing. Like all Eighth Air Force Groups its aircraft carried specific markings; until July 1944 a black 'W' in a white triangle identified the 398th, but this was changed to a white 'W' in a black triangle painted on the tail, which was coloured red as a 'Wing' marking, as were the wing tips. Each squadron had its own code painted on the rear of the fuselage along with the aircraft's individual identification letter; the Group's squadron codes were N8, 30, K8 to N7 for 600th to 603rd respectively. In any case the Group was most distinctive as all of their B-17s were resplendent in the original all-silver finish.

The crews were detailed for their first mission on 6th May 1944, which promised to be a reasonably easy introduction into the air war, nothing more than a short trip across the English Channel to bomb a large V1 rocket site at Sottevast in the Pas de Calais – one of the so-called 'No-Ball' operations. However, the planning and logistics involved in mounting any bombing operation was a complicated affair, and sadly things went rather awry at the airfield on this important day. It all started with the kitchen staff not being informed of the impending operation, with the result that when the crews arrived for briefing they had not been fed. This resulted in the briefing being a rather hurried and disjointed affair, with the crews having little time to assimilate the various formation instructions and the correct signals that were being used. Then the transport to take the crews to their aircraft failed to appear, so the crews wandered about on foot with all their flying equipment, looking for their aircraft. The Group managed to finally take off, but some of the aircraft had not received their full bomb load, and others had scratch crews, while some arrived too late over the assembly area with no less than ten crews joining other formations. In the end it mattered little because heavy cloud obscured the targets, and all of the force returned without bombing.

The following day the Group's Commanding Officer, Colonel Frank P. Hunter, made very certain that all of the pre-operation arrangements and plans went well. After all, his inexperienced crews were about to be thrown in the deep end with Berlin as their target. On this occasion he, no doubt, breathed a huge sigh of relief as the B-17s left the airfield without a hitch, and what is more they all managed to return home from this formidable mission without a single loss. The German capital would be the crews' objective on another three days in the month, but they were not blessed with their initial success. The first aircraft to be lost in action came on the 19th over Berlin, followed by another two five days later. By the end of May the crews could be considered well and truly 'blooded' with 18 missions completed, and besides Berlin they had been in action over Stettin, Metz, Ludwigshafen, Dessau and Kiel, as well as the feared oil targets at Merseburg and Ruhland – a really harsh indoctrination into the war.

As with all of the Eighth's Groups, be they Bombardment or Fighter, June 1944 was a very hectic month with many operations to strategic targets in North-West France during the first two weeks, in support of the Allied invasion of Normandy. On the 18th of the month the Eighth returned to German targets, and on this day the Harburg oil refinery at Hamburg was attacked; out of the 18 aircraft that failed to return, one came from the 398th. By the end of June, in less than two complete months, the crews had completed 37 missions, for the loss of six B-17s; this was a most commendable performance, considering the losses suffered by far more experienced Groups.

In theory, at least, any of the Group's crews that had flown on every single mission, would now be on their way home back to the States. Originally a Combat tour had comprised 25 missions in total, but in April 1944 the figure was increased to 30. It was then decided that with

B-17 of 398th Bomb Group badly damaged over Cologne, 15th October 1944. (USAF)

the rapid increase in the number of operations being mounted and the number of 'relatively safer operations to France' (according to Headquarters!) the number of missions to constitute a tour would be increased to 35. Those fortunate crews that managed to survive 35 missions found that it could take up to four to five months before they left for 'Stateside' and home leave. Unlike the majority of RAF crews, few American airmen returned for a second tour of operations, they were mainly engaged on training duties in the States.

July proved to be a particularly harsh month for the Group, with nine crews lost in action and another four B-17s being written-off in crashes. Two of the missing aircraft had actually collided whilst going in over the Dutch coast outward bound for Leipzig. Such unfortunate accidents were an ever present risk given the close formation flying that was the hallmark of the Eighth's Bomber Command. In nearly 1,000 days of operations there were over 100 such collisions involving heavy bombers, most of which occurred over England during the involved assembly procedures.

The Eighth Air Force chiefs had been rather surprised by the relatively light Luftwaffe forces that opposed most of their operations during October. Indeed the view was expressed that perhaps the Luftwaffe had now become a spent force, although the following month showed that this pious hope was far from being a reality. In the middle of October

1944, Cologne was attacked on three separate days, the 14th, 15th and 17th. The first mission was relatively uneventful, but on the following day a B-17 crashed at Anstey, to the south-west of the airfield, shortly after take-off with all ten crewmen killed. On return to Nuthampstead one heavily damaged aircraft was safely brought back by 1/Lt Lawrence De Lancey – the photograph clearly shows the amount of damage a B-17 could sustain and still survive; it is no wonder that the crews had an unbounding faith in their 'ships'! In this instance a flak shell directly hit the chin turret and exploded, causing the failure of the cockpit instruments and oxygen system; the bombardier alone was killed. Two days later two damaged aircraft crashed in France, also victims of flak. Then on the 28th of the month when the 1st Division sent just five Groups – 190 B-17s in total – to attack the marshalling yards at Münster, merely a token force considering the strength and power of the Eighth at this time, only three aircraft were lost in action, and all belonged to the 398th. A case of being in the wrong place at the wrong time.

However, it was in November that the Group suffered their heaviest losses of the war. It was also in this month that the 398th passed a major milestone, its 100th mission. On the Eighth's first operation in the month (2nd) some 680 B-17s were despatched to attack the large synthetic oil refinery at Leuna near Merseburg. Most crews considered this to be the most heavily defended place in Germany bar none, 'one that sent shivers down the spine', as one crewman recalled later. The Merseburg operation involved a long flight over hostile territory (about 500 miles) before facing a fearsome corridor of heavy flak batteries on the approach to the target. Having survived all that, the crews were faced with another long haul for home often in aircraft that had been damaged. It was felt that such missions should count as double towards a combat tour. On this day it was estimated that the Luftwaffe had some 400 fighters in action – so much for being a spent force! However, they were opposed by over 700 American fighters, and the ensuing action has become known as 'the biggest air battle of the war'. The Eighth's gunners and fighter pilots claimed to have destroyed 153 enemy aircraft (the 55th FG claimed 17½) for the loss of 54 aircraft with another 500 being damaged; three of the missing B-17s came from Nuthampstead. On the 21st over the same target the 398th suffered more heavily with five crews missing in action, with another crew being compelled to force-land in Belgium. By the end of the month twelve crews had been lost, all on operations to oil targets. Although only about 20% of the Group's missions were to oil targets, they resulted in about 45% of its total wartime losses. The bomber crews paid a very high price indeed for the Eighth's concentrated and critical bombing offensive against the German oil industry.

For the next four months, whilst mounting over 60 missions, the 398th would 'only' lose the same number of aircraft in total as were lost in November. Unfortunately its Commanding Officer, Colonel Frank Hunter, went missing in action on 23rd January 1945 whilst the crews were attacking railway yards at Neuss near Düsseldorf. He was flying in the leading PFF aircraft, which belonged to the 91st Group, and it proved to be the sole B-17 loss. His replacement, Lt Col Lewis P. Ensign, only remained in command for some two and a half months. Even in these last months of the war, the flak batteries that defended Berlin (some 1,000 in number) were still a potent and frightening force to encounter. On 3rd February when over 1,000 B-17s attacked the Templehof railway yards at Berlin, 23 were shot down by flak, two of which were from the 398th.

It was somewhat ironic and very galling that in the last complete month of the war, April, the 398th suffered more heavily than most other Bomb Groups. On the 8th, whilst engaged over the Stendal marshalling yards, one crew was lost and another aircraft crashed heavily on its return to the airfield. Then on two consecutive missions, on the 10th and 11th, two more crews failed to return. Two days later whilst in action over the railway yards at Neumünster, some 30 miles north of Hamburg, two B-17s were lost in unusual circumstances. One of the Group's B-17s failed to release its bombs on time, but about two minutes later the full load was discharged, and within 400 feet of the aircraft two bombs touched and detonated. The resultant explosion not only crippled the B-17 that dropped the bombs but also a nearby aircraft, with another four aircraft also being heavily damaged. The damaged aircraft made forced-landings on the Continent and all were written-off. The operation had caused the loss of six aircraft and cost the lives of 25 airmen, a very sad occasion for the Group, especially as it was clear that the end of the war was in sight.

The Group completed its final operation on 25th April when the

Fine memorial stone to the 398th Bomb Group.

Skoda motor plant at Pilsen in Czechoslovakia was attacked; six aircraft were the victims of flak and two of them belonged to the 398th. This brought the total losses in action to 58 in 195 completed missions. Towards the end of May the B-17 crews left to make their long flights back to the States, and the ground crews finally left Nuthampstead for Greenock on 22nd June to sail home in some comparative style on the *Queen Elizabeth*.

The airfield was transferred back to the RAF on 10th July; it was taken over by Maintenance Command, who used it as an ordnance depôt for the next nine years or so, and it finally closed in March 1959. The airfield site was later considered, amongst others, as a possibility for the third London airport. However, most of it has now returned to farming, although there is still a small strip of grassed runway, which is used by light aircraft. Also on the old airfield site is a VOR radio navigation ground station used by London Heathrow and Stansted airports. Thankfully the elegant memorial, which was dedicated in September 1982, will ensure that the sacrifices of the Group's airmen will never be forgotten.

12

PODINGTON

Although the airfield at Podington began to take shape in 1941, it would be another two years before it became fully operational as an Eighth Air Force heavy bomber base. This was an unusual and inordinate length of time, especially as it was during a period of the war when airfield space was at a great premium. The site had been tentatively allocated to the USAAF in November 1941 and officially confirmed six months later, with the first American airmen moving in during late July 1942.

These airmen proved to be the precursors of a number of detachments of American units, who would merely use Podington as a temporary and expedient home. They were attached to the 60th Troop Carrier Group and brought just a handful of their aircraft, C-47s or Skytrains; the main body of the Group was housed at Chelveston in Northamptonshire, to which Podington acted as a satellite airfield. The men had barely time to unpack their bags and settle in before, in a week or so, they moved off to another new base at Aldermaston, from where they would later leave for service in Operation Torch – the invasion of North Africa.

On 20th August 1942 the ground crews of the 352nd Bomb Squadron of 301st Group arrived to take up residence, followed the next day by its B17Fs. The reason for their detachment at Podington, was that at the time the USAAF had a policy that each Bomb Group would occupy two

Boston III – 'F for Freddie' – of No 15 Bomb Squadron (Light) but left behind at Podington when they left for North Africa. (USAF)

airfields. The rationale behind this thinking was that, compared with a RAF heavy bomber squadron, which then comprised two Flights, the four squadrons of a Bomb Group with its greater complement of men and aircraft, would require two airfields to house the aircraft and operate satisfactorily. However, it was soon discovered that the theory of detached squadrons did not really work in practice, so early in September the 352nd squadron left to join the rest of the Group at Chelveston, although, in November, it would also move abroad to serve with the Twelfth Air Force in North Africa.

The next American combat unit to use the airfield as a temporary base was No 15 Bomb Squadron (Light), thus Podington became the squadron's third station in a matter of just four months; they had previously been based at Grafton Underwood and Molesworth. The squadron had originally been sent to the United Kingdom to train as a night-fighter unit, but suddenly its role was changed to low-level daylight intruder bombing. Its crews had been given the honour, albeit in borrowed RAF Bostons, of opening the Eighth's bombing offensive. The day was most appropriate – American Independence Day (4th July) – although two of the six taking part in this first operation failed to return. These were the first fatalities in action for the Eighth, and the operation also resulted in the award of the first decorations of the war – three American DFCs and a Distinguished Service Cross to Captain Charles C. Kegelman, who led the American crews. Since that date the crews had completed three more missions but now they flew American Bostons, which carried the famous American national insignia – a white star enclosed in a blue circle centred in a blue outlined white bar.

The Douglas DB-7 was one of the most versatile combat aircraft of the war, with over 7,380 being produced, of which some 3,000 were supplied to the Soviet Union. It operated as a make-shift RAF night-fighter, had been adapted to Turbinlite duties (as noted under Hunsdon), and Boston IIIs or DB-7Bs were being used by the RAF as daylight intruder bombers as replacements for the Bristol Blenheims. Later the Ninth Air Force would use another version of the aircraft, known as A20-Gs or Havocs, on bombing missions both prior to and after D-Day. The squadron's Boston IIIs were capable of carrying up to 2,400 pounds of bombs and were armed with five .303 machine guns, with an operational cruising speed in the region of 240 mph over a range of 200 miles.

The crews arrived at Podington on 13th September, and were informed the following day that they had also been allocated to the Twelfth Air Force in North Africa. In fact they only undertook one operation from Podington; on 2nd October 1942 just twelve Bostons left to bomb a large German merchant vessel in Le Havre docks, all returned safely. In the middle of November 13 Bostons left for Predannack in Cornwall as a staging airfield en route to the Mediterranean. Ten of their Bostons were left behind at Podington, which were then used by the Eighth Air Force for target-towing and general communications duties.

Some other detachments of American airmen used the airfield during the winter of 1942/3. They belonged to two Photographic Reconnaissance Squadrons, each equipped with Lockheed F4s, an unarmed version of the P-38 Lightnings. The decision was taken to improve the airfield, with two of the runways being extended, additional hard standings constructed, and the provision of extra accommodation blocks. Whilst the construction work was still going ahead, a B-17 Group, No 100, arrived on 2nd June, for the briefest of stays – just eight days – before moving on to its permanent base at

Thorpe Abbots in Norfolk. (This Group would become a living legend in the Eighth Air Force, to be known as 'The Bloody Hundredth' because of appalling losses of aircraft and crews during certain periods of time, and their history is covered in greater detail in my *Norfolk Airfields in the Second World War*.) Other than being used occasionally for training and trialling purposes by units from Bovingdon, the airfield was relatively quiet during the summer of 1943. But this situation would drastically change by the middle of September.

It was the oldest Bomb Group in the Eighth Air Force – the 92nd – that came to Podington to make the airfield its home for the rest of the war. The Group had originally served at Bovingdon before moving away to Alconbury, where it had been engaged on training duties up until 14th May 1943, when it returned to operational flying. The reason for the Group's move was the formation, at Alconbury, of a new PFF Group – the 482nd. Not only had the 92nd lost its Commanding Officer, Colonel Baskin R. Lawrence Jr, to the new Group, but also many of its experienced crews. Furthermore, only days before its move to Podington seven crews had been lost in a disastrous raid to Stuttgart.

The Group was dubbed 'Fame's Favored Few', and perhaps the 'Few' was rather appropriate in this instance because by the end of September, Lieutenant Colonel William M. Reid, the Group's CO, had only 23 crews available for operations, although its complement of operational B-17s (mainly 'G's) was 41. The Group's first operations mounted from Podington went out on 23rd September, one in the early morning to Nantes, when unfortunately a B-17 exploded during assembly killing three airmen. The second operation left Podington in the late afternoon to attack V1 rocket sites on 'the rocket coast', as the Pas de Calais was dubbed by the crews. This was the first occasion that the Eighth Air Force mounted two heavy bombing missions on a single day. All of the aircraft returned safely to Podington.

Matters were somewhat different in October when the Group completed seven operations but sadly for the loss of eight aircraft; most of them fell on the 14th when the Eighth Air Force returned to Schweinfurt, where it had lost 60 aircraft two months previously. The 1st Bomb Division, in which the 92nd served, despatched 149 B-17s and of these 45 (30%) were lost in action, with another five being written-off. The 92nd, which had survived the previous Schweinfurt raid with only

182

B-17 of 327th Bomb Squadron of 92nd Bomb Group taking off in wintry conditions. (Smithsonian Institution)

two losses, now paid a heavier price. It was one of the three Groups that comprised the 40th Combat Bomb Wing, and it was this Wing that suffered the brunt of the Luftwaffe attacks; out of 53 aircraft, 29 were shot down (55% loss!) of which six came from Podington, and another of its B-17s crashed at Aldermaston on return.

From then until the last day of 1943, the Group's missions went reasonably smoothly with fairly minimal losses. However, on 31st December, the Eighth sent just under 300 heavy bombers to attack airfields in South-West France. It was a long and extended flight with bad weather hampering the formations for most of the journey; 33 aircraft were lost either in action or in crashes, largely as a result of the atrocious weather conditions and an acute shortage of fuel. Perhaps the Group could consider itself fortunate in the circumstances that only three of its aircraft were lost.

During early November the Group had to share the airfield with the B-24s (Liberators) of the 479th Anti-submarine Group, which had moved in from Dunkeswell in Devon, where it had been engaged on U-boat patrols over the Bay of Biscay. The Group was quickly disbanded with most of its aircraft and crews being seconded for 'special operations' – the dropping of supplies and arms to Resistance forces in occupied Europe – first from RAF Tempsford, then Alconbury and Watton, and later more famously from Harrington in Northamptonshire.

The New Year started on a dismal note for the 92nd. On the first day of the month a B-17 was being ferried to Little Staughton for repair when it crashed on landing and was so badly damaged that it was written-off; another four aircraft would be scrapped during the month. In addition seven aircraft were lost in action, two of which went missing over Kiel on the first operational mission of 1944 (4th January). A week later the 1st Division attacked Focke-Wulf components and assembly plants at Oschersleben and Halberstadt. The Luftwaffe opposed the force in the greatest strength since Schweinfurt in the previous October. To make matters worse the weather seriously deteriorated during the operation with the presence of high clouds, sometimes exceeding 28,000 feet, which made it difficult for the American escort fighters to maintain contact with their charges – the bomber formations – a situation which the Luftwaffe fighter pilots exploited to the full, accounting for most of the 42 B-17s (14%) lost. Considering such heavy losses the 92nd escaped relatively lightly, with two crews missing in action. All eleven Bomb Groups that took part in this memorable mission were awarded a Distinguished Unit Citation. The USAAF reserved this highly-prized commendation for a Group's meritorious achievement on a single mission or a succession of operations. Only 27 were awarded for operations throughout the war, so they were highly regarded and cherished by the Group's personnel, and were formally presented to the Groups with full military ceremony.

In the next three calendar months the 92nd went through a most horrendous time, which would prove to be its worst period for losses throughout the war. In each month the Group lost the equivalent of virtually a bomb squadron, on average some 160 airmen missing or killed in action with a number also being wounded. Despite the fact that there was now a ready supply of replacement crews arriving almost

B-17 landing at Podington, passing the runway controller's chequered trailer. (Smithsonian Institution)

daily from the States, to fill the vacancies, the overall shock of suffering continual losses over a long period was difficult to dispel, and morale on the base suffered. It had almost become an acceptable fact of combat flying that most Bomb Groups would experience abnormally heavy losses on at least one or two operations, when luck decreed that their aircraft would happen to be in the wrong place at the wrong time; but to lose crews on a steady and regular basis was quite a different matter.

The Group's 'bad patch', if indeed it can be so described, began on 4th February 1944 when its crews were in action over the Main railway yards at Frankfurt. Two aircraft were lost in action with a third crashing at Matching airfield in Essex, killing five airmen. Four days later over the same target another three crews went missing. There was now a blessed lull of nine days free of operations, whilst the Eighth Air Force geared itself up for Operation Argument – the joint bombing offensive with RAF Bomber Command on the German aircraft industry. Starting on the 20th the Group was engaged over Leipzig, airfields in Germany, Oschersleben, Schweinfurt and Augsburg, and in these five operations ten crews were lost, three of them at Schweinfurt (yet again!) on the 24th.

Seven days of rest from operational flying followed the 'Big Week', as Operation Argument became known in the Eighth Air Force, but on 2nd March Frankfurt was the target once again. It also proved to be the downfall of another two crews, Frankfurt appearing to have become the *bête noire* of the 92nd. However, Berlin or 'Big B' beckoned the Eighth Air Force and the four missions mounted to the German capital in March resulted in the loss of six of the Group's aircraft. Then on the 22nd when Münster was the main target for the Division, just six B-17s were lost in total, five of them from Podington. This brought the Group's total operational losses in the month to 16; since the 92nd began operations in September 1942, 83 aircraft had been lost in action with another 20 written-off.

April did not bring any relief at all, and although the crews were not detailed for operations until the 10th, another 16 aircraft would be lost during the month. On 11th April the Eighth launched a massive attack on aircraft assembly and component plants in Eastern Germany at Sorau near Stettin, and the 'old favourite' targets of Oschersleben and Bernburg. Despite a most effective bombing operation, the cost was heavy; 64 bombers were lost, including nine landing in Sweden. Over half of the aircraft fell to a series of strong and determined attacks by enemy fighters. The 92nd effectively lost eight crews, seven missing in action with an eighth landing in Sweden. Four missions then passed without a single loss, but on the 24th of the month, whilst engaged in attacking Luftwaffe targets near Munich, five crews failed to return to Podington; one crew was interned in Switzerland this time. On the last day of the month when bombing Bron airfield in France, the 92nd suffered the only loss of the whole operation.

During the next frantic three months – May, June and July – only 13 aircraft would be lost in action, although the targets were as diverse as Berlin, Merseburg, Stettin, Kiel, Leipzig, Munich, Bremen, the Pas de Calais and Mannheim. Perhaps it could be thought that at long last the Group's luck had changed for the better. However, on 20th May there was a tragic accident at the airfield. Thirty-six crews had been detailed for the operation against Orly airfield near Paris. The take-off was timed for the early morning and there was a heavy ground mist with very poor visibility. Eighteen B-17s, each loaded with six 1,000 pound bombs, had taken off at 90-second intervals, when the next aircraft failed to become airborne and ran off the runway into woods alongside the boundary of the airfield. The following B-17 stopped half-way along the runway and, for some unaccountable reason, the pilot turned his aircraft to taxi back

*New B-17 of 92nd Bomb Group under camouflage netting at Podington.
(USAF)*

up the runway. The next pilot, who was totally unaware of what was
happening, carried on with his take-off procedures. The two aircraft
collided head-on, 21 airmen were killed in the massive explosion, and
the runway was so badly damaged that it took 72 hours to repair;
although on the 22nd the Group was still able to mount an operation to
Kiel.

It would not be until late August that the 92nd suffered a further
unfortunate and costly mission. On the 25th when the Peenemunde
Experimental Rocket Station (first bombed by the RAF on 17th/18th
August 1943) along with Anklam and Neubrandenburg airfields were
the targets, just five of the Division's B-17s failed to return, four
belonging to the 92nd. No fewer than seven of the Eighth's aircraft on
the day's operations landed in Sweden, including one from Podington.
The whole question of crews landing in neutral Sweden had become
quite a concern for the Eighth Air Force chiefs. The majority were
genuine forced landings, the aircraft having been so badly damaged that
the crews' chances of surviving a North Sea crossing were very slim.
Some of the landings, however, were thought to be more an opportunity
for the crews to opt out from combat flying, as all the crews were
interned and the aircraft impounded by the Swedish government. In the
early days crews were strictly ordered to set fire to their aircraft if forced

to land in a neutral country. Certainly since the Eighth Air Force began its operations to Berlin and further east, the number of aircraft landing in Sweden had increased, so much so that an appreciable 'American colony' had sprung up, and subsequently a special Air Attache was appointed to look after their interests. The crews still received flying pay during their internment, and were housed in quite comfortable camps. Towards the end of the year a party of American ground personnel were allowed into Sweden to repair the damaged aircraft, and ultimately an agreement was reached, whereby the aircraft and crews were released provided neither were used again in any operations over Europe.

The day after the Peenemunde mission, the 1st Division's Groups found themselves attacking the oil refineries of Buer and Nordstern at Gelsenkirchen in the Ruhr. The plain statistics of the operation – three aircraft lost and another 89 damaged with 26 airmen killed or missing in action and five wounded – do not reveal the practical effect the mission had on the 92nd. Although the Group did not lose any aircraft, amongst the five wounded airmen was its Commanding Officer, Lt Colonel William Reid, whose injuries were sufficiently serious to prevent him continuing in command; one month later he was replaced by Lt Colonel James W. Wilson.

In September 1944 the 92nd would again suffer grievously in just two separate operations. On the 11th the Lutzkendorf oil plants at Merseburg were the targets for a major Eighth Air Force operation. It so happened that the Luftwaffe, despite all the Eighth's herculean efforts to destroy its fighter force, was able to put up its strongest opposition since the end of May; it was estimated that over 450 enemy fighters were in action. The 92nd was flying in a low group that had lagged a little behind the main formations, and for a short period of time this group was left unprotected by its fighter escort. The Luftwaffe struck with a vengeance and in just five brief minutes 19 B-17s were shot down; eight came from the 92nd but eleven belonged to the 100th Group. The damage could have been even more disastrous but for the sudden appearance of some squadrons of P-51s. As it was, another four of the Group's aircraft were so badly damaged that they were forced to land on the Continent. Two days later, it was the same target and almost the same story, although on this occasion four of the Group's B-17s went missing, with a fifth making a crash landing at Woodbridge, killing three

Crew members of 92nd Bomb Group beside their badly damaged B-17, 9th February 1945. (National Archives & Records Administration)

of the crew. And yet for all that, in November, when the Eighth Air Force generally, and many Groups in particular, suffered heavy losses in several major air battles, the 92nd managed to escape unscathed, that is until the last day of the month when just one aircraft went missing…on a trip to the dreaded Merseburg!

For the final five months of the war the 92nd piled up the number of operations with a steady regularity, passing a major milestone in early April 1945 – its 300th operation. Most of the missions passed uneventfully, at least as far as aircraft losses were concerned. The harsh and costly days of twelve months ago, seemed now to be a matter of history. In February the Group became involved in a rather innovative type of bombing. During the previous autumn Colonel Cass Hough and his team at Bovingdon had been conducting trials into methods by which the Eighth could use the 'Disney' rocket bombs, which had been

'Big Picture' completed by S/Sgt Waldschmidt of 92nd Bomb Group, now on display at the Imperial War Museum, Duxford.

designed and developed by the Royal Navy for use in penetrating and destroying the heavy reinforced concrete pens of the U-boats and E-boats. These 4,500 pound bombs were 14 feet long, and were dropped in the conventional manner, but at an altitude of 5,000 feet the rocket motors would ignite, to propel the bombs at a speed of 2,400 feet per second. Because of the bomb's length no Allied bomber could carry it internally, so two special racks were devised and constructed to attach under the wings of a number of B-17s. The 92nd was selected to use the bombs operationally.

A number of crews trialled the bombs over a captured V1 rocket site at Watten in Northern France, and then on 10th February, just nine of the Group's B-17s were loaded with two Disney bombs each and the E-boat shelters at Ijmuiden were selected as the first target. The operation was led by Colonel Wilson, with Colonel Hough sitting alongside as an observer. Subsequent photographic evidence showed that only one bomb had directly hit the target, but the damage was considerable, which was felt to sufficiently merit another 'Disney' operation. This took place in March (14th) against the same target with encouraging results. Later in the month the three Groups of the 40th Wing took part in another 'Disney' operation against the U-boat pens at Farge. However, by now the war was rapidly coming to an end and no further 'Disney' operations were thought necessary.

The Group's long and bitter war ended on 25th April 1945 when its 308th and last mission was mounted against the Skoda motor works at Pilsen. As befitting the oldest Bomb Group in the Eighth, the 92nd was given the honour of leading this final bombing operation, but sadly one crew failed to make it back to Podington – a victim of enemy flak. This final casualty brought the total of aircraft lost in action to 154, and most of the Group's operations (274) had been mounted from Podington. By early June all of the B-17s had left Podington for Istres in Southern France, where the crews were engaged in ferrying US troops over to Casablanca for their final repatriation to the United States.

The *Illustrated London News* in September reported that: 'Silence reigns over the once crowded runways at Podington...They [the American airmen] had been here long enough to get to know their neighbours and the rural English pretty well, to their mutual benefit and friendship. Some have married the local girls and the little village had become a second home to them.' This friendship has continued over the years since those grim wartime days, and, in 1985, the Group's Memorial Corporation restored the organ in the local church, 'in the hope that the voice of this instrument will speak for them – the living and the dead – to the people of Podington every time it is played.' In a corner of the church is also a memorial to the 92nd below which stands a blade of a B-17 propellor. Further afield is another memorial to 'Fame's Favored Few' – a fine wall painting of a B-17 completed by S/Sgt Waldschmidt, which was removed from the 325th Bomb Squadron's briefing room at Podington, and is now on display at the Imperial War Museum at Duxford.

Podington, which is one of the better preserved wartime airfields, is now far better known as Santa Pod, the major European centre for drag racing; part of one of the original runways is used as the race track. The two wartime T2 hangars have survived, and are used as workshops, and the old control tower is one of the few to have been converted into an unusual private house.

13

SAWBRIDGEWORTH

This airfield, rather like Topsy, just grew and grew; from a small and basic landing ground of some 40 acres in the summer of 1940, it increased in size to well over 600 acres by the end of 1942. This slow but steady expansion ultimately encompassed the site of a night landing ground used during the First World War, and then known as Mathams Wood. From 1937 a small grassed site, to the north-west of this early landing ground, had been used intermittently by several squadrons of Army Co-operation aircraft, but the eventual wartime use of the airfield may be said to be due to one man, Wing Commander A. J. W. Geddes, the Commanding Officer of No 2 (Army Co-operation) squadron.

During June 1940 Wing Commander Geddes was seeking a suitable landing ground for his squadron, which was temporarily based at nearby Hatfield. Back in 1938 when Geddes was a Major in the Royal Artillery and a very experienced Army pilot, he would probably have been aware of the small landing ground used by Army Co-operation aircraft, and now he felt it was worth a closer examination. His aerial reconnaissance of Mathams Wood convinced him of its potential and merit, providing the landing area could be slightly enlarged. Thus, on 15th June, the Flight office was established at a requisitioned farmhouse, and the necessary work put in hand to make the site more suitable. A hedge was removed and some ditches filled in, enabling a team of Royal

Engineers to put down an all-weather runway 950 yards in length, comprised of coir matting overlaid with Sommerfeld track. Although a form of this tracking dated from the First World War, it had recently been developed by an Austrian engineer, Kurt Sommerfeld, for runway construction at grassed landing grounds. It was basically 13 gauge, 3 inch mesh wire netting secured by metal pickets and strengthened by flat steel bars; its great advantage was that it was cheap, easy and quick to lay. Although it was used at a number of airfields in the United Kingdom, the tracking was particularly successful in North African deserts, where it became known as 'tin lino'!

By October 1940 the site had been increased to some 77 acres, and the provision of the single runway allowed the squadron to fully move into RAF Sawbridgeworth (as Wing Commander Geddes now insisted on calling the airfield). For the next three and a half years Sawbridgeworth would become No 2 squadron's wartime home, although by the very nature of Army Co-operation duties the pilots and crews would spend considerable periods away on detachment to other airfields, whilst mainly engaged on a variety of air exercises.

The squadron is one of the most famous in the RAF. It was formed on 13th May 1912 out of the Air Battalion of the Royal Engineers, and was then known as 'No 2 Aeroplane Company'. It was the first squadron to be sent to France in August 1914 and one of its airmen, Lieutenant W. B. Rhodes Moorhouse, was awarded (posthumously) the first air Victoria Cross, with a second being awarded to 2nd Lieutenant MacLeod in March 1918. From its inception the squadron had been engaged in Army support duties and nothing had changed. The squadron's motto 'Hereward' is derived from Hereward the Wake and signifies the Guardian of the Army. In October 1939 the squadron was sent to France as part of No 71 Wing, and it had been forced to withdraw on 19th May. It regrouped at Bekesbourne in Kent and from there still continued to operate over France until well after the fall of Dunkirk. On 22nd May the squadron claimed two enemy aircraft – a Henschel Hs126 and a Junkers Ju87 – and during this period lost only one aircraft due to engine failure.

The squadron was equipped with Westland Lysander IIs. This aircraft had been designed by Westland Aircraft Ltd in response to an Air Ministry specification A39/34 for a specific Army Co-operation aircraft to replace the Hawker Hectors. The 'P8' or Lysander made its first flight in June 1936,

Westland Lysanders of No 4 (AC) squadron in the summer of 1939.

and entered the Service with No 16 squadron two years later. The Mark Is were powered by Bristol Mercury XII engines, which gave them a top speed of about 220 mph, and were armed with two forward machine guns in their wheel spats, and a single gas-operated gun from the cabin. The Mark IIs, however, were equipped with Bristol Perseus XII engines, which had slightly increased their performance especially at altitude. The 'Lizzies', as they were familiarly known, had certain advantages, in that they afforded an excellent field of vision for their crews, and were particularly suited to small or improvised landing grounds, as they could take off and land on a very short run – about 240 yards. Seven Lysander squadrons had gone over to France to serve with the British Expeditionary Force where their inadequacies were harshly exposed; 118 were lost up to the end of May 1940, almost 20% of the total force.

The crews of No 2 squadron, like other Lysander units, were engaged in a nightly patrol of the coasts searching for any signs of an enemy invasion. The patrols left at dusk and returned early the following morning. The entire coastline from Land's End to Duncansby Head had been divided into separate 'beats', which were continually patrolled by Lysanders throughout the hours of darkness; these night patrols lasted until the end of December. The squadron also had a few Boulton & Paul Defiants, a fighter which had entered the Service in December 1939, and was the first to be supplied with a heavy power-driven turret. The Defiants proved to be very vulnerable to frontal attack and had suffered heavily during the Battle of Britain. They ultimately became more than useful night-fighters.

Army Co-operation squadrons had always been the Cinderella of the RAF, and the Service had strongly fought off every demand from the Army for more squadrons to be allocated to Army support. Indeed, in 1937, the Chief of the Air Staff, Sir Cyril Newall, thought that Army Co-operation was 'a gross misuse of air forces.' The AC squadrons were placed in No 22 Group of Fighter Command, and it must be admitted that they did not sit easily in a Command dedicated, as it was at that time, to the air defence of the country. However, on 1st December 1940, the Army Co-operation Command was formed, comprising two Groups, Nos 71 and 72; although in one contemporary writer's view, 'there was an air of unreality in the role of the Army Co-operation Command.' Its first and only AOC-in-C was an experienced officer, Air Marshal Sir Arthur S. Barratt, KCB, CMG, MC, who had commanded the RAF squadrons, or the BAFF, in France and who had been dubbed 'Ugly' by his airmen! It would appear that the Air Marshal had very little operational control of his twelve or so AC squadrons, as they were largely at the beck and call of the Army. However, at this stage of the war, and for the next year or so, the main task for Barratt's squadrons was photographic reconnaissance.

The squadron was now equipped with Mark III Lysanders, wherein the single manually operated gun had been replaced by a twin .303 machine gun. Like all RAF squadrons, No 2 had its own unique identification code, which since 1938 had been 'KO'. These letters were applied to the aircraft's fuselage to the aft of the RAF rondel, with the aircraft's individual letter on the other side of the rondel. During 1941 the 'KO' was changed to 'XV', though in late 1943 the squadron's aircraft remained unmarked until 1945 when the code 'OI' was carried by its Spitfires.

It was with these Lysander IIIs that the squadron began training pilots for No 419 Flight, which had been formed in August 1940 as the operational arm of the Special Operations Executive (SOE). This Flight had been established to land and pick up agents operating in occupied France. It is thought that Wing Commander Geddes made the first such flight on 3rd September 1940 to deliver an agent to a field near Tours in France, although the official records show the first clandestine operation taking place about a month or so later (19th/20th October).

In December 1940 the Wing Commander was requested by the Air

195

Ministry to select a small number of good and well experienced Lysander pilots to serve with the Flight. They would be trained in the techniques of landing and taking off in very short distances (about 75 yards) mainly at night and this training was undertaken with the assistance of a few torches, conditions they would expect to face when landing in France. The training, which was cloaked in the greatest of secrecy, commenced in January 1941 and on 11th/12th April one of the squadron's pilots, Flying Officer F. M. Gordon Scotter, picked up an agent from Châteauroux, followed a month later with another pick-up near Fontainebleau. After these two successful operations F/O Scotter was awarded the DFC, and although he was seconded to the Flight, he actually remained with No 2 squadron. One of the most celebrated Lysander pilots operating on such subsequent missions, Squadron Leader J. Nesbitt-Dunlop, was trained at Sawbridgeworth. The Flight was renumbered No 1419 in March 1941, and became No 138 (SD) squadron in late August. It would ultimately operate from Tempsford, and its operations will be detailed under that airfield.

By the early summer of 1941 the Army Co-operation Lysanders were reaching the end of their operational life, and the decision was taken to replace them with an American aircraft – the Curtiss Tomahawk. For this reason some further construction work took place at the airfield. The original runway was lengthened, and a second one was added, each strengthened with Sommerfeld track, also a concrete perimeter road was laid to connect the two runways. With this new work completed, the size of the airfield had now increased to almost 300 acres.

It was not until the end of August 1941 that the squadron had about half a dozen Tomahawks to enable its pilots to start their conversion training. The Tomahawk had been introduced into the US Army Air Corps in late 1939, and was known as a P-40 or Warhawk; at the time of Pearl Harbor it was the main American fighter in service. The RAF had ordered 140, as well as taking those produced for the now non-existent French Air Force. The Tomahawk was intended to act as an escort fighter, but the aircraft's overall performance proved to be rather disappointing, especially its rate of climb and manoeuvrability, and it was not considered very suitable as a bomber escort. The aircraft were relegated to training duties until transferred to the army support role, and ultimately twelve AC squadrons were equipped with Mark Is. The

196

Curtiss Tomahawk of No 26 squadron. (RAF Museum)

aircraft later served admirably in North Africa, where their ability to absorb considerable punishment became almost legendary.

The squadron's experiences with their new aircraft were anything but successful and there were a series of training accidents during September, some of them due to failures with the Allison V-1710 33 engines. The conversion programme was halted until the engine problems were sorted out, so the pilots returned to their old faithful Lysanders, and used them on the first major Army Co-operation exercise, 'Bumper', which took place at the end of September 1941, when the squadron operated from Wattisham. The squadron's last operational Lysander sorties were made in March 1942. It was during this period that the first of many squadrons, mainly AC, arrived to use Sawbridgeworth as a detached base. The first two squadrons, Nos 241 and 286, were equipped with both Lysanders and Tomahawks, and they remained at the airfield until early December.

It was now decided that the airfield would be further extended, with the provision of a third runway and improved permanent facilities,

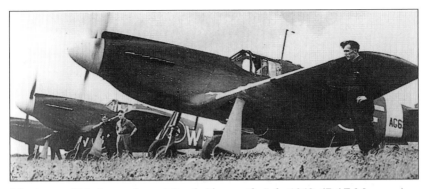

Mustangs of No 2 squadron at Sawbridgeworth, July 1942. (RAF Museum)

including a number of hangars. In the middle of March 1942, W. & C. French & Co moved in to start the construction work. Whilst this work was going ahead, the first North American Mustang I appeared at the airfield on 19th April. This aircraft had been selected to replace the unsatisfactory Tomahawks, and would revolutionise Army Co-operation duties, with No 2 squadron operating with them until after D-Day.

The Mustang, which was destined to have such a dramatic effect on the European air war, owed its very existence to the British Air Purchasing Commission in America. In April 1940 the Commission had ordered more P-40s than Curtiss-Wright could deliver on time, so it was suggested that North American Aviation might set up a supplementary production line for 'substitute P-40s'. However, the American company responded to the challenge with some alacrity, and its chief designer, Edgar Schmued, a German-born Austrian, produced a prototype of a new fighter in no less than 102 days. After certain modifications, it first flew in September 1940 and was designated the P-51. It is perhaps with some poetic justice that this aircraft, which would cause such havoc with the Luftwaffe day-fighter force, was actually designed by a German-born aviation engineer!

The Air Ministry was most impressed with the P-51's design and specifications, and it certainly possessed some striking similarities to the Tomahawk; it was even dubbed by one American aviation engineer 'the first cousin to the P-40'. From the outset the P-51 looked a winner; it had

Mustang – AG550 – XV-U – of No 2 squadron, lost 26th May 1943. (RAF Museum)

clean fine lines, an ideal cockpit layout, good performance, and, unusually, squared wings. However, the Americans showed little interest in the new fighter, a decision they would rue later. The Air Ministry immediately placed an order for 320 aircraft, and the first Mustang ('Apache' had been its original tentative name) arrived in Britain in October 1941. The RAF trials showed that although the aircraft had an impressive performance at low altitudes, this tended to fall away at higher altitudes. The reason, it was thought, was its under-powered and 'asthmatic' Allison engine, and like the Tomahawk it did not quite fit the bill for escort duties, so it too was seconded to the AC squadrons. Of course, the aircraft's salvation came with the experiment of replacing the Allison engine with a Rolls-Royce Merlin.

During June and July 1942 several AC squadrons of Mustangs used the airfield on detachment whilst engaged in Army Co-operation exercises. On 24th July, No 2 squadron was selected to introduce the Mustang to a large press gathering where numerous photographs were taken of the aircraft on the ground and in the air, and another official display was given in the following month. The squadron's pilots were still, however, working up towards an operational readiness. Then in the middle of September a detachment of Fairey Fulmar 2s from No 809 squadron of the Fleet Air Force arrived at Sawbridgeworth to gain some experience in army support duties prior to the squadron's departure to North Africa. This aircraft had entered the Fleet Air Arm in June 1940 as a replacement for the Navy's rather antiquated bi-planes. Although they were superseded by Supermarine Seafires from 1943, Fulmars operated with the FAA until February 1945.

Finally on 14th November, No 2 squadron was considered operational when an unsuccessful photo/reconnaissance sortie ('Popular') was made to a radar station at Doburg, on an island off the Dutch coast; a return visit had to be made four days later. For photographic duties an oblique camera was sited in the aircraft behind the pilot on the port side. In the following month the squadron left for a short exercise at Martlesham Heath, and it returned accompanied by another squadron, No 182, which was equipped with Typhoon Mk 1bs; these rugged 'Bomphoons' (they carried a 250 pound bomb under each wing) stayed at the airfield until the end of January 1943. On the same day No 2 squadron left for Bottisham in Cambridgeshire; it was now commanded by Wing Commander P. W. Stansfield. The pilots were mainly engaged on 'Lagoons' – shipping patrols in pairs along the Dutch coast, and sometimes they used the airfield at nearby Fowlmere.

In the squadron's absence from Sawbridgeworth, their place was taken during February and March 1943 by the Taylorcraft Austers of No 652 (AOP) or Air Observation Posts squadron under the command of Major R. M. Coble of the Royal Artillery, which had been formed at Old Sarum in May 1942. The Austers (the name came from the Middle English for a 'southerly wind') were of an American design and produced by Taylorcraft Aeroplanes (England) Ltd under licence. They were the direct military version of their very popular civilian sports aircraft, which, in 1938, had sold for £450. The aircraft was exceedingly light in construction, blessed with the ability to need a very short take-off and landing run. Although they appeared to be very fragile they proved to be quite rugged, and Austers saw service in North Africa, Italy and in Europe after the Normandy invasion, with No 83 Group of the 2nd Tactical Air Force. Nearly 1,600 in varying marks were produced during the war and they became quite indispensable for Army support duties. Before the squadron left for Almondbank near Perth at the end of

March, two of its Mark 3s had been destroyed in training accidents.

Really from now until the middle of November the airfield would be greatly under-utilised. At the end of May 1943 the Army Co-operation Command was disbanded in anticipation of the formation of the 2nd Tactical Air Force later in November. Air Marshal Barratt was placed in charge of Technical Training Command, which seemed to waste his long and valuable experience of army support flying. Sawbridgeworth now passed into the control of Fighter Command, though not a single fighter squadron would use the airfield. No 211 Maintenance Unit, which had moved into nearby Great Hyde Hall in December 1942, would be the only permanent residents. In fact in August the airfield was placed on a care and maintenance basis, although No 2 squadron would return 'home' on several occasions after detachments away at airfields further south. On one of these spells at Thruxton in Wiltshire during late May, the squadron tragically lost three pilots in crashes in Dorset when they were returning from a 'Ranger' operation over Northern France in bad weather.

From November until April 1944 the airfield once again returned to life, with the arrival of several squadrons of Mustangs – Nos 63, 168 and 170. The first two only stayed for a couple of weeks, but No 170 remained until 15th January 1944, when it was disbanded, only to be reformed later (in October) as a Lancaster squadron. Another squadron made its first appearance at Sawbridgeworth during November 1943 – No 4. It could lay claim to a history almost as old as No 2 squadron, having been formed in September 1912 from part of No 2. No 4 had always operated on army co-operation duties, and had been the first squadron to use air-to-ground radio. The squadron was now employed in low-level photographic reconnaissance duties mainly equipped with Spitfire PR X1s and Mustangs, though it would later receive some Mosquito PR16s for high-altitude operations.

Both squadrons, except for some absences away, would operate from the airfield until early April 1944, and along with No 268 squadron, would form No 35 (Recce) Wing of the 2nd Tactical Air Force. Both finally left Sawbridgeworth on 4th April to operate from Gatwick under Group Captain P. L. Tonkin, the Wing's Commanding Officer. The two squadrons have survived into the 1990s: No 2 is at present serving at RAF Marham flying Tornado GR.1As, whereas No 4 is a Harrier

Austers of No 652 squadron arrived in February 1943. (RAF Museum)

squadron operating from RAF Laarbruch in Germany.

The days of flying at Sawbridgeworth were not quite finished. Three weeks later, on the 26th April, No 80 squadron moved in, having recently returned from service in the Middle East, followed by No 126 squadron, which had been operating in Italy. Both were to be re-equipped with Spitfire IXs. The former would leave to join a Spitfire Wing at Hornchurch early in May, whilst No 126 left on the 22nd of the month. Its departure brought to a close Sawbridgeworth's operational life, although most Service airfields were then very active in the run-up to D-Day. Indeed, it was said that in June 1944 a rather dispirited airfield controller at Sawbridgeworth had suggested tying a bottle of whisky to the windsock to attract visitors!

On 30th November 1944 the airfield was placed under the control of No 42 Group of Maintenance Command with Squadron Leader H. F. G. Tristram as Station Commander. No 211 MU remained at Sawbridgeworth until the Unit closed down in September 1945, although the last RAF unit to use the airfield was No 3 MU, which dealt with the disposal of surplus Service stores, until it also closed in June 1947. Travelling along the Much Hadham road, which once bisected the wartime airfield, it is now difficult to visualise a time when the surrounding fields echoed to the sounds of Lysanders, Tomahawks, Mustangs, Typhoons and Spitfires, so comprehensively has the airfield site been returned to farming, although the odd wartime building can still be sighted. However, in this respect, Sawbridgeworth is no different from hundreds of other wartime airfields dotted throughout the countryside, where virtually nothing remains of that transient period when they were the scenes of intense action, great bravery, joy and deep sadness.

14

TEMPSFORD

Tempsford...the name conjures up images of Lysanders droning away on moonlit nights to land on some isolated field in occupied France in order to deliver or pick up Resistance leaders and agents, all in total secrecy and right under the noses of the German occupation forces. These clandestine flights were the very epitome of excitement, daring and bravery, and yet they were really only a minor part of the operations mounted from Tempsford; the vast majority involved the dropping of vital supplies and arms and ammunition to the Resistance forces, as well as agents, which continued right up to March 1945. These operations were conducted at low-level and mainly during the full moon period, so they also required cool nerves and a high degree of navigational skills in order to pinpoint the exact dropping zones. It was a unique and special kind of air war that was waged from Tempsford.

The airfield, which had been built by John Laing & Son and Balfour Beatty, came to life in December 1941, when Wellington ICs of No 11 Operational Training Unit used the newly constructed concrete runways, whilst the Unit's base at Bassingbourn was being improved. Early in the New Year some other Wellingtons arrived, belonging to the Wireless Intelligence Development Flight of No 109 squadron, then engaged in gathering information on German navigational beams. By March 1942, No 1418 (Experimental) Flight had also moved in with a handful of Wellington IIIs; this Flight was involved with experiments with TR 1335 or GEE. In retrospect it can be seen that the use of Tempsford by these rather secret Flights really determined the airfield's future wartime existence as the home of two Special Duties squadrons devoted to secret operations.

One by one the various Wellingtons left, the training aircraft returning to Bassingbourn and Steeple Morden, with the others moving away to Gransden Lodge and Stradishall. Tempsford was now commanded by Group Captain A. H. MacDonald and was placed under No 3 Group of Bomber Command for administrative purposes, although the two SD squadrons would in fact be controlled by the Assistant Chief of Air Staff Intelligence at the Air Ministry. It was in the middle of March 1942 that the airfield's first permanent squadron appeared – No 138 (Special Duties). The squadron was operating as the air arm of the Special Operations Executive, which had been largely the brainchild of Dr Hugh Dalton, the Minister of Economic Warfare, who intended that it would be used as a 'Fourth Arm' or 'Secret Army'. The Executive's intention was to undertake 'irregular warfare in all forms, to include industrial and military sabotage, propaganda, riots and strikes.' Winston Churchill thought that this Fourth Arm would 'Set Europe ablaze'!

The squadron was equipped with Lysanders, Whitley Vs and a few

Westland Lysander III modified for 'special duties'.

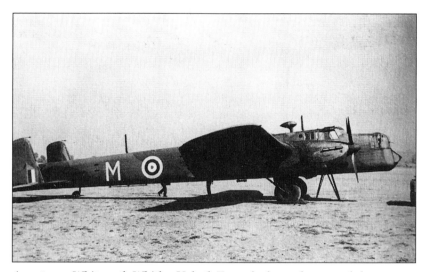

Armstrong Whitworth Whitley V: both Tempsford squadrons used these aircraft.

Halifax IIs; by the end of January 1942 it had completed six successful Lysander landings in France with another two failing. It had operated from Stapleford Tawney, Newmarket Heath and Stradishall. During the second week of April, No 161 (Special Duties) squadron also moved in from Graveley. It had only recently been formed and was commanded by Wing Commander E. H. Fielden, MVO, AFC, better known as 'Mouse', who had been King George VI's personal pilot as well as captaining the King's Flight. The squadron had been formed because of the huge demand placed on No 138 for these special operations, the original intention being that No 138 would be used by the SOE and No 161 by the military. Actually No 138 took on the task of parachuting supplies and agents, whereas No 161 was now given the duty of landing and picking-up 'passengers', equipped with seven Lysander IIIs, a number of Whitley Vs for dropping supplies, and a solitary Lockheed Hudson. The squadron had two very skilled Lysander pilots – both ex-138 members – Squadron Leader Alan M. Murphy, DFC, and Flight Lieutenant W. Guy Lockhart – who had completed six successful Lysander pick-up missions.

Guy Lockhart, who would take over the Lysander Flight from 'Sticky' Murphy in June, was quite a remarkable airman. As a pre-war officer, he had been court-martialled and dismissed from the Service for low-flying over an airfield. Then with the outbreak of the war he re-enlisted as a Sergeant pilot and had a spell in fighters before joining No 138 squadron. Lockhart would complete nine Lysander pick-up missions before being promoted to a desk job at the Air Ministry. He later commanded No 692, a PFF Mosquito squadron, with great verve and daring, before moving over to command another PFF squadron, No 7, flying Lancasters from Oakington. As a Wing Commander with the DSO, DFC, Croix de Guerre, he was killed on a raid to Friedrichshafen in April 1944. Lockhart was described by Air Vice-Marshal Bennett as, 'fanatically courageous and "press on" at all times, and in all circumstances. Virtually nothing would stop him...his determination passed all bounds..'.

The squadron's Lysander IIIs had been lightened to improve their range and speed; the machine guns, long-range radios and armour plating had been removed. They had also been specially modified for their moonlit operations. A fixed ladder, with its rungs painted yellow, had been provided to afford easier access to the rear cockpit, the floor had been extended so that four passengers and their luggage could be fitted into the rear cockpit, and a large 150 gallon fuel tank was fitted under the fuselage. These Lysanders had originally been painted matt black overall in the belief that this would help to make them invisible at night, but it was found that the colour gave a sharp silhouette against low cloud, so now only the lower surfaces were painted black, with the upper parts of the fuselage and wings being camouflaged in dark green and pale grey.

The Halifax B Mk II Series 1s operated by No 138 squadron, and later by No 161, had also been adapted; a parachute hatch was fitted, as was a winch for the recovery of static lines, and special fairings were added to protect the tailwheel, fins and rudders from static lines and containers. Large asbestos exhaust shrouds were fitted to shield the tell-tale glow from the exhausts. Both squadrons would later operate Halifax V Srs 1s, which were virtually the same as the Mk IIs except for a change of undercarriage from the British Messier to Dowty landing gear. They would retain their Halifaxes until the late summer of 1944.

Halifax B Mk II – W7773 – of No 138 (SD) squadron, lost in action October 1942. (via J. Adams)

Within two weeks of its arrival at Tempsford No 138 squadron lost a Whitley V, whilst dropping Dutch agents, the aircraft was believed to have crashed into the sea. Almost a month later (20th/21st April 1942) the squadron lost two aircraft; a Whitley returning from dropping leaflets over France crashed at Porton in Wiltshire in thick fog, killing four of its five-man crew. The second aircraft, a Halifax B II, crashed into a hillside in Bavaria in dense fog and the eight airmen were killed. The squadron's Commander, Wing Commander W. R. Farley, DFC, was the only British member of the crew, the rest belonging to the Polish Air Force. Farley had been an original member of No 419 Flight back in late 1940, and is credited with the first *official* Lysander pick-up in October.

There had always been a number of Polish crews serving with the squadron, and in March 1943 when No 301 (Polish) bomber squadron was dissolved, seven crews were transferred to No 138, where they were formed into a Polish Flight. Back in late 1941 the squadron had made several attempts to drop supplies to the Polish Resistance forces, a 2,000 mile round trip which took in the region of 14 hours, and although it was within the range of a Halifax the squadron did receive a few Liberator IIs to undertake these longer missions. In October 1942 three Halifaxes were lost on operations to Poland, with another four lost in September 1943 and all were crewed by Polish airmen. In November the Polish crews were withdrawn from the squadron and they were formed into a Special Duties Flight (No 1586) operating first from Tunis and then later from Italy, to carry supplies and arms to Poland and the Balkans.

No 161 lost its first Lysander on 29th May 1942 when the aircraft became bogged down at a field to the south of Issoudon in Vichy France. The pilot, Flight Lieutenant A. J. Mott, although captured by the police, later escaped from a prison camp, and returned to England but not to Tempsford. During the summer of 1942 when there were no pick-up operations, the Lysanders joined the Whitley crews in bombing a variety of targets in France. Towards the end of August the Lysander pilots returned to their more familiar duties, Squadron Leader Guy Lockhart successfully landing an agent and picking one up at a field at Thalamy in Southern France. The next operation on 31st August/1st September was not so successful, as his Lysander landed in a ditch and had to be fired. Lockhart was posted missing, but less than two weeks later he was back at Tempsford, having escaped via Gibraltar.

Another 28 missions were mounted to the end of the year, of which about 50% were successful. Bad weather or the pilot's inability to locate the landing field caused the failures, although occasionally the 'passengers' did not arrive at the pick-up point. During this period some famous Lysander pilots began their service with No 161 squadron – Pilot Officers P. E. Vaughan-Fowler, J. C. Bridger, J. A. McCairns, MM, Flying Officer F. E. 'Bunny' Rymills, DFC, DFM, and Squadron Leader Hugh Verity – all would be engaged in these dangerous missions during 1943.

The training of the new pilots, who were required to have at least 250 hours of night-flying experience, was usually undertaken at Somersham, a small and secluded grassed airfield in Cambridgeshire, perfectly suited to practise night-landings and take-offs. The pilots also flew several cross-country flights at night, and at least one night-flight over France without passengers. The Flight also conducted a short course for 'Joes' – the universal name for agents. The name is said to have derived from 'Joe Soap', the slang for a person landed with a rotten job. They were driven around the local countryside to pick out fields that would match the Flight's specification for emergency landing strips. They also received ground instruction in the arrangement of lamps that would light the temporary 'runway'.

The cleared landing strip, where possible, should be about 500 metres long and maybe 75 to 100 metres wide, with an agreed set pattern of three lamps, A, B, and C; these indicated to the pilot not only the direction of the wind but also established the windward end and width of the landing area. The main signal lamp, A, would become the first torch in the 'flarepath', placed near to where the 'reception committee' (agents and passengers) stood to the left of the lamp, and the pilot touched down to the right. He would know that he had sufficient runway to use as far as the lamp B, before turning across the strip close to lamp C and taxiing back to the point where the group were waiting, when the aircraft would then be ready to take off into the wind. If everything went well the whole operation could take less than five minutes. Later in the war the pilots would be guided into the landing strip by a beacon signal from a 'S-phone', which was worn on the reception organiser's chest. The signal had a range of about 40 miles and it also provided radio-telephone communication with the pilot once the aircraft was within a few minutes of the landing strip.The Lysander Flight used Tangmere airfield in Sussex as the final setting-off point for France. The pilots would arrive a week before each full moon period (13 in the year) and remain there for about a week afterwards. They, along with their passengers, occupied Tangmere Cottage, a 17th century house, which was well hidden by tall hedges and was opposite the main gates of the RAF station.

On 1st October 1942 Wing Commander E. H. Fielden was promoted to Group Captain and took over the command of RAF Tempsford. His replacement as No 161's Commander was Wing Commander P. C. Pickard, DSO Bar, DFC, one of the most famous and charismatic airmen of the war. He had gained early popular fame as the pilot of a Wellington of No 149 squadron – 'F' for Freddie – which featured in the successful war film *Target for Tonight*. Pickard led his Whitley squadron, No 51, on the audacious Bruneval raid in February 1942 when a company of paratroopers had captured parts of the German Würzburg radar installation. His old English sheepdog Ming was a constant companion, and became almost as famous as his owner; when he went missing in London in January 1944, the news made the national press! In the eight months Pickard served at Tempsford he flew over a dozen pick-up operations in both Lysanders and Hudsons, before being promoted to Group Captain.

Towards the end of 1942 the squadron used a Lockheed Hudson for a pick-up operation for the first time; on this occasion it was flown by

Group Captain P. C. Pickard, DSO Bar, DFC, with his faithful dog 'Ming'.

Group Captain Fielden. The Hudson had been developed from the company's successful 14 Super Electra airliner, and had first flown in July 1937. The initial Service order was placed by the British Purchasing Committee in Washington in June 1938. It was primarily intended for service with Coastal Command as a maritime/reconnaissance bomber to replace the Command's bi-planes, and had a cruising speed of about 125 mph with an endurance of some six hours. The aircraft could carry 1,000 pounds of bombs and was armed with seven .303 machine guns; on 8th October 1939 a Hudson of No 224 squadron had shot down a Dornier 18 flying boat, the first enemy aircraft to be destroyed by an

Lockheed Hudson: these aircraft were used by No 161 (SD) squadron for 'pick-ups' from the end of 1942.

aircraft flying from the United Kingdom. The Hudsons were increasingly used on pick-up operations during 1943; they were faster than the Lysanders, and their twin Wright Cyclone engines were quieter on the landing approach. Their undercarriage was of stouter construction, more suited to the uneven landing strips, and furthermore they could carry up to twelve passengers. The Hudsons were particularly suited to the 'Ascension' flights, flown by No 161 squadron, when they would fly at about 20,000 feet above the French and Dutch coasts to maintain radio contact with intelligence agents in the field. The squadron also used a number of Havocs in this role, although they mainly operated from St Eval in Cornwall.

During 1943 both squadrons were fully extended in their many and varied operations to France, the Low Countries, Denmark, Norway, Poland and Czechoslovakia. The year proved to be the busiest period of the war for the Lysander Flight with 178 attempted pick-up missions, of which 125 were successful with 200 passengers landed and over 400 picked up. The Flight was now commanded by Squadron Leader Hugh Verity, DFC, as Lockhart had moved to A12C, Air Ministry, the branch of

Air Intelligence that vetted and approved requests for air operations by the various secret agencies. Verity would remain with the squadron almost to the end of the year when he had completed well over 30 pick-up operations; the story of the squadron's secret landings are closely detailed in his fine book, *We Landed by Moonlight*.

In February 1943 another famous airman, Wing Commander Ken Batchelor, DFC, arrived to take over the command of No 138 squadron. He had taken part in Bomber Command's first operation of the war as well as the costly raids in the following December, when serving with No 9 squadron. Since then he had commanded No 311 bomber squadron, which was mainly manned by refugee Czechoslovakians, so he was well used to commanding Eastern European airmen. One of the most crucial operations of 1943 undertaken by the squadron was a number of missions to Norway, code-named 'Gunnerside', to drop Norwegian agents to sabotage the Norsk Hydro factory at Vermork, which was producing heavy water for Germany's nuclear programme. Some of these agents had been trained in sabotage methods and techniques at the SOE's training school at Brickendon Grange near Hertford. The plant was eventually successfully put out of action, dealing a severe blow to the German nuclear programme.

The dropping operations required the Halifax crews to fly at low-level, and mainly during the full moon periods in order to locate the dropping zones, which were invariably nothing more than small fields or clearings in woods. Usually leaflets were dropped in an attempt to disguise the real object of the flights. The warnings of impending drops were put out on the BBC World Service as coded personal messages, one early in the day and then repeated later to confirm the drop was taking place. In the early days the dropping zones were located by dead reckoning navigation, so considerable expertise was required, with perhaps a few hand-held torches to indicate the spot. By 1943 GEE was being used for navigation, and an absolute radio altimeter was essential to determine the correct height for the drop – 700 feet or so for both agents and containers – and at a speed of about 130 mph or less. Later the S-phone was used by the reception committee, as was 'Rebecca' – an airborne radar directional air/ground device. Rebecca worked in conjunction with 'Eureka', a ground beacon set, which was supplied to agents. When the Eureka set was switched on, radar impulses sent from the Rebecca apparatus in the aircraft were returned as directional blips on the navigator's grid screen thus providing an accurate location. Because the Eureka sets were heavy and cumbersome to carry, as well as being difficult to secrete, there was a certain and understandable reluctance on behalf of the agents to use them.

The supplies were dropped mainly in eight-foot long metal containers, which were later designed to break down into sections to make them more easily transportable.They included portable radio equipment, specialised tools, money, forged documents, foodstuffs, clothing, compasses, flashlights, batteries, first aid kits and medicines, printing inks and presses, cigarettes, soap, boots, folding bicycles...the list seemed endless. Arms, ammunition, ordinary and plastic explosives, along with detonators, were normally supplied in separate drops.

In a year of most hectic operations, heavy losses were sustained by both squadrons. No 138 lost 33 Halifaxes and one Liberator, with No 161 losing 13 Halifaxes and five Lysanders. Without doubt the blackest night for the two squadrons occurred on 16th/17th December 1943 when six Halifaxes (three from each squadron) came to grief in thick fog whilst trying to locate and land at Woodbridge emergency landing ground in Suffolk. On the same night two Lysanders, on return to Tangmere, crashed in the fog, and both pilots were killed along with two of the four agents. During December a detachment of Lancaster IIIs of No 617 (Dambusters) squadron were based at Tempsford, along with Short Stirlings of No 214 squadron; they assisted in the dropping of arms and supplies. Two Lancasters were lost on 10th/11th, and a Stirling crashed near the airfield shortly after it had taken off. On the same night a Lysander was lost over France and a Halifax from No 138 squadron came down over Denmark.

During November 1943 the first six American crews of the 36th and 406th Bomb Squadrons had arrived at Tempsford to gain experience of night-flying and dropping operations. These squadrons would operate on behalf of the Office of Strategic Services, the American counterpart of the SOE. The Eighth Air Force code-named their secret operations as 'Carpetbaggers' – a name recalling the opportunist travelling salesmen of post-Civil War days! Each member of the crew was required to complete two missions with the RAF squadrons; on 11th November a 1/Lt B. W. Gross, an American bombardier, was amongst the crew of a

Halifax V of No 161 squadron that failed to return from France. The Americans sent out their first operation from Tempsford on 4th/5th January 1944.

In the months leading up to D-Day, the two Tempsford squadrons were unable to cope with the tremendous and seemingly insatiable demand for arms, ammunition, supplies and agents. For this reason several Stirling squadrons from No 3 Group of Bomber Command became engaged in the dropping operations. In the first three months of 1944 over 6,100 supply containers were dropped and by the beginning of June over 1,500 sorties had been made for the loss of 14 aircraft – a mixture of Halifaxes and Stirlings. In June both 138 and 161 were engaged in a variety of dropping operations, and in the early hours of D-Day eight crews of No 138 took part in Operation Titanic I, which included the dropping of fake paratroopers.

But it was in their normal operations that the squadrons suffered heavily; for instance, on one night (7th/8th June) four Halifaxes (all from No 138) went missing with 20 airmen killed. By the end of August No 138 squadron had completely re-equipped with long-range Stirling IVs, with No 161 following suit in September. The last Stirling bombing sorties were flown on 8th September, but really since the beginning of the year the aircraft's main role had been that of a glider tug and transport. The Mark IVs had the nose and dorsal turrets removed, but the four-gun tail turret was retained. There was a large opening in the underside of the rear fuselage for dropping paratroopers or agents, and the bomb cells had been retained for dropping supplies; up to a maximum of 18 containers. For the remainder of the year most of the squadrons' operations took place over Denmark and Norway.

In March 1944, No 161 squadron was commanded by Wing Commander A. H. C. Boxer, who had replaced Wing Commander L. McD. Hodges, DSO, DFC Bar. Both airmen would have distinguished post-war Service careers, the latter reaching the rank of Air Chief Marshal with Boxer retiring as an Air Vice-Marshal. Although no pick-ups had been made in January 1944 because of bad weather, on 4th/5th February three Lysanders and two Hudsons were in action over France. The Flight's operations did not now seem quite so secret, because on the 9th of the month, the *Daily Telegraph* carried a report under the headline 'Allied Planes Secret Landings in France'! However, until early

September, some 80 pick-up sorties were made by Lysanders and Hudsons, the last four, all Hudsons, being flown on the night of 5th/6th September with both Group Captain Fielden and Wing Commander Boxer in action.

In about four years over 320 sorties had been made with 455 'passengers' landed and over 650 picked up, and in those operations just 13 Lysanders had been lost, from which seven of the pilots had been recovered – a quite remarkable record. The aircraft were now mainly used on courier flights to and from the Continent, although on 26th/27th November a Hudson was shot down over Belgium, whilst returning from a parachute operation over Germany; its pilot, Squadron Leader R. E. Wilkinson, DFC, was the Flight's Commander. Also during November 1944 the RAF Film Unit was at the airfield and Somersham filming a Lysander, R9125, for a Central Office of Information film, *Now It Can Be Told*, which was first shown in February 1947.

At the end of 1944 Group Captain Fielden was promoted to Air Commodore, and his replacement as Station Commander was an Australian airman, Group Captain E. J. Palmer. Special operations continued on a greatly reduced scale and in February 1945 No 138 relinquished its special role; from 9th March it became a Lancaster bomber squadron operating from Tuddenham in Suffolk. It had carried out more operations in support of Resistance groups than any other squadron, at least 2,560 sorties, dropping more than 40,000 packages and containers and almost 1,000 agents. No 161 squadron, now commanded by Wing Commander L. Ratcliff, DSO, DFC, (an ex-Lysander and Halifax pilot), made the last Resistance supply drops of the war, when, on 8th/9th March five Stirling crews were in action over Norway and Denmark. Although, on 20th/21st March most of the crews and agents were killed when three Hudsons were shot down by night-fighters on their way to drop agents in Germany. From May onwards the crews flew out supplies to liberated countries and brought back British prisoners of war. No 161 was disbanded on 2nd June 1945, having made at least 1,749 sorties for the loss of 49 aircraft.

The airfield was placed under care and maintenance in June 1947, and in April 1961 many of the original buildings were auctioned, with the airfield site being sold in early 1963. Some of the wartime buildings and lengths of runways have survived as has the perimeter road. There is a

Memorial at Bletterans, France dedicated in June 1998. (via Jean Perraudin, le Maire de Bletterans)

board on the outside of an old barn belonging to Gibraltar Farm, which is on the airfield site, and it records, 'the brave deeds of the men and women of every nationality, who flew from this wartime airfield to the forces of the Resistance in France, Norway, Holland and other countries during the years 1942 to 1945. The equipment for their dangerous missions was issued to them from this barn.' Further afield, in France, there are several memorials to the bravery of the squadrons' aircrews, Resistance fighters and agents. The latest to be unveiled is at Bletterans, near the Franco/Swiss border, which was dedicated in June 1998.

15

THURLEIGH

The massive development of Thurleigh in the immediate war years, and subsequently, has virtually obliterated the old wartime airfield, which for over three years was the home of one of the most renowned Bomb Groups in all the Eighth Air Force. From early October 1942, the 306th or 'The Reich Wreckers' mounted a long, arduous and very costly bombing offensive operating with B-17s from Thurleigh. In the process the Group gained two Distinguished Unit Citations, one of its airmen was awarded the Congressional Medal of Honor, and sadly over 730 airmen were killed in action. They are remembered by the fine stone memorial, which is situated on a roadside site to the north of the village of Thurleigh, and on the eastern boundary of the present large airfield.

The original airfield was built by W. & C. French Ltd in 1941 and was sited about two miles to the north-west of the village, with most of the 16 living and communal sites dispersed to the east of the airfield and north of Thurleigh. The bomb store was placed in woodland to the north-west of the flying field and well away from the technical sites that were to the east of the field. In common with most airfields built in the early war years, the concrete runways were later lengthened and additional hard standings laid down, to bring it up the Class A Standard bomber base. Rather unusually the airfield was provided with four T2 hangars rather than the normal two.

Colonel C. B. Overacker takes over Thurleigh from the RAF. (Smithsonian Institution)

Thurleigh had originally been allocated to No 2 Group of Bomber Command, but within weeks the airfield was transferred to No 8 Group, which had just been formed to control the light bomber squadrons. In fact the Group never became operational, but it would be later re-activated to control the Pathfinder Force. In January 1942 No 160 squadron was re-formed with the intention of being equipped with Liberator IIs for ultimate service in India. In less than a month the squadron's personnel would move away to Polebrook. Then, for a brief period, the airfield was used by training Wellingtons of No 18 Operational Training Unit based at Bramcote in Warwickshire. One of its Wellingtons crashed at the airfield on 18th May whilst engaged in night-flying practice. By May 1942 the future of the airfield had been settled when its transfer to the USAAF was officially confirmed. In early June the Unit's detached personnel left the airfield in the hands of the building contractors, who were busy improving its facilities.

On 7th September 1942 the 306th's ground personnel arrived from Greenock, where they had recently disembarked from the *Queen Elizabeth*. During the following week the Group's B-17Fs began to arrive from Prestwick, although two had been lost on the ferry flights across the Atlantic. The 306th had been assigned to No 1 Bomb Wing, and its four squadrons' aircraft carried the Group's identification letter, a black H in a white triangle on their tail fins, with their squadron codes, GY, BO, WW and RD, on the fuselages for the 367th to 369th and 423rd squadrons respectively.

In just under a month the crews were considered ready for their first operational mission, but already the Group had suffered the loss of six airmen killed when a B-17 had crashed near Spalding on 2nd October whilst on a training flight, while another aircraft would be written-off later in the month. On the 9th, Colonel Charles B. Overacker, the Commanding Officer, led 24 B-17s to the Fives-Lille steel works in Belgium; the crews joined another 'freshman' Group, the 93rd, which was based at Alconbury with B-24s. This was the first time that the Eighth Air Force had managed to despatch over 100 heavy bombers, a feat that would not be repeated until April 1943. The Luftwaffe opposed this force in more numbers than on any earlier mission, and four aircraft were lost; one from the 306th fell in France. The British press acclaimed the operation as a great success, although in truth the bombing was not very accurate. The press reports implied that the gunners' claims of 56 enemy aircraft destroyed were rather an exaggeration – 'typical American hyperbole'! Although the claims were later reduced to 21, they were still well in excess of the actual Luftwaffe losses.

On 20th October 1942 a new Command directive was issued whereby the U-boat yards on the French Atlantic coast were made the Eighth's top priority. During the next four months the Group's crews would be mainly engaged over Lorient, La Pallice and St Nazaire. The latter target was considered to be the most heavily defended area outside Germany and became known as 'Flak City', proving the downfall of a number of the Group's crews in the coming months. The Group's first mission to St Nazaire on 9th November resulted in three aircraft missing in action with another crashing at RAF Portreath in Cornwall. When the same target was attacked on the 23rd, another B-17 was lost, the seventh crew to be lost in action, which made it the highest loss rate in the Eighth. On this operation a B-17 named *Banshee* piloted by 1/Lt William 'Wild Bill' Casey, returned with claims of seven FW190s shot down in twelve minutes. This was then a record for a single aircraft and would remain so until well into 1943.

The whole question of gunner and fighter pilot claims was to be a

'Man o' War' *of 367th Bomb Squadron, was lost on 9th November 1942.*
(Smithsonian Institution)

contentious issue for the Eight Air Force throughout the war, although at this stage of proceedings the Eighth's chiefs were not overly concerned about the problem. However, in 1943 intelligence officers were given strict criteria to apply to all such claims: the pilot of a fighter must be seen to abandon his aircraft, or else the aircraft should be seen to crash or explode in the air. Nevertheless, the nature of the Eighth's air battles with very close bomber formations resulted in several individual gunners claiming the same fighter destroyed, and the speed and ferocity of the fighter attacks made accurate claims almost an impossibility. The RAF had a similar problem during the Battle of Britain. It is now generally accepted that the claims of enemy aircraft destroyed could be as much as treble the actual Luftwaffe losses. But whether the claims were accurate or not, the numbers of enemy aircraft thought to be shot down did wonders for the crews' morale, they were convinced that they were making serious inroads into the Luftwaffe fighter force, which helped them to bear the losses of their friends and colleagues. By the end of the war the Group had claimed 332 enemy aircraft destroyed, a fine performance notwithstanding the probable over-assessment.

Towards the end of the year the performance of the 306th was causing General Eaker no small concern. The Group's losses were high (eleven in action and a number more written-off), the crews' formation flying was ragged and undisciplined, bombing results were poor and reports had reached him that the crews' morale was low with a defeatist attitude. Even discipline at the base was lax. On 30th December 1942 all but one of the Group's aircraft abandoned the mission before the start point, thus endangering the rest of the formations. This proved to be the last straw for Eaker, and he decided to replace the Commanding Officer. Eaker selected his right-hand man, Colonel Frank A. 'Army' Armstrong Jr, to be the troubleshooter and to try to bring the 306th up to an acceptable standard. Armstrong had led the Eighth's first heavy bombing operation in August whilst in command of the 97th Bomb Group, and although not a martinet, he was a firm but fair commander, who led by example. He took over command of the Group on 3rd January 1943.

On 27th January Armstrong flew in the Group's lead aircraft to Wilhelmshaven for the Eighth Air Force's first raid on Germany; hence why the 306th proudly claimed to be the 'First USAAF Unit Over

Germany' – the inscription on the Group's memorial stone. The Luftwaffe's opposition to this mission proved to be surprisingly light, only three aircraft were lost, but all the B-17s returned to Thurleigh safely. Colonel Armstrong remained at Thurleigh only until 17th February, but in that short time he greatly improved morale, discipline and the standards of performance. He was promoted to Brigadier General to command the newly formed 101st Combat Bomb Wing. After the war Major Sy Bartlett and Colonel Bernie Lay Jr wrote a novel based around Armstrong's move to Thurleigh, which in turn became a successful and excellent film, *Twelve O'Clock High*; the central character, General Frank Savage was primarily based on Armstrong. Armstrong would later command the 1st Bomb Wing, as well as a B-29 (Superfortress) force in the States, and had a successful post-war USAF career.

In the first three months of 1943 another ten B-17s were lost, and 'Flak City' had become the crews' *bête noire*, accounting for ten missing crews since early November. In April only four operations were mounted, and on the 5th Anderson returned to Thurleigh to fly in the lead aircraft for an attack on Antwerp. His subsequent report estimated that at least 25 head-on fighter attacks were made on the leading aircraft, and although his B-17 sustained heavy damage, its pilot, Major James Wilson, the Group Executive, managed to bring it back safely, although four other crews were not so fortunate. After this raid the Belgian Ambassador to the United States complained to the President about the inaccurate bombing which had resulted in heavy civilian casualties.

The Antwerp mission also meant that T/Sgt Michael Roscovitch, known as the 'Mad Russian', became the first Eighth Air Force airman to complete a tour of 25 operations – it had taken him six months. At this stage of the war only about 25% of crews had the chance of completing a tour, but with the losses experienced by the 306th the chances of its airmen making the magic figure were even slimmer. Roscovitch did not return to the United States, but was commissioned and completed another eight operations before being sent back home for publicity purposes. Tragically, he was killed when the aircraft returning him to the States crashed in Scotland.

Twelve days later, on 17th April, the Eighth managed to send over 100 aircraft (115) for the first time since early October. The situation of replacement aircraft and crews had greatly improved during the early spring, and each bomb squadron had about twelve aircraft on complement with maybe about ten operational crews. On this day's operation the target was the large Focke-Wulf factory at Bremen rather than the port area. This plant produced the FW190s, which were causing such havoc and mayhem amongst the Eighth's bomber formations. Once again the 306th was leading the Wing and its crews, along with those from the 91st Group, bore the brunt of sustained and co-ordinated attacks by waves upon waves of FW190s. The two Groups lost 16 B-17s, ten of which belonged to 306th. This represented a loss of 38% for the Group, which was then the highest loss to be sustained by any Group on a single mission. One of the B-17s that went missing was *Banshee* but at least Lt 'Wild Bill' Casey survived as a prisoner of war.

The Group's ill-fortune continued to dog the crews, especially on 1st May 1943 when St Nazaire was again the target. Thick cloud over the target area had greatly hampered the bombing and when the Group turned for home the lead aircraft made a navigational error. Instead of turning out over the Atlantic the crews flew too close to the Brest peninsula, which they mistook for the Cornish coast, and heavy accurate flak brought down three aircraft and damaged a number more. One of these, flown by 1/Lt Lewis P. Johnson of 423rd squadron or 'The Grim Reapers', received several direct hits, starting fires in the tail wheel housing and the radio room, as well as damaging the oxygen supply, which only fanned the flames to an intense heat; the aircraft seemed to be doomed to a watery fate.

The ball turret gunner, S/Sgt Maynard 'Snuffy' Smith, who was on his first mission, emerged from his turret to see three of the crew taking to their parachutes. However, Smith decided to remain and try to fight the fires. He then found the injured tail gunner and administered first aid. For the next 90 minutes or so Smith desperately fought the fires, and despite the intense heat and thick and acrid fumes, he still managed to keep an eye on the injured crew member. Then when the ammunition boxes started to explode in the heat, he began to jettison them out through the gaping hole in the fuselage. In all this mayhem he still found time to fire the waist gun when some enemy fighters closed in for the kill. As the aircraft neared the English coast Smith began to throw out items of equipment to lessen the strain on the aircraft, and Lt Johnson

Presentation of the Congressional Medal of Honor to S/Sgt Maynard H. Smith by the US Secretary of War, Henry L. Stimson at Thurleigh on 15th July 1943. (National Archives & Records Administration)

managed to land the stricken aircraft at RAF Predannack in Cornwall.

Without doubt Smith's actions had saved both the aircraft and the remaining crew members. A few weeks later he was awarded his country's highest decoration, the Medal of Honor, which was presented to him at Thurleigh in July 1943 with due military ceremony. Smith was the first living Eighth Air Force airman to receive the MOH, and one of only 17 in the Eighth. He completed only four more missions and was then given a desk job. He married a Bedford girl and died in Florida in 1984 aged 73 years; Smith is buried in Arlington National Cemetery in Washington.

The 306th, along with 91st, 303rd and 305th, became known as the 'Pioneer' Groups because in the early months they were *the* Eighth's

Bomber Command. Their crews had led the way and had initiated, developed and perfected combat formations and bombing techniques that would later became standard Eighth operational procedures. The Groups had also suffered all the early setbacks and between them they had lost 99 aircraft in action, with the 306th bearing the heaviest losses – 45. One of its squadrons, the 367th, known as 'The Clay Pigeons' had the unenviable record of having the highest squadron losses in the whole of the Eighth; whereas the 369th or 'Fitin Bitin' squadron had not lost a crew to enemy action since January. However, on 29th June 1943 this amazing record came to an end when the 369th lost two crews over the Kiel shipyards. On this raid not only were over 200 tons of bombs dropped but also three quarters of a million propaganda leaflets.

The Group was now commanded by Colonel George L. Robinson, who would remain in charge until September 1944. From the Kiel operation the Group's fortunes seemed to have taken a turn for the better. August and September passed with very minimal losses, just three in fact, and the Group sent 30 crews (the highest number) on the first infamous Schweinfurt raid in mid-August. All managed to return intact to Thurleigh with not a single crewman killed, but only two other Groups managed to make such a miraculous escape from this horrendous blood-bath. However, all this changed in October 1943; four crews went missing over Bremen and Gdynia early in the month, and then on the 14th when the Eighth returned to Schweinfurt, ten of the 18 crews from Thurleigh failed to return, and only five had managed to bomb. It was the second time for the Group that 100 airmen went missing on a single day, and sadly it would not be the last.

The second Schweinfurt operation, which incurred the exact same losses of aircraft as the first raid, was hailed in both Britain and America as a mighty air victory, mainly due to the claims of 288 enemy fighters destroyed (later reduced to 186). General Arnold, the USAAF Commander in Washington, said, 'the opposition isn't nearly what it was and we are wearing them down'! Although the damage to the ball bearing plants was severe, and it was six months before they returned to full production, the loss of American aircraft and crews had been prohibitive. Morale in the Eighth Air Force was at a low ebb, with the bomber crews incurring a casualty rate far higher than any other branch of the US forces. The Eighth Air Force was at a critical point, and as one

HRH Princess Elizabeth at Thurleigh, 6th July 1944 to name B-17, 'Rose of York'. (National Archives & Records Administration)

of its Generals, Curtis LeMay, famously said, 'The more Fortresses we have here the shorter the war is going to be and the more fighters we have to protect the Forts the smaller the losses will be.' No doubt all the bomber crews said 'amen' to the latter point!

One of the features of the Eighth Air Force's aircraft, both bomber and fighter, was the strange and sometimes exotic names given to them by their crews or pilots. The names were usually accompanied by a pictorial representation painted on the nose, and this 'nose art' has rightly become famous. Much of the artwork depicted scantily clothed ladies in a variety of poses, much in the style of Vargas, the famous calendar 'pin-up' artist. Some of the names of B-17s that served at Thurleigh were, *Man o' War, Joan of Arc, Sons of Fury, Piccadilly Commando, Satan's Lady, Belle of the Brawl* and *Impatient Virgin*. But perhaps the most famous B-17 was *Rose of York*, which had been officially named by HRH Princess Elizabeth, when she and the King and Queen visited the airfield in July 1944. The original name, *Princess Elizabeth* was rejected by the Eighth's chiefs on the grounds that it would provide too much propaganda material for the Germans should the aircraft be shot down. In fact this B-17 managed to make 62 successful missions, only to ditch in the North Sea in February 1945 after a Berlin operation; at the time a senior BBC war correspondent, Guy Byam, was on board.

The last two months of 1943 were relatively quiet periods for the Group. Several missions were abandoned because of bad weather and the 306th survived with the loss of 'just' six crews, and two of these had collided before reaching the target.

By 1944 the 306th had been in action for almost 15 months and it was nearing its one hundredth mission. Two operations to Kiel on 4th and 5th of January resulted in the loss of two aircraft. But on the 11th of the month when the 1st Bomb Division (it had been upgraded from a Wing in the previous September) despatched over 290 B-17s to aircraft assembly plants at Oschersleben and Halberstadt, the outcome was rather different. The Luftwaffe opposed this force in the greatest numbers since the ill-fated Schweinfurt operation in October, another reminder that the Luftwaffe was far from being a fighter force in demise! The Group, which was now part of the 40th Combat Bomb Wing, had been allocated Halberstadt as its target. Heavy cloud formations hampered the fighter escorts in locating the bomber formations and the

Luftwaffe fighter pilots took full advantage and managed to bring down no less than 42 B-17s. Four came from the 306th, including two that collided during the fierce fighter attacks. Like the other ten Groups taking part in this operation, the 306th was awarded its first Distinguished Unit Citation.

The following month proved to be the most costly of the war for the Group. In total 18 crews went missing in action, mainly lost in the 'Big Week' – the massive assault by the Eighth and RAF Bomber Command on the German aircraft industry. Early in February three operations to Frankfurt railway yards resulted in the loss of four B-17s, but on the 22nd when Aschersleben and Bernburg were bombed, the 306th, once again, suffered heavily – seven aircraft. For the crews' actions on this operation, when they faced most severe fighter opposition and all in very unfavourable weather conditions, the Group was awarded its second DUC. But there was precious little respite for the battered crews, because two days later they were in action over Schweinfurt, followed the next day by Augsburg, these two missions bringing about the loss of another five crews. In just five days twelve aircraft had gone missing, which meant the loss of many friends and colleagues, only emphasised by the number of empty beds in the living quarters; morale at Thurleigh was understandably low.

In truth there was really little time for the crews to reflect on the losses because the pace of operations and action was decidedly quickening. During March and April 1944, 31 operations were flown from Thurleigh including five missions to Berlin, which mercifully passed with only light casualties. But the most costly mission mounted during this period occurred on 24th April, when the Division attacked aircraft targets in Southern Germany – Landsberg, the Dornier factories at Oberpfaffenhofen near Munich, and an air depôt at Erding. Ten aircraft failed to return to Thurleigh, two of which had crash-landed in Switzerland where the crews were interned. As the Eighth Air Force had increasingly struck at vital targets in Southern Germany, the numbers of damaged aircraft that were forced to seek refuge in this neutral country had been growing steadily, but on this operation no fewer than 18 crews would land in Switzerland.

During May another 19 missions were flown, with airfields and marshalling yards in France figuring large, but also three trips were made

Formation of 306th Bomb Group bound for Berlin. (Smithsonian Institution)

to the 'Big-B' or Berlin, which caused the downfall of six crews, one of which ended up in neutral Sweden. Oil targets at Merseburg, Ruhland and Posen were attacked but without a single loss. Indeed it would not be until September that the 306th would suffer heavily on a single operation. The Group was now one of the most experienced units operating in the Eighth, having passed its 150th operation, whereas there were a few Bomb Groups just entering the European air war for the first time.

From 21st June until 15th July 1944 the Group managed to mount 15 missions without a single aircraft being lost, quite a record for 306th. Then on 18th July the Eighth attacked the Experimental Rocket Station at Peenemunde, about eleven months after the RAF had famously bombed it for the first time; one of the Group's crews was forced to land in Sweden. Two days later aircraft industry targets at Dessau and Leipzig in deepest Germany were attacked, and two of the Group's aircraft were lost on the long return flight home. One ditched in the English Channel about 20 miles north of Dunkirk and nine of the crew were saved by the air-sea rescue services. It was thought that a B-17 would float for about one and a half minutes, so there was precious little time for the crew to escape into their dinghy. During the war over 450 of the Eighth's bombers ditched and over 1,500 airmen were rescued, or a survival rate of some 35%; so the nine airmen could consider themselves rather fortunate.

Hitherto the Group had escaped relatively unscathed from the Eighth's

231

Memorial stone at Thurleigh – 'Always First'.

heavy bombardment of German oil targets, which had commenced in May, but on 12th September 1944, which was the second day running that the Eighth had launched a major oil operation, it was a different story. The previous day the Leuna refinery at Merseburg had been bombed, now it was the refineries at Ruhland and Brüx that were the primary targets. The 1st Division lost 19 B-17s of which the 306th sustained the heaviest casualties, eight aircraft missing in action with a ninth badly damaged crashing at RAF Manston on return, killing two of the crew.

Eleven days later a new Commanding Officer, Colonel James S. Sutton, was appointed to the Group. The Colonel had, during 1942/3, commanded the 92nd Group. He would be destined to stay at Thurleigh almost to the end of the war; little did he realise at the time that the days of heavy losses for the 306th were over. In fact in November when a seemingly resurgent Luftwaffe took quite a toll of the Eighth – 128 bombers – on four separate operations, the 306th lost just a single B-17 to enemy action, and only another three crews would go missing up to the end of the year.

Although one B-17 was lost on the first day of 1945 when the Henschel marshalling yards at Kassel were attacked, the final four months of the

232

war were blessed with very few losses, indeed the Group had one of the safest operational records and lowest loss rates in the whole of the Eighth during this period. What a vast difference from two years earlier. Just two operations in February marred what would have been a most remarkable run. On the 3rd the Templehof railway yards in Berlin were bombed and the City's flak batteries, even at this late stage of the war and despite the heavy bombardment by the RAF and the Eighth, were still potent enough to bring down 24 B-17s. Four were lost by the Group, one landed in Sweden and another on the Continent, killing seven airmen; a further two crews were lost over Dresden on the 14th. Before the month was over the 306th passed 300 operations, quite a milestone.

The Group finally completed their long war on 19th April 1945, which was their 342nd mission, the second highest for a B-17 Group. During its time at Thurleigh over 9,600 sorties had been flown for the loss of 171 aircraft in action and over 22,500 tons of bombs dropped. Unlike most of the Eighth's Groups the 306th did not return to the United States, it had been selected to serve with the Allied occupational air forces in Germany. Many of the B-17s were detached to Germany before the whole of the Group moved out of Thurleigh to Giebelstadt in early December, thus establishing another record. The 306th had been stationed in England, and at Thurleigh, for longer than any other Eighth Air Force Group. In 1946 construction work began on the airfield site to turn it into what is now known as the Royal Aeronautical Establishment Bedford.

16

TWINWOOD FARM

This wartime airfield, a little over three miles to the north of Bedford, will be forever linked with Glenn Miller. It was from here, on 15th December 1944, that the legendary American bandleader left on his last and fatal flight to France. The old wartime control tower where he had waited patiently for the aircraft to land, has quite remarkably survived, although the building now stands somewhat desolate and forlorn against a background of trees, which form Twin Wood from whence the airfield gained its name.

The airfield, some 330 acres in extent, was requisitioned early in the war by the Air Ministry, although a few years earlier the site had been seriously considered as a possible location for a civil aerodrome for nearby Bedford. It was not until mid-1941 that the RAF began to use the grassed field; some of the Oxfords from No 14 Service Flying Training School, then based at Cranfield, made circuits and the student pilots practised their landing and take-off skills. In order to relieve some of the pressure on Cranfield's airfield and airspace, it was decided to develop the basic landing ground into a satellite airfield, with the provision of three concrete runways, additional temporary buildings and accommodation huts. The newly refurbished airfield was ready for use by April 1942.

Twinwood Farm was known as a 'Beaufighter base' to American airmen.

From that time onwards until the end of the war, the Blenheims, Beaufighters, Beauforts and Mosquitos of No 51 Operational Training Unit, which now operated from Cranfield, used Twinwoods, as it was more generally known. But really it was the Unit's Beaufighters that were mainly in evidence, so much so that the US servicemen referred to the airfield as a 'Beaufighter base'. It has already been mentioned how the Beaufighter proved to be the salvation for Fighter Command's night-fighter force from late 1940 right up until the time they were replaced by the Mosquito night-fighters. Though in this context it is interesting to note that Lettice Curtis, the ATA ferry pilot, who had flying experience of both aircraft, preferred the Beaufighter. As she commented in her book, 'I liked the roomy cockpit with its centrally placed seat, the rugged trimmers and throttle levers, and its solid wide-spread undercarriage.' However, she did concede that getting in and out of the cockpit was not the easiest of operations, indeed the aircraft's Handling Notes devoted 'the best part of a page' to describing the rather complicated manoeuvre!

The Beaufighter, despite the fact that it owed its very existence to a somewhat hybrid and improvised development, served the RAF very well throughout the war; the final British version of the aircraft was the XIC, which operated with Coastal Command. A total of over 5,600 were produced in this country, with some 360 being built under licence in

Australia, where they saw service in the Pacific war theatre and where they gained the name 'Whispering Death'! The last Beaufighter was produced by the Bristol Aeroplane Co Ltd on 21st September 1945 from its Weston-super-Mare factory. After the war some Beaufighters were converted to act as target towers, and the aircraft was not finally withdrawn from the Service until 1960 – 20 years of sterling service.

During March 1943 the airfield saw an unprecedented amount of action when five squadrons of RAF Mustangs – Nos 164, 169, 239, 268 and 613 – used Twinwood Farm at various times during the month. They were all engaged in Operation Spartan, which was the last grand scale air exercise or manoeuvres undertaken before D-Day. The Operation's main objective was to judge how effectively the various air forces could be in supporting the Allied land troops after the invasion. It had been assumed for the sake of Spartan that the Allied air forces had gained 'a marked air superiority', and the exercises were intended to test the speed, mobility and adaptability of the many RAF squadrons. Forward moves between airfields of about 30 to 40 miles distant were practised by the squadrons, which is the reason why so many Mustang units appeared at the airfield in such a short time span.

Even before that fateful December day, Twinwood Farm had established an association with Glenn Miller and his American Band of the Supreme Allied Command, as it was known originally; the more famous name '..Band of the AEF' (Allied Expeditionary Forces) came directly at General Eisenhower's request. The band's links with the airfield really dated from the time that it became based in Bedford in early July 1944. Miller and the band used the airfield on a couple of occasions as their main take-off and landing point as they undertook their exhausting tour of USAAF bases and hospitals throughout the country from the middle of July until early October. In recognition of these links Glenn Miller and the band gave a concert at the airfield on Sunday 27th August before they left the following day from Twinwoods for RAF Harrowbeer in Devon and their concerts in Plymouth.

It was during November that a six week tour of American bases and field hospitals on the Continent was authorised, with the tour planned to commence on 15th December 1943. Miller told his band members that they would be playing 'for 30,000 to 40,000 GIs of the fighting forces of the AEF, giving them a "Hunk O' Home".' The order detailing Major

A famous publicity photograph of Major Glenn Miller.

Noorduyn C-64 Norseman, similar to the one that was lost with Glenn Miller on board. (NASM)

Miller's journey to France was issued on 12th December, but the British weather now intervened, as thick fog covered most of England and the near Continent. The regular American military ferry flights to Paris left from Bovingdon, and they had been cancelled, so Miller knew that once the weather lifted there would be a long back-log to make up, and he would be at the back of the queue. He was desperately keen to precede the band to ensure personally that all the necessary travel arrangements to Paris were in order.

One of his friends at Milton Ernest Hall, which was the headquarters of the Eighth Air Force Service Command, was Lieutenant Colonel Norman F. Baessell. When he heard of Miller's urgency to get to Paris, he offered him a lift in one of the Command's aircraft; Baessell had a trip to France planned for the 15th as he was responsible for the establishment of advanced air depôts in France, and frequently travelled there. Baessell had met Miller at the Hall, where the band had given several concerts, also the members of the band messed at the Hall, which, of course, is close to Twinwood Farm.

Glenn Miller, along with Lieutenant Don Haynes, the band's manager, joined the Colonel for lunch at Milton Ernest on the 15th whilst they awaited news that the proposed flight to France had obtained the necessary meteorological clearance. The aircraft that would be used for the trip was a Canadian-built Noorduyn UC-64A Norseman, which was

238

The control tower at Twinwood Farm in the summer of 1998.

probably the most utilised small transport aircraft operating with the Eighth Air Force. It was based at the Strategic Air Depôt at Abbots Ripton adjacent to Alconbury, which was about 20 miles north of Twinwood Farm. The aircraft, piloted by Flight Officer John R. S. Morgan, arrived safely at Twinwood Farm but it remained on the runway with its engine running. Haynes drove Glenn Miller and Lt Colonel Baessell out to the aircraft. He later recalled that it was 'a cold, rainy, foggy afternoon' and that Glenn Miller had said to him just as he was boarding the aircraft, 'Haynsie, even the birds are grounded today.' The aircraft took off at 1.55 pm, and it was never seen again.

During the week before Christmas all reports of single-engined aircraft were checked and every possible airfield both in the United Kingdom and France was investigated but not a single trace of the aircraft was found. On Christmas Eve, Miller's wife in America was informed that he was missing, a press release was then issued and later on the same day the BBC announced the sad news. The band went ahead with their Christmas Day concert from Paris, which was heard in this country as well as in the United States. The Eighth Air Force inquiry into the aircraft's disappearance, which was held in January 1945, decided that the most likely explanation was that the aircraft had 'iced up' and had crashed into the English Channel, where nobody would have survived very long in such freezing conditions. It was also pointed out that the Norseman was not equipped to deal with icing. Since then a number of rather fanciful stories have been written about Miller's disappearance. In March 1945 Major Alton Glenn Miller was posthumously awarded the Bronze Star for his service in the European Theater of War, and it was presented to his widow, Helen, in New York. The band remained on the Continent for over six months and returned directly to the USA.

Twinwood Farm airfield closed down in June 1945, and it was then thought that it would be linked to the Research Station being established at nearby Thurleigh, some few miles to the north, but the scheme did not materialise. Although the airfield site returned again to agriculture, it has since become a mecca for Glenn Miller enthusiasts. On the fiftieth anniversary, the Glenn Miller (UK) orchestra re-enacted the concert of 27th August 1944, which was followed by a Service of Remembrance on 15th December, held close to the control tower with the USAF providing an Honor Guard. A scarlet oak was planted where the original station flagpole had been sited.

17
OTHER AIRFIELDS

There were several other airfields in the two counties, which although never used operationally, are certainly deserving of notice. Without doubt the two most important were Radlett and Leavesden, both in Hertfordshire, each fully engaged in the manufacture of aircraft – Halifaxes and Mosquitos. They made a considerable contribution to the war effort.

The country's aircraft production was one of the most outstanding success stories of the Second World War. In 1938 there were just 19 aircraft companies operating from 54 factories of various sizes, and they produced some 3,000 aircraft for the Service. But the Air Ministry 'Scheme L' provided for the production of 12,000 new military aircraft in three years; in fact at the end of 1941 well over 40,000 had been built. By March 1944 the number of aircraft factories and dispersed sites had increased to some 370, employing over 1.7 million people, of whom the majority were women. In that year alone 26,500 Service aircraft were built, an increase of nearly 800% on the pre-war figures – a phenomenal growth by any standard! However, sheer numbers were not the sole consideration, as Sir Stafford Cripps, the Minister of Aircraft Production, made clear in 1943: 'Quality is more important than quantity. Nothing but the best and most up-to-date is good enough for our magnificent airmen.' During the war years over 120,000 aircraft were produced, which accounted for more than one third of the wartime budget. Of this total, almost 10% were constructed or assembled at Hatfield, Leavesden, Luton and Radlett.

Radlett

Handley Page Ltd, which had been formed in 1909, was the first limited company incorporated in Great Britain for the purpose of aircraft production. In the late 1920s the company had bought a site of about 150 acres at Colney Street to the north of Radlett for their new aerodrome and to serve their rapidly expanding aircraft production programme, both civil and military. The new airfield was built by James Turner, one of the few engineering companies that then specialised in aerodrome construction. In those days the building of aerodromes followed a very similar and rather simple pattern, there were few engineering problems and, of course, no concrete runways. By the summer of 1929 the new aerodrome was ready for use, but it was not officially opened until the following July.

Handley Page Ltd had built a fine reputation for producing bomber and transport aircraft for the Service, which went back to December 1914. In the immediate pre-war years the company was fully engaged in producing their latest bomber – the HP52 Hampden – and the first production model flew from Radlett in May 1938. It was specifically designed to be constructed in separate units, and most of these were built at the old factory at Cricklewood and removed by road to Radlett for assembly and testing. Along with Wellingtons and Whitleys, the Hampdens comprised Bomber Command's front-line force at the outbreak of the war. Because of a sadly inadequate defensive armament, a new role was found for the aircraft, that of a mine layer, and although Hampdens continued to serve as bombers until September 1942, by then they were mainly operating as torpedo bombers with Coastal Command. The 500th and last Hampden built by Handley Page left Radlett in July 1940. The company was now fully engaged on the development and production of its most famous wartime bomber, the HP57 Halifax.

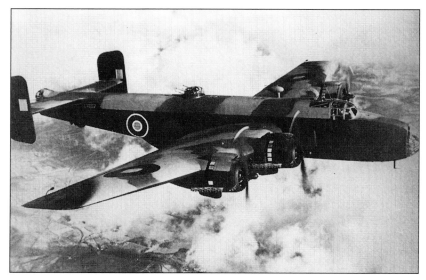

Halifaxes were built both at Radlett and Leavesden.

The aircraft owed its existence to an Air Ministry specification B13/36 for a twin-engined heavy bomber to be powered by Rolls-Royce Vulture engines. When the Vulture engine production ran into technical problems, the company looked for a suitable alternative. The original aircraft was redesigned to take four Rolls-Royce Merlin engines, and made its maiden flight on 25th October 1939. The second prototype, fitted with nose and tail turrets, first flew from Radlett on 17th August 1940, and was then passed over for Service tests and acceptance trials. The first production Halifax was ready in October, almost twelve months to the day since the aircraft had taken to the air. One month later a few Halifaxes were delivered to No 35 squadron, which had been specially re-formed to introduce the Halifax into the Service. The first Halifax operation was mounted on 10th/11th March 1941, and two nights later the Halifax became the first four-engined bomber to drop bombs on Germany.

The Halifax B Mark I had a maximum speed of 255 mph but cruised at just under 200 mph, it had a service ceiling of 18,000 feet and an operational range of 1,850 miles. The aircraft had a bomb capacity of

13,000 pounds and was armed with six .303 inch Browning guns in the nose and turrets with Vickers K guns in the beam position. Without doubt the Halifax was a large and heavy aircraft, 70 feet long with a wing span of 98 feet and its laden weight close to 24½ tons, and later models were even heavier. Within a year a new Mark had been introduced with improved performance and operational range, and provided with a Boulton & Paul dorsal turret. The aircraft went through considerable development up to a Mark IX and the major visual differences, other than engines, concerned the shape of the aircraft's nose and the presence or not of an upper turret. The most numerous Mark III came into the Service in February 1944. The Air Ministry's doctrine was that modifications and new equipment for operational aircraft, should be introduced as soon as possible whatever the effect on production figures; which was why aircraft like Halifaxes and Mosquitos went through so many changes in a relatively short period of time.

The Halifax was one of the most versatile of wartime aircraft. Of course its primary use was as a front-line heavy bomber but it also operated with No 100 Group on radio counter-measures duties. Halifaxes served in Coastal Command, where they were employed on reconnaissance, meteorological and anti-submarine patrols. They also operated as paratroop and supply-droppers, as well as casualty, freight and personnel transporters. Additionally the Halifax acted as a glider tug, in fact it was the only RAF aircraft capable of towing the large Hamilcar glider. They remained in service until late 1947.

The Halifax had been officially named by Lord Halifax at Radlett on 20th September 1941 – in his speech he quoted an old Yorkshire prayer, 'From Hull, Hell and Halifax, good Lord deliver us'! Although the production of the Halifax was first undertaken by the Cricklewood and Radlett factories, they quite soon became the subject of a group production effort of a unique kind. Four separate assembly and production lines were laid down in addition to those of the parent company, who also acted as technical advisers and consultants. The first member of this group to come into production was the English Electric Company of Preston, which had earlier produced the majority of Hampdens. It was followed by the London Aircraft Production Group at Leavesden. Then Fairey Aviation took over a factory in Stockport to

The Memorial to Handley Page Ltd at Colney Street near Radlett.

245

build Halifaxes and finally Rootes Securities, the motor car company, produced over 1,000 Halifaxes at Speke. At its peak the 'Group' employed over 50,000 workers at 45 different sites, and it was estimated that a Halifax was completed at the rate of one per working hour! Ultimately 6,176 Halifaxes were produced, of which only 1,590 were produced by the parent company, the last one leaving the Cricklewood factory in November 1946. The Halifax was a splendid successor to Handley Page's first military bomber, 0/400, the 'bloody paralyser of an aeroplane' of First World War days.

The airfield at Radlett had been greatly extended during the early war years with increased workshops to accommodate the new Halifax production lines, and concrete runways had been laid to cope with the heavy Halifaxes. In October 1944 the company released details of their new HP68 Hermes, a civil airliner or a transport carrier. This aircraft did not make its maiden flight until 2nd December 1945 from Radlett, when sadly it crashed near to the airfield killing the two test pilots. The disaster delayed the Hermes project for about two years. In February 1956 the first Victor B1 entered the Service, but after Sir Frederick Handley Page, CBE, died in April 1962, aged 77 years, the days of his company and the airfield seemed numbered. In March 1970 Handley Page Aircraft Ltd was wound up, and shortly afterwards the airfield was closed. There is, however, a memorial stone at the former entrance to Colney Street works remembering Handley Page Ltd and its founder.

Leavesden

The site of this airfield, which lies to the north-west of Watford towards Abbots Langley, had originally been spacious playing fields known locally as Mile Field. The 300 acre site was purchased by the Ministry of Aircraft Production in 1940, and was provided with a 1,000 yard concrete runway, along with workshops, fitting shops and hangars. It was then leased by the Ministry to two Groups for aircraft production – the London Aircraft Production (LAP) and the Second Aircraft Group (SAG).

The LAP was made up of Chrysler Motors, Duplex Bodies and Motors, Express Body and Motor works, Park Royal coachworks, and the London Passenger Transport Board works. Each member of the Group was responsible for a different part of the Halifax production. For instance, Chrysler and Duplex built the rear and forward fuselages respectively, whereas Express and Park Royal constructed the inner and outer wings. London Passenger Transport Board made most of the interior equipment and fittings, as well as undertaking the final assembly and testing. Indeed it was said that the 'Halibag' crews (as they dubbed the aircraft) knew immediately which Halifax had been built at Leavesden because of the very comfortable green leather seats (redolent of London buses!). They also maintained that the rivetting being far smoother increased the aircraft's air speed by ten to fifteen knots!

The LAP Group started to build Halifax BIIs from late 1941 and by the end of July 1942 35 had been produced with each aircraft being given a serial number in the 'BB' series. It was normal practice for contractors to provide their aircraft with a separate series number different from that used by the main manufacturer, and these changed for different marks of aircraft. It was during 1942 that the Air Transport Auxiliary set up their four-engined conversion training for their ferry pilots at Leavesden, having acquired one of the earliest Halifax BIIs built by LAP; manufacturers were allowed to retain a certain number of their production aircraft for trials and tests with the agreement of the Ministry of Aircraft Production. Lettice Curtis well remembers her conversion training at Leavesden and 'the long 1,000 yard runway which sloped down towards the hangars.' Just over 700 Halifaxes were produced by LAP.

SAG came under the general administration of the de Havilland Company, and Geoffrey de Havilland had originally considered using Leavesden for building Armstrong Whitworth Albemarles under contract. However, by September 1941, it was clear that Hatfield would not be able to cater for the Service's demand for his 'wooden wonder' – he anticipated that in 1942 at least 200 would be needed (in fact 442 were produced in that year) – therefore de Havilland decided to set up a second production line at Leavesden. The first Mosquitos built at Leavesden were TIIIs – the dual-control trainers. Later in 1942 the plant

247

A Halifax at Leavesden showing the height of the aircraft compared with a London bus. (London Transport)

produced FIIs, the day/night long-range fighters, of which almost 500 were built, and almost a half of them were converted to night-fighters (NFXIIs and XVIIs).

During its first complete year of production (1942) SAG produced 53 Mosquitos, but in the following year the number had increased to over 370, and by 1944 over 580 were produced, many of which were NFXXXs, which had made their first appearance in March of that year. Of the 6,710 Mosquitos built during the war, almost 1,400 came from Leavesden – 20% of the Mosquito production – which was second only to de Havilland's main plant at Hatfield. Production continued at Leavesden until 1946 with TR33s, the torpedo/reconnaissance bombers, coming off the line along with T3 trainers; ultimately a total of 1,476 Mosquitos were produced there.

DH Tiger Moth: one of the finest training aircraft of all time – over 8,000 were built.

Panshanger

This small grassed airfield to the east of Welwyn Garden City, first known as Holwell Hyde, had originally been used as a relief landing ground for the Tiger Moths of No 1 E&RFTS at Hatfield. But in 1940 it became a 'decoy' airfield for Hatfield. The idea of establishing dummy airfields to lure the enemy aircraft away from authentic operational airfields was first conceived in September 1939, and towards the end of the year the project was activated with Colonel John Turner placed in charge. He set up his new department at Shepperton film studios, and his team set about constructing the first decoy airfields. There were basically two types, one for day coded 'K' and one for night coded 'Q'; the latter would be provided with lighting. The dummy workshops, sheds and hangars were built mainly of wooden frames covered with canvas, and painted to add a touch of realism, in many cases even dummy aircraft were provided. By the end of January 1940 the first K site was ready and another 30 or so decoy airfields had been completed by July.

Holywell Hyde was rather more than a decoy airfield, it was one of four dummy aircraft factories completed during the Second World War. A complete mock-up of an aircraft factory, complete with canvas sheds and workshops, was erected along with a number of dummy aircraft dotted around the landing field. Official figures suggest that these dummy factories were attacked by the Luftwaffe on over 20 occasions, which certainly justified their existence. By the summer of 1941 the airfield had returned to its original use, and in September 1942 No 1 EFTS moved in completely from Hatfield bringing its large complement of Tiger Moths.

One year later the airfield became known as Panshanger, and by now the School was fully engaged on what were known as 'grading courses'. During 1941 because of the rapid growth of operational requirements, and the introduction of more sophisticated and faster aircraft, there was demand for a higher standard of pilot training. Flying Training Command had been deeply concerned about the high wastage rate at the Elementary Flying Schools, so it was decided that another check to the pilot selection procedures would be applied, hence the grading courses.

Under this new system the aspiring pilots would be given twelve hours of dual instruction to bring them up to the time that they would be ready to fly solo, and at this stage they were assessed as to whether they were suitable for further flying training, only then would they pass on to the next stage of training. Invariably three weeks was set aside for grading courses, which No 1 School at Panshanger mounted for the rest of the war. The School then reverted to elementary flying training, and in May 1947 it was redesignated No 1 Reserve Flying School and remained so until disbanded in March 1953. At the time of writing, the small grassed airfield is still used by private aircraft.

Satellite Landing Grounds

In the autumn of 1940 Sir Alan Cobham was asked by Lord Beaverbrook, the first Minister of Aircraft Production, to make a tour of the country to locate suitable sites for use as landing grounds. Sir Alan was given a small team of RAF pilots along with a chartered surveyor.

Aerial view of Woburn Abbey and Park in the late 1940s.

These landing grounds were to be used for the storage of operational aircraft, because the RAF's Maintenance Units were already becoming rather overcrowded as the country's aircraft production began to accelerate dramatically. Cobham and his team identified over 100 likely sites, although in the end only about a half were actually prepared and developed. The first Satellite Landing Ground (SLG) to be used, in December 1940, was sited at Slade Farm in Oxfordshire.

The SLGs were developed under the direction of a firm of consultant engineers, Rendall, Palmer & Tritton. They were basically rather primitive grassed landing areas with few facilities and buildings deliberately kept to the minimum, often existing farmhouses and cottages being requisitioned to house the small number of Service personnel based there. At many sites almost miniature hangars, known as Robins, were provided and they were often camouflaged to resemble houses or farm buildings. The SLGs were expressly forbidden to be used for emergency landings, and they did not appear on any aeronautical charts. The aircraft stored there were heavily camouflaged and most of the sites were guarded by local Army units or Home Guard companies, although some SLGs were also protected by guard dogs, the first use of RAF guard dogs.

There were two SLGs in Bedfordshire, one at Beechwood Park, to the south of Luton, and the other at Woburn Park. Each SLG was numbered; Beechwood Park (No 12) was certainly in use from May 1942, storing aircraft for No 5 Maintenance Unit at Kemble in Gloucestershire, as well as being used by No 15 MU at Wroughton. Beechwood mainly housed fighters – Hurricanes, Spitfires and later Seamews – although in 1944 Stirlings were stored there, and even as late as October 1945 the SLG was still being used.

Woburn Park (No 34) was the largest satellite landing ground of them all, owing its selection as a SLG to the pre-war flying days of the late Duchess of Bedford. The landing strip at Woburn ran uphill to the west of the Abbey from the lake at the south end of the Park. Although the date of its first use is not accurately recorded, certainly in 1941 it was used for the storage of Spitfires. There is a story that 'WOBURN' in large white letters was painted on the roof of the indoor riding school, which obviously dated from the days of the 'Flying Duchess', and the name was not removed until 1941! The Landing Ground was shared by No 6 MU at Brize Norton and No 8 MU based at Little Rissington. As well as Spitfires, Halifaxes, Stirlings and the odd Lancaster were stored there, and it is known that surplus Stirlings were housed there well into 1947, when they were scrapped.

Minor Airfields

Four other small pre-war airfields came into use during the war. Barton-in-the-Clay, as has already been noted, was used for flying training purposes. Broxbourne was engaged in the repair and rebuilding of Percival aircraft, as well as modifying Canadian-built North American Harvards. Old Warden aerodrome came under the umbrella of the nationwide Civilian Repair Organisation, which had been established by Lord Nuffield to co-ordinate the repair, rebuild and conversion of operational aircraft. The tiny airfield at Elstree, near to Aldenham Country Club, was used by Fairchild Aviation for the modification of a number of aircraft, but most notably Westland Lysander IIIs.

18

CIVILIANS AT WAR

On that fateful September Sunday morning when Neville Chamberlain informed the Nation that it was now at war with Germany, the solemn and dire announcement did not occasion any great surprise; to some it came as 'a mild shock', but for most it brought 'a strange sense of relief after all the strains and tensions of the previous week'. The majority of the country had considered that the war had really started two days earlier.

In the early hours of 1st September 1939 German troops entered Poland, and from that moment, it may be said that the Nation's future was sealed. ARP wardens were mobilised, and the BBC merged its National and Regional networks into a single Home Service to broadcast from 7 am to 12.15 am. The black-out regulations came into force from sunset; a State of Emergency had been declared and people reacted by crowding desperately into shops to buy extra supplies of sugar, flour, tinned goods, tea and candles. But perhaps the most ominous sign of the impending war was the mass evacuation of children from London that commenced at sunrise.

The sight of thousands upon thousands of children with labels tied around their necks, their gas masks in cardboard boxes, and carrying their few precious possessions in bags, produced the most evocative and

Some of the 17,000 evacuees allotted to Bedford pass the Royal County Theatre

in Midland Road. (Bedfordshire & Luton Archives & Records Services)

poignant images of the war. Walter Elliott, the Minister of Health, described the evacuation as 'an exodus bigger than that of Moses. It is the movement of ten armies, each the size of the Expeditionary Force.' The plans called for the relocation of more than 3½ million individuals, although the actual number was less than 1½ million – over 800,000 schoolchildren, 520,000 mothers and children under school age, and 103,000 teachers and helpers.

Although not all of the towns were considered suitable as reception areas, both counties received their share of evacuees and over 36,000 were found new homes in Bedfordshire. Other than the billeting of children and families in private houses, which became a quite contentious issue, especially when refusal could lead to a £50 fine, one of the biggest problems was schooling, and by the middle of September most schools had introduced a shift system, with local children and evacuees being taught on alternate days (Saturday included). The evacuation caused an upheaval on a grand scale, not only for the children but also for the receiving families, but after the first week in September, the Mayor of Bedford was able to report that 'the whole proceedings passed off entirely without a hitch.' However, by the spring of 1940 almost 75% had left for home, although many would return later in the year as the London blitz intensified. One shocking fact to emerge from the mass evacuation operation was the depth of poverty and hardship suffered in many areas of London.

There were some other evacuations to the area, which did not receive the same glare of publicity. Giant pandas, elephants, yaks and some water deer were moved from London Zoo in Regents Park to new pastures at Whipsnade. The BBC moved its religious and music departments to Bedford in 1941, and many concerts were broadcast from the Corn Exchange. Several companies left London to set up their headquarters offices in large country houses dotted around the countryside. One of the major consequences of the People's War, as it has been called, was the movement of people. At least two million were officially evacuated, many more made their own private arrangements with relatives or friends, and well over one million were forced to move because their homes were destroyed; it was reported that during the whole of the war, there were over 60 million changes of address in a total civilian population of about 34 millions.

For the remainder of September the British people were beginning to come to terms with major changes to their everyday lives. The vast majority considered that the black-out was the most irksome and restrictive, more so even than food rationing. The rate of road accidents increased by 100% in the month and during the war there were thousands of minor injuries to pedestrians as a result of the lighting restrictions. The ARP wardens on their regular nightly 'lights' patrols could be a little over-zealous in ensuring that the black-out was enforced in homes; 'put that light out' became an all too familiar cry! The same complaint was often voiced about their officious attitude to the compulsory carrying of gas masks; certainly many ARP wardens, with their distinctive white helmets, were not, at least in the early days, the most popular members of the Civil Defence!

Over 38 million gas masks had been issued to the civilian population, and it was estimated that less than one in five actually carried them to work. Nobody who was compelled to wear one of these gas masks, if only during the regular practice drills, has ever forgotten the chilling experience; the clammy breathlessness they induced and the very distinctive smell of rubber and disinfectant! The Government considered that the threat of poison gas was very real, posters giving information of what to do in the event of gas attack were prominently displayed in offices, and the tops of GPO post boxes were coated with yellow gas detector paint.

The month also saw the imposition of petrol rationing (on the 22nd), the first ominous signs of things to come, though in truth this affected only a small percentage of the population as just one family in ten possessed a car. Five days later the first of the many War Budgets was introduced, bringing a sharp increase in Income Tax to 7s 6d with additions to the taxes on beer, wine, spirits, tobacco and sugar. And although most people felt the Budget to be 'drastic', they accepted the punitive taxes because, 'after all, this war must be paid for'. In the coming years taxation would rise dramatically, but it would be borne with calm stoicism by the public, to some degree because of the lack of consumer goods on which to spend their hard-earned wages!

National Registration Day was set for 29th September and the establishment of a National Register enabled the Government to issue a National Identity card to every person, and also brought the introduction of food rationing that much closer. The National Identity card and the Ration book became the two most important documents of the war. In the following month the insistent wartime motto 'Dig for Victory' was introduced. The Minister of Agriculture, Sir Reginald Dorman Smith, demanded that all gardens should to be given over to the culture of vegetables, and furthermore that every able-bodied man and woman should dig an allotment in their spare time. Helped by the introduction of Double British Summer Time in May 1941, this became a major occupation and the number of allotments grew from 815,00 in 1939 to almost 1½ million by 1943.

Relatively quickly the civilian population had 'slipped very easily into war habits', as one wartime diarist recorded. Of course, this was helped by what had become known as the 'Phoney' or 'Bore' war; the expected air bombardment had not materialised, and there was a lack of wartime activity anywhere. This also engendered a general unease in the country, as everybody seemed poised waiting for the 'war to begin and get it over with'. Places of entertainment that had closed immediately on the outbreak of the war, now reopened; cinemas, especially, were well attended as they would be throughout the war, despite air raids, and the epic film *Gone with the Wind* became the outstanding box-office success.

The winter of 1939/40 proved to be the most severe of the century, with weeks of hard frosts and heavy snowfalls; although coal was not rationed, it was nevertheless in short supply due largely to supply problems caused by the atrocious weather. Food rationing, which had been first introduced in November, was extended in early January, and queuing had become a constant and unwelcome feature of this long and harsh winter; the habit of queuing became so ingrained in people that it became a national obsession! The majority of people who lived through this first wartime winter, later readily agreed that it was probably the worst period of the war. The complete uncertainty of what the future held for them and their families only added to their misery and suffering.

It was the BBC that became the country's chief solace during these very dark and cold winter days. The news bulletins had settled into a regular pattern and they became essential and compulsive listening throughout the war years. From June 1940 when the newsreaders identified themselves – Alvar Lidell, Frank Phillips, Stuart Hibberd and Bruce Belfrage – they became celebrities, as did the novelist and playwright, J. B. Priestley, for his 'homely fireside talks', which had a regular audience of ten million. But it was the comedy shows such as *Band Wagon*, *Hi Gang* and *It's That Man Again* (later *ITMA*) that became firm favourites, bringing humour into the drab and dreary wartime years. In 1942 over 16 million listened to *ITMA*'s fifth series.

On 9th April 1940 a diarist recorded, 'Well, well, this blinking war has started at last. Now we expect things to happen.' He was referring to Germany's invasion of Norway and Denmark. The 'Funny' or 'Strange' war had come to an abrupt end. On the last day of the month the first fatal casualties in England as a result of air action occurred; a Heinkel III crashed into a house at Clacton-on-Sea in Essex, killing two persons – the People's War had started. For the next three years civilians would bear the brunt of the war, sustaining more fatalities and injuries than the whole of the armed forces.The invasion of Belgium and Holland on 10th May brought the war front far closer to home, and marked a great difference in the war situation with the mood of the country reflecting this change.

The tired and terminally ill Neville Chamberlain resigned, and was replaced by Winston Churchill, in charge of an all-party National Government. The arrival at the helm of this most inspiring and charismatic war leader occasioned one writer to record, 'We should now have no complaint about the speed of prosecution of the war', a view that was echoed throughout the country. Described in October 1939 as 'the best talker we have', Churchill's 33 wartime speeches (or broadcasts, as he preferred to call them) greatly inspired the country during its darkest days. He seemed able to express the feelings of the British people in the most stirring and unforgettable words. Throughout the war no less than 78% of the public approved of his conduct of the war. Without doubt the country was fortunate to be led during its extreme trial by a great man.

On 14th May 1940 Anthony Eden, the new Secretary of State for War, made a radio appeal for men between the ages of 17 and 65 years to enlist for a new force to defend the country; it was to be known as the Local Defence Volunteers. The response was immediate and remarkable, within 24 hours a quarter of a million men had come forward, and by the

The Hatfield Home Guard in training about 1943. (Hertfordshire Archives & Local Studies)

end of June over one million were on the register. At first they received little more than their LDV armbands – these initials were jokingly said to be short for 'Look, Duck and Vanish'! Soon almost every town and village in the two counties had their own platoon, with the various battalions being commanded by retired senior Army officers.

In August the LDV was renamed the Home Guard, at the insistence of Churchill, and slowly it was placed on a more military footing. Uniforms were provided and the men were armed, although at first weapons were rather scarce until one million First World War rifles were purchased from the United States. The Home Guard's primary function was to deal with any parachute troops that landed, and they took their duty very seriously. They also manned road-blocks, patrolled their territory and inspected the identity cards of persons moving during the hours of darkness. By the summer of 1943 there were over 1,100 battalions throughout the country comprising some 1¾ million men with the average age of under 30 years; less than 10% were ex-

Servicemen. Contrary to the comic images created by *Dad's Army*, the Home Guard became quite a professional force, with many manning anti-aircraft batteries as well as undertaking regular army duties later in the war. Over 130 medals were awarded to Home Guardsmen including two George Crosses.

With the fall of France in June 1940 the threat of invasion became a distinct and frightening possibility. Most people in the country were convinced that invasion was imminent, it was more a matter of *when* rather than *if*. The Government issued a pamphlet, *Rules for Civilians in case of Invasion*, to every household. It instructed people to stay indoors rather than block the roads, hide maps and guides, food, petrol and bicycles, and moreover they were told, 'Do not panic' (shades of *Dad's Army*!). Even in March 1941 a further leaflet, *If the Invader Comes*, was issued, with additional and more explicit instructions. Road signs were removed, as were the names on railway stations; maps and guides were removed from sale. From 13th June church bells were silenced and would only be rung as a warning that the expected paratroops had landed. Pill boxes, anti-tank traps and concrete blocks appeared throughout the towns and countryside. Some little publicised preparations were put in hand. Each town and village had its own Invasion Committee and had a designated 'inner keep' where soldiers and the Home Guard would make a last stand; at Letchworth it was the Spirella corset factory! Reserve stocks of food were hidden away – at the small Bedfordshire village of Willington there were three such food dumps, each containing biscuits, corned beef, tinned soup, sugar, margarine and tea.

The Treachery Act had been passed in May designed to deal with enemy agents and 'Fifth Columnists' – described as Fascists and aliens who might assist the Germans. Thousands of aliens were rounded up and placed into 'protective custody', with the national press demanding that the Government 'Intern the Lot'! All foreigners were treated with the gravest suspicion, and posters carrying such slogans as 'Careless Talk Costs Lives' and 'Be Like Dad, Keep Mum' could be seen everywhere. Even the carrying of a camera could lead to arrest. As was the case throughout the war, the radio programme *ITMA* captured the spirit of the nation, with its character 'Funf' the spy, whose catch phrase, 'This is Funf speaking' entered the language of the time.

The arrest of the German spy, Karl Richter, in May 1941. (Hertfordshire Archives & Local Studies)

However, spying was a serious matter and in May 1941 the first 'real' spy was captured in the area. In the early hours of 13th May SS Obersturmführer Karl Richter landed by parachute in a field not far from Salisbury Hall near London Colney. This was, of course, close to where the de Havilland Mosquito was being developed, but whether this was by pure coincidence or deliberate intent is not known. Richter remained in hiding for two days before he started to walk along the road towards London Colney. He was soon stopped by a lorry driver, who sought directions from him. The lorry driver became a little suspicious of the well-dressed foreigner carrying a suitcase, so when he saw a policeman he mentioned 'the man with a strong foreign accent.' When apprehended Richter produced an identity card with an address in London, but he said he was ill. The police constable offered to telephone the local hospital but instead rang the St Albans police station for help. Richter was arrested and his suitcase was found to contain a considerable amount of British and American money, a map of the eastern counties and a compass. The following day Richter led the police to the spot where he had buried his parachute, flying suit, automatic pistol and radio equipment. He was ultimately sentenced to death and was executed in Wandsworth prison in December 1941.

The country had been preparing itself for the threatened aerial bombardment since the outbreak of war. By the end of September 1939 most towns had built public shelters, though invariably the number provided would only accommodate about 10% of the total population. The town of Bedford had provided a number of public basement shelters, which were sufficient to house over 6,000 persons. At many of the schools throughout the area trenches had been dug and blast walls erected. Air raid shelters had been offered to all households at the cost of £7 but free to those where their annual income was less than £250. These shelters were of a curved corrugated sheet design, intended to be sunk several feet into the ground, and then covered with earth or sandbags. They became known as 'Anderson' shelters supposedly from Sir John Anderson, who in 1938 had been in charge of the nation's Civil Defence, although their name actually derived from their designer, David A. Anderson. One historian wrote, 'To be inside an Anderson shelter felt rather like being entombed in a small, dark bicycle shed, smelling of earth and damp.' However, they were acceptably safe and could withstand considerable damage except for a direct hit. When it was found that many people would not use such shelters, preferring to stay inside their houses, the Government produced an indoor shelter – the Morrison – which was named after Herbert Morrison, then in charge of Civil Defence.

The first bombs fell on Bedfordshire on 27th June 1940 at Pertenhall, but it was the Vauxhall factory at Luton, which was producing Bedford military trucks and Churchill tanks, that suffered the first heavy raid on 30th August. Considerable damage was caused as well as fatalities and injuries, but the factory was back in production within six days. Later in September (the 22nd) the area of Park Street, Luton sustained damage. During the winter of 1940/1, which also turned out to be very cold, few towns or areas of the countryside in the two counties escaped air raids, some like Hatfield, St Albans and Luton to a greater extent than others. On 20th October Hockerill Training College at Bishops Stortford was

The Grosvenor Hotel, Bedford after the air raid of 23rd July 1942.
(Bedfordshire & Luton Archives & Records Services)

bombed, killing three students. Then in January the school at Long Marston, Hertfordshire received a direct hit; three evacuee children were dug out of the rubble but the headmistress was killed. Almost nightly the air raid siren or 'Wailing Winnie' was sounded as hordes of enemy aircraft passed overhead bound for targets in the Midlands. It was a time when, according to one wartime diarist, 'Sleep is now elevated to a position of national importance'. Most of the male civilian population was engaged in some kind of Civil Defence work...ARP wardens, rescue workers, special policemen, auxiliary firemen, drivers, fire watchers etc, and after their night duties which afforded little opportunity for sleep, the following morning they were back at their daytime work in the factories, shops and offices.

Although the intensity of the night raids lessened from May 1941, sporadic attacks continued throughout the war. Bedford suffered several raids during the summer of 1942, and the bombardment was renewed with a vengeance from June 1944 when the first V1 rockets or 'Doodlebugs' began to arrive, followed by the V2 rockets. And yet everything is relative, a couple from London visiting friends in Bedfordshire in 1942 remarked on 'the blessed relief, the peace and quiet of the countryside compared with the hell of London...it is almost like pre-war England'!

In retrospect 1941 can be viewed as the nadir of the country's fortunes. By the end of the year over 40,000 civilians had been killed in air raids with another 50,000 injured – the Home Front was bearing the brunt of the war. As the U-boats in the Atlantic took their deadly toll on the Allied shipping convoys, food rationing became more stringent. The weekly ration of cheese was cut to 1 oz, meat reduced to 1s per week, eggs were a rarity being replaced by the powdered egg sustitute, and milk was rationed for the first time. Although bread was never rationed during the war, the white loaf disappeared to be replaced by the National Wheatmeal Loaf, which was universally detested and described as 'nasty, dirty, dank and coarse.' Towards the end of the year a points system was introduced for canned goods, and the purchase of clothing and footwear was severely restricted by coupons. In such a climate of shortages and austerity the black market flourished, and it was from this time the word 'spiv' entered the vocabulary; the person who could provide anything from petrol and clothing coupons to scarce consumer goods, but 'at a price'.

One saving grace to come out of this time of grave shortages and harsh austerity was the appearance of the British Restaurants run by local authorities and subsidised by the Government, where good and wholesome food could be obtained for 1s per head. They filled a gap for those people who did not have the opportunity of obtaining their main meal at a works or office canteen. The number of industrial canteens had risen from 1,500 in 1939 to 18,500 in 1944; these canteens received extra allowances of meat, cheese, butter and sugar, and went some way to subsidise the weekly ration. The first British Restaurant to be opened in Bedford in September 1941 was sited at the Full Gospel Tabernacle, where smoking was strictly forbidden! It was quickly followed by others in the towns throughout the area. Within two years there were over 2,000 British Restaurants serving over 600,000 mid-day meals daily. They were certainly not everybody's choice; one woman recalled her first experience of this way of eating out: 'Even wartime difficulties did not make me enjoy this method of serving oneself; pick up a tray, slide it

The Women's Voluntary Service at Bromham.

along the bars, receive a slop of meat (not *too* bad, but a bit gristly), far too much potato and gravy and masses of cabbage. Next three prunes and a half and not too bad custard...the coffee was vile, so I left it.'

As 1941 came to a close, conscription for unmarried women between the ages of 20 and 30 years was introduced. The conscripts were given the choice of serving either in three female auxiliary armed services, the civil defence or industry. Thousands of women were already filling jobs vacated by men serving in the forces – bus drivers and conductors, milkmen, postmen, railway workers – and by mid-1943 the number of women engaged on war work was in excess of three million, mostly employed in aircraft and munitions factories. This was one of the major social changes brought about by the war.

However, since the outbreak of the war women had taken up voluntary war work, either in Civil Defence, the Red Cross, the Women's Land Army, or the Women's Voluntary Service. The WVS had been formed in 1938 by the Dowager Marchioness of Reading with the original intention of encouraging women into the Civil Defence. The Service could be said to be essentially middle class, which its uniform of a grey-green tweed suit, beetroot-red jumper, and felt hat, only seemed to further proclaim. By 1941 there were over a million WVS volunteers with only 200 paid staff. Often they jocularly referred to themselves as 'Widows, Virgins and Spinsters', though to the public and servicemen they were simply known as 'the women in green'. Throughout the war they made an immense and magnificent contribution to the Home Front, often operating under most trying and distressing conditions. From helping with the evacuation of children and families in 1939 to aiding victims of the air raids, they operated canteens, reception and rest centres for servicemen, ran mobile canteens at airfields, and organised the wholesale distribution of clothes and other items to bombed-out people. No task seemed too difficult or onerous for the 'women in green'.

The other most conspicuous female war workers were the girls of the WLA, which had been revived by Lady Gertrude Denman in June 1939. In Bedfordshire the numbers of Land Army girls rose from 85 in 1939 to over 1,000 five years later. They, too, had their own uniform – green jersey, brown breeches, wide-brimmed brown hat and a khaki overcoat. All were volunteers and they came from all walks of life, becoming an essential part of the wartime farming scene. After about a month's training, the girls were sent to one of the many hostels dotted throughout the area. Their hours were long and the work hard and poorly paid. They had to face considerable suspicion from farmers, before ultimately gaining their grudging respect. At its peak, in 1943, the WLA numbered over 87,000 and survived well after the war, not being disbanded until October 1950.

Considering the high levels of taxation (in April 1941 income tax rose to 10s in £1), one of the outstanding success stories of the Home Front was the National Savings Movement. It had all started back in November 1939 as the War Savings Scheme, which aimed to collect £475 million in a year, and actually £463 million were raised. The start of regular and on-going National Savings proved to be an outright winner. There were savings groups in every street, office, factory and school, and such was the importance that the BBC news bulletin reported details of the total weekly contributions. It was said that at least 25% of the average weekly income was given up to savings compared with a mere 5% before the war.

National Savings plaque on display at Harpenden Public Hall. (Courtesy St Albans City & District)

But the most dramatic success of the Savings Movement came with the special drives organised on a national basis throughout the war: from the Spitfire Fund in the summer of 1940 through to War Weapons Week, Warships Week, Wings for Victory and Salute the Soldier Week. Every town and village took part in these drives, which were usually introduced to the accompaniment of fancy dress parades and sports events, and the inevitable large barometer was located at some prominent position to record the progress of the amount of money collected. For example, in May 1943 St Albans collected almost £656,000 for Wings for Victory. There was often great rivalry between neighbouring towns; Luton challenged Watford to raise more money for Warships Week. Luton won by collecting £1.4 million, £200,000 more than Watford! Special plaques were issued to local authorities to acknowledge successful achievements in these special Weeks, but to my knowledge only Harpenden in Hertfordshire still has them on public display.

The austerity of the wartime years was reflected in the continual exhortations from the Government to save everything from rags, bones, jam jars, glass, rubber, old pots and pans to waste paper; 'Waste Not Want Not' and 'Make Do and Mend' were the guiding principles. The symbol of this era of thriftiness and scrimping was the Squander Bug, a cartoon figure liberally daubed with German swastikas which appeared in newspapers, magazines and on posters. Salvage drives were organised from street level upwards with schoolchildren actively involved in the collections. Newspapers and magazines ran regular salvage competitions awarding prizes of National Savings certificates (what else?) for the best hints. By the end of the war some six million tons of salvage had been collected, the majority of it scrap metal. Although coal was never rationed during the war, limits were imposed on supplies to householders, and in the long 'Battle of Fuel' the country was urged to follow the King's example and use no more than five inches of water in their baths. They were also continually pressed to consider, 'Is my journey really necessary?'; though few people would wish to use the over-crowded, irregular and unpunctual trains unless their journeys were essential!

As the country entered the fourth year of war, HM King George VI appointed 3rd September 1942 as a day of prayer, and it was marked by religious services throughout the country. Factories and offices stopped work for a quarter of an hour at 11 am for a broadcast service. Most people felt that the war had already lasted for an eternity, and there was precious little to celebrate or be thankful for. The war news from the Far East had been disastrous, Hong Kong and Singapore had fallen to the Japanese; the Russian Front was equally grave, and the situation in North Africa was less than promising. Closer to home, the Dieppe fiasco in August had pushed the notion of a Second Front into the very far distance, the so-called Baedeker air raids in the summer brought fresh sufferings and civilian fatalities, and only the RAF seemed to be hitting back at Germany. Nevertheless the majority were convinced that 'the tide must turn soon', which it finally did in October with El Alamein – the first land victory of the war. Churchill was cautious in his praise: 'This is not the end. It is not even the beginning of the end. But it is, perhaps, the end of the beginning.' On 15th November church bells rang once more to celebrate the victory. Perhaps now there was a glimmer of light at the end of a very long tunnel, and after all 'the Yanks had arrived'!

The first American servicemen or GIs (Government Issue) arrived in the area in the summer of 1942, and it could be said that they made an immediate impact; for those local communities close to the American bases it would prove to be the biggest event for many a long year. Suddenly, as if by magic, many scarce goods that had all but vanished from the shops, began to filter out from the American PX stores – razor blades, cheap cigarettes, sweets (or candies), tinned fruit and ham, chewing gum, and a new commodity – nylons. Soon the lanes and roads were crammed with their large lorries and little omnipresent jeeps. The streets of the nearby towns echoed to the sounds of American accents and became crowded with servicemen, along with their own American police, who were dubbed 'snowdrops' because of their white helmets. Bedford, especially, became an off-duty mecca for the GIs with its several American Red Cross clubs, and, from the summer of 1944, as the base for Glenn Miller's band.

There was a certain amount of resentment at first, especially when the Americans drunk the precious stocks of wartime beer dry, in spite of regularly complaining about its strength and quality! The friendly and generous nature of most American servicemen soon broke down local reserve and antipathy, and generally a very good relationship was established. Families welcomed the Americans into their homes and the air bases organised Christmas parties for local children where they shared their rations and distributed gifts. Strong links of friendship were made with local communities which have survived down the years.

During 1943 there was 'a very hopeful outlook' in the country, the news from the various war fronts was much more encouraging. The Ministry of Food, under the control of the ebullient Lord Woolton, the most famous wartime politician after Churchill, was able to report that the nation's diet was now healthier and better than it had been pre-war, despite the fact that rationing was again tightened. It was during this period that the very popular Radio Doctor with his sound and practical advice delivered in his inimitable style, tried also to keep the nation healthy. He was, of course, Dr Charles Hill, later Lord Hill of Luton, who could claim to have 14 million patients – his regular audience!

The growing might of the RAF and the USAAF could be witnessed by the sight and sound of their heavy bombers passing overhead both by day and night. During this time there was a greater risk to life and limb from friendly aircraft crashing than at the hands of the Luftwaffe. In fact on 24th March two young children were killed at Yelden when an American aircraft crashed shortly after take-off. The country 'hungered for the Second Front' and bets were made in pubs, offices and works as to the likely date. It was the familiar voice of John Snagge that announced the historic news at 9.30 am on 6th June 1944: 'D-Day has come. Early this morning the Allies began the assault on the north-western face of Hitler's European fortress.' According to reports there was 'an almost tangible release of tension in the country.'

However, the euphoria soon evaporated as the first V1 rocket landed on 12th/13th June. Within days the newspapers were reporting that 'Pilotless planes now raid Britain', and on the 16th of the month a statement was issed by the Ministry of Home Security: 'When the engine of the pilotless aircraft stops and the light at the end of the machine is seen to go out, it may be that explosion will soon follow'! The arrival of the V1s and V2s brought about a mini-evacuation of children and families away from London and the south-east. Hertfordshire suffered more rocket attacks than Bedfordshire – 154 in total

USAAF airman helping with the harvest near Bletsoe, August 1943.
(Bedfordshire & Luton Archives & Records Services)

compared with 13 – with the rural districts of Hatfield, Hertford, Hitchin and Cheshunt having the greatest number of incidents but mercifully with relatively light casualties. The worst V1 incident was at Watford on 30th July when 38 persons were killed (including two GIs) and another 64 injured. In all the air raids it was Luton that sustained the heaviest damage and highest casualties, 107 persons were killed and 500 injured.

During the autumn of 1944 things on the Home Front were slowly returning to some semblance of normality; the black-out restrictions were partially lifted to universal approval. On 1st November the Home Guard was stood down, and in early December the men paraded for the last time. Christmas was a time, at long last, for modest celebration;

extra rations of sweets, sugar, margarine and meats had been allowed, and the clear, bright and sunny weather seemed to reflect the optimistic mood of the country. But it would be almost the end of March 1945 before the dread sound of the wailing sirens was heard for the last time, and 24th April before black-out restrictions were fully abolished.

Every village, street and town in the country celebrated VE Day on 8th May 1945 with parties, bonfires, firework displays, fancy dress parades and sports events, with the celebrations continuing well into the early morning. One newspaper commented that the celebrations were more 'a conscious sense of relief from strain rather than a triumphant exultant.' After almost six long years of unremitting hardship, privation and sacrifice the People's War had ended, but the civilian population had paid a heavy price for their victory – more than 60,000 killed with another 86,000 seriously injured and well over 2 million people made homeless. As Winston Churchill later wrote, 'The People's will was resolute and remorseless. I only expressed it…They had the lion's heart. I had the luck to be called upon to give it the roar.' Richard Brown of Ipswich, who had religiously kept a wartime diary, entered for Saturday 8th June 1946, 'It is Victory Day and we deserve to celebrate. We won, just, but we won well and are rightly proud of our achievements. We've escaped something.'

BIBLIOGRAPHY

During my research I consulted a number of books. I list them below with my grateful thanks to the authors.

Air Ministry, *Target: Germany. The USAAF's Official Story of the VIII Bomber Command First Year over Europe*, HMSO, 1944

Armitage, Michael, *The Royal Air Force: An Illustrated History*, Cassell, 1993

Asworth, Chris, *RAF Bomber Command, 1936–1968*, Patrick Stephens, 1995

Bannerman, Kenneth P., *A Towering Control: The Story of British Airfields*, ISE, 1958

Barker, Revel, *Field of Vision: Cranfield University the First 50 years*, Cranfield University Press, 1996

Bennett, Don, *Pathfinder*, Frederick Muller, 1958

Bishop, Edward, *Mosquito: The Wooden Wonder*, Airlife, 1980

Bowyer, Chaz, *Royal Air Force, 1939–1945*, Pen & Sword Books, 1996

Bowyer, Michael J. F., *Action Stations: 6. Military Airfields of the Cotswolds and the Central Midlands*, Patrick Stephens, 1991

Calder, Angus, *The People's War; Britain 1939–45*, Pimlico, 1992

Chamberlain, Geoffrey, *Airships – Cardington*, T. Dalton, 1984

Chorley, W. R., *RAF Bomber Command Losses in the Second World War; Vols 1 to 5*, Midland Pubns, 1992–97

Cooper, Alan, *Air Battle of the Ruhr*, Airlife, 1992

Curtis, Lettice, *The Forgotten Pilots: The Story of the Air Transport Auxiliary*, G. T. Foulis, 1971

Doyle, Paul A., *Where the Lysanders were: The story of Sawbridgeworth's airfields*, Forward Airfield Research Pubs, 1995

Embry, Sir Basil, *Mission Completed*, Methuen, 1957.

Franks, Norman, *Fighter Command, 1936–1968*, Patrick Stephens, 1992

Freeman, Roger A., *The Mighty Eighth*, Arms & Armour, 1989

Freeman, Roger A., *The Mighty Eighth War Manual*, Janes Publishing Co, 1984

Freeman, Roger A. with Alan Crouchman & Vic Maslen, *The Mighty Eighth War Diary*, Janes Publishing Co, 1990

Golley, John, *Aircrew Unlimited: The Commonwealth Air Training Plan during World War II*, Patrick Stephens, 1993

Hamilton, Alexander, *Wings of Night: The Secret Missions of Group Captain Pickard DSO 2 Bars, DFC*, W. Kimber, 1977

Harris, Sir Arthur, *Bomber Offensive*, Collins, 1947

Jackson, Robert, *Guinness Book of Air Warfare*, Guinness Publishing, 1993

James, John, *The Paladins*, Macdonald & Co, 1990

Longmate, Norman, *How We Lived Then: A History of Everyday Life during WWII*, Hutchinson, 1971

Lutt, Nigel, *Bedfordshire at War*, Alan Sutton, 1997

Maynard, John, *Bennett and the Pathfinders*, Arms & Armour, 1996

McIntosh, Dave, *Terror in the Starboard Seat*, General Pub Co Ltd Canada, 1980

Middlebrook, Martin, *The Berlin Raids*, Viking, 1988

Millgate, Helen D (Editor), *Mr Brown's War: A Diary of the Second World War*, Alan Sutton, 1998

Mondey, David, *British Aircraft of World War II*, Hamlyn, 1992

Moyes, Philip J. R., *Bomber Squadrons of the RAF*, Hutchinson, 1981

Musgrave, Gordon, *Pathfinder Force: The Story of No 8 (PFF) Group*, Macdonald & Jane, 1976

Penrose, Harold, *British Aviation: Widening Horizons: 1930–1934*, HMSO, 1979

Penrose, Harold, *British Aviation: Ominous Skies: 1935–1939*, HMSO, 1980

Rawlings, John, *Fighter Squadrons of the RAF*, Crecy Books, 1993

Rawnsley, C. F. & Wright, Robert, *Night Fighter*, Collins, 1957

Richards, Denis. & Sanders, H., *The Royal Air Force, 1939–45*, HMSO, 1953

Scutts, Terry, *Lions in the Sky*, Patrick Stephens, 1987

Smith, David J., *Britain's Military Airfields, 1939–45*, PSL, 1989

Terraine, John, *The Right of the Line*, Hodder & Stoughton, 1985

Townsend, Peter, *Duel in the Dark*, Harrap, 1986

Turner, John Frayn, *VCs of the Air*, Harrap, 1960

Verity, Hugh, *We Landed by Moonlight:Secret RAF landings in France, 1940–44*, Airdata Pubs, revised ed 1995

INDEX

Air Transport Auxiliary 58,
110–111, 112–113, 162–164, 247
Airfields 47–57
Airspeed Anson 32, 110, 111; *Horsa*
114; *Manchester* 145–146;
Oxford 31, 32, 83, 84, 107, 112,
113, 158, 160–161, 164, 234;
Queen Wasp 124
Aldenham 13
Anstey 118, 176
Arlesey 127
Armstrong Whitworth Albemarle
247; *Whitley* 22, 126–127, 205,
206
Avro Lancaster 26, 27, 29, 32,
96–102, 145–147, 149–156, 214,
216

Barrage balloons 73–78
Barton-in-the Clay 15, 16, 161,
162, 252

Bedford 14, 254, 256, 263, 264,
265, 270
Beechcroft 45F 58, *AT-7* 58
Beechwood Park 18, 251–252
Bishops Stortford 263
Bletsoe 272
Boeing B-17 (Flying Fortress) 18,
37, 38, 39, 40, 42, 45, 46, 58–62
passim, 144–145, 172–178, 181,
182–191, 220–233
Bomber Command 19, 21, 22–29,
43, 59, 79–83, 91–93 and *passim*
Boulton & Paul Defiant 136, 194
Bovingdon 18, 63, 58–70
Bristol Beaufighter 85–86, 137,
235–236; *Beaufort* 86, 88;
Blenheim 17, 22, 24, 32, 80–81,
85–86, 235
Bromham 266
Broxbourne 12, 16, 18, 252

Cardington 9, 17, 71–78, 124
Chestnut 272
Colney Street (see Radlett)
Consolidated B-24 (Liberator) 37,
  38, 58, 62, 184, 208, 214, 220
Cranfield 17, 18, 48, 49, 53, 55, 57,
  79–90, 234
Cuffley 10, 111
Curtiss Tomahawk 196–197

de Havilland Air Company 9, 12,
  14, 18, 106–119, 247, 248
de Havilland School of Flying 16
de Havilland Albatross DH91 15;
  Comet DH106 9, 119; *Dominie*
  87, 106; *DH 108* 119; *Gipsy
  Moth* 12, 13; *Hornet DH103*
  118; *Leopard Moth* 14; *Moth
  Minor* 106; *Queen Bee* 106, 124;
  Tiger Moth 32, 83, 106, 107, 110,
  113, 158, 161, 249, 250; *Vampire
  DH100* 118, 119; and *see
  Mosquito*
Dornier Do 17 130; *Do 217* 137
Douglas Boston 38, 180–181; *C-47*
  58, 69–70, 170; *C-53* 58, 69, 70;
  Havoc 85, 86, 130–131, 132–134,
  181, 212
Dunstable 51

Edgware 12
Elstree 13, 14, 55, 252

Fairchild UC 61A 58, 59
Fairey Battle 17, 24, 82, 101;
  Fulmar 2 200

Flying Training Command 29–34,
  52, 83
Focke-Wulf FW190 135, 139, 225

Goldington 12
Gransden Lodge 18, 53, 57,
  91–105, 205

Handley Page Ltd 9, 12, 18,
  242–246
Handley Page Halifax 9, 18, 25, 58,
  94–96, 98, 112, 127, 206–216,
  242–248, 252; *Hampden* 9, 242;
  Hannibal 9; *Harrow* 9; *Hermes*
  246; *Heyford* 9; *Hudson* 127,
  128, 206, 210–212, 215–216
Harpenden 268, 269
Hatfield 9, 12, 14, 15, 16, 18,
  106–119, 192, 249, 260, 263, 272
Hawker Hind 17, 79–80; *Hurricane*
  24, 124–126, 128, 130, 132, 133,
  252; *Tempest* 141; *Typhoon* 128,
  136, 138, 200
Heinkel He 111 131, 259
Henlow 9, 12, 17, 57, 120–128
Hertford 14, 272
Hertingfordbury 106
Hitchin 13, 272
Hockerill Training College 263
Hoddesdon 55
Holwell Hyde (see Panshanger)
Hunsdon 18, 54, 57, 129–142

Johnson, Amy 112
Junkers Ju 88 106

Kempton 13

Leavesden 18, 118, 244, 246–248
Leighton Buzzard 14
Letchworth 261
Lewsey Farm 13
Little Gransden (see Gransden
 Lodge)
Little Staughton 18, 53, 54, 55, 57,
 143–156
Lockheed P-38 (Lightning) 39, 41,
 42, 58, 65, 166–172
London Colney 11, 262
Long Marston 264
Luton 14, 15, 17, 18, 57, 113,
 157–164, 263, 269, 272

Martin B-26 (Marauder) 42, 58
Mathams Wood (see
 Sawbridgeworth)
Messerschmitt Me 163 45; *Me 262*
 45, 46
Miles Magister 32, 83; *Master* 32,
 112; *Martinet* 87
Miller, Glenn 234, 236–240, 270
Minor airfields 252
Mosquito 9, 18, 29, 87, 90, 99,
 101–105, 107, 113–119, 128, 134,
 137–141, 147–156, 163, 164, 235,
 247–248

Noorduyn UC-64A Norseman
 238–239
North American Harvard 32; *P-51
 (Mustang)* 42, 44, 45, 46, 58, 65,
 90, 141, 198–199, 201, 236
Nuthampstead 18, 39, 47, 53, 57,
 165–178

Old Warden 11, 18, 252

Panshanger 16, 54, 56, 57, 113,
 249–250
Pathfinder Force 18, 27, 28, 29
Percival Aircraft Ltd 16, 18,
 157–164
Percival Gull 16, 157; *Mew Gull*
 16, 158; *Petrel* 159, 160; *Proctor*
 158–159, 164; *Vega Gull* 158
Pertenhall 263
Podington 18, 47, 53, 54, 57,
 179–191
Potters Bar 11

R101 airship 9, 11, 71–73, 128
Radlett 9, 12, 112, 242–246
Republic P-47 (Thunderbolt) 39, 45,
 58, 65
Royal Air Force 19–34, 47–57 and
 passim
Royston 14

St Albans 16, 262, 263, 269
Salisbury Hall 114, 115, 116, 262
Satellite Landing Grounds
 250–252
Sawbridgeworth 11, 17, 53, 54, 55,
 57, 192–203
Sharnbrook 145
Short Stirling 25, 214, 215–216, 252
Supermarine Spitfire 24, 37, 38,
 201, 252

Taylorcraft Auster 200–201, 202
Tempsford 18, 57, 127, 184,
 204–218

Thurleigh 18, 47, 51, 53, 57, 145, 219–233
Twinwood Farm 18, 54, 57, 84, 87, 234–240

USAAF 34–47, 52, 59–70, 144–145, 165–178, 179–191, 214, 219–233, 236, 238, 240

V1 rocket 29, 45, 78, 138, 139, 140, 150, 173, 264, 271–272
Vickers Vimy 122; *Virginia* 126;

Wellington 22, 24, 87, 91–93, 204, 205, 220

Watford 269, 272
Westland Lysander 87, 111, 113, 193–196, 197, 205–215, 252
Whipsnade 256
Willington 261
Woburn 13, 18, 252

Yelden 271

SQUADRONS, UNITS ETC

2 111, 192–200, 201
3 129, 132–136
4 194, 201
XV 17
21 137–139
23 122, 123
26 197
29 139
35 (Madras Presidency) 82
43 122, 123
56 11
62 79, 80, 81
63 201
80 202
82 (United Provinces) 79, 80, 81
85 129–136
87 125
97 96
105 117
108 79, 80
109 204, 147–156

116 113
126 202
138 (SD) 127, 196, 205–218
142 101–105
151 141
157 117, 136
160 220
161 (SD) 127, 128, 205–218
164 236
168 201
169 236
170 201
182 200
192 (SD) 93
198 138
207 (Leicester) 82
214 214
239 236
241 197
268 201, 236
286 197

405 (Vancouver) 93–105
409 139
410 137, 139
418 (City of Vancouver) 140
441 (Silver Fox) 142
442 142
464 137–139
487 29, 137–139
488 141
501 (County of Gloucester) 141
515 136
530 132
571 117
582 145, 146, 149–156
613 236
617 214
652 (AOP) 200, 202
809 200
ATA No 5 Ferry Pool 111–113, 162, 164
ATA Cross-Country Flight 162
ATA Training Unit 162, 164
1 Balloon Training Unit 74–78
1 Bombing Development Unit 93
1 EFTS 16, 107–109, 113, 250
24 EFTS 161
29 EFTS 17, 158–159
1418 Experimental Flight 91, 92, 93, 204

Light Night Striking Force 101
3 MU 202
5 MU 252
6 MU 252
8 MU 252
13 MU 124, 126, 127, 128
15 MU 252
211 MU 201, 202
Officers Engineering School 123
11 OTU 204
18 OTU 220
51 OTU 85–90, 235
Parachute Test & Training Section 126
Pathfinder Navigation Training Unit 93, 96
8 (PFF) Group 93–105, 145–156
102 Personnel Despatch Centre 78
3501 Pilot Replacement Unit 90
Pilotless Aircraft Section 124
6 Repairable Equipment Unit 128
3501 Servicing Unit 88, 90
14 SFTS 83–85, 234
Training Aids Development Unit 78
1451 Turbinlite Flight 132
1459 Turbinlite Flight 132
1474 Wireless Investigation Flight 92

USAAF

91st BG 64
92nd BG 37, 59, 62–63, 182–191
97th BG 37, 62
100th BG 181–182
301st BG 59, 179
306th BG 145, 219–233
379th BG 64, 144
381st BG 64
398th BG 165, 172–178
467th BG 36
15th BS 36, 38, 180
36th BS 214
325th BS 191
326th BS 60, 63
327th BS 183
352nd BS 179–180
367th BS 222, 227
369th BS 227
406th BS 214
407th BS 60

422nd BS 41
423rd BS 225
20th FG 169
31st FG 37
55th FG 41, 166, 168–172
361st FG 44
38th FS 166, 167
338th FS 166
343rd FS 166
Air Technical Section (8th Fighter
    Command) 65–69
479th Anti-Submarine Group 184
1 Combat Crew Replacement Center
    63, 69
15th Photo Mapping Sq 64
Reclamation Unit 145
Strategic Air Depot No 2 144–145
60th Troop Carrier Group 179
US Air Transport Service (Europe)
    69